# Oil Price Shocks, Market Response, and Contingency Planning

# Oil Price Shocks, Market Response, and Contingency Planning

**George Horwich
and David Leo Weimer**

American Enterprise Institute for Public Policy Research

Washington and London

George Horwich is professor of economics at Purdue University, special assistant for contingency planning in the Department of Energy, and an adjunct scholar at AEI. David Leo Weimer is associate professor and deputy director of the Public Policy Analysis Program at the University of Rochester.

*This report was prepared with the support of U.S. Department of Energy Grant DE-FG01-83PE70502. Any opinions, findings, conclusions, or recommendations expressed herein, however, are those of the authors and do not necessarily reflect the views of the Department of Energy.*

**Library of Congress Cataloging in Publication Data**

Horwich, George.
    Oil price shocks, market response, and contingency planning.

    (AEI studies ; 405)
    1. Petroleum industry and trade—Government policy—
United States.  2. Petroleum—Reserves—Government policy
—United States.  3. United States—National security.
I. Weimer, David Leo.    II. Title.
HD9566.H67  1984      333.8'232'0973      84-2997
ISBN 0-8447-3555-8
ISBN 0-8447-3554-X (pbk.)

1 3 5 7 9 10 8 6 4 2

AEI Studies 405

*Printed in the United States of America*

# Contents

TABLES

FIGURES

# Foreword

Since the oil shocks of the past decade, the question of how government should respond to the next oil market disruption has been a key public policy issue. Although at this writing oil experts predict stable prices for the near future, we have learned from recent history that energy market forecasts must be viewed cautiously. Oil remains the world's leading energy resource, and the largest concentration of low-cost reserves is still located in areas susceptible to political turmoil. Given the costly and pervasive effects of disruptions on the economy, we considered this issue serious enough to deserve further attention. We were pleased when George Horwich and David Weimer agreed to make a detailed assessment of the traditional policy of government price controls and allocations in contrast to market-oriented approaches for coping with oil supply disruptions. Their work builds upon a previous conference whose papers were later published as *Policies for Coping with Oil-Supply Disruptions* (1982), edited by George Horwich and Edward Mitchell and published by AEI.

Dr. Horwich is a professor of economics and holder of the Burton Morgan Chair of Private Enterprise in the Krannert Graduate School of Management, Purdue University, and an adjunct scholar at the American Enterprise Institute. Dr. Weimer is an associate professor and deputy director of the Public Policy Analysis Program at the University of Rochester. He is the author of *The Strategic Petroleum Reserve: Planning, Implementation, and Analysis* (1982). In addition to their work as academic economists, both authors have had firsthand government experience during an oil supply disruption. Dr. Weimer served as a senior economist in the policy office at the Department of Energy, in 1980–1981, as did Dr. Horwich in 1978–1980. This year Dr. Horwich is serving at the department as a special assistant to the assistant secretary for policy, safety, and environment.

The authors provide new insights into the effects of oil supply disruptions and offer an innovative proposal for policies government should pursue in the event of another disruption. As support for their market-oriented contingency plan, the authors review the experiences with oil price controls and allocations in the 1970s and compare their effects with what might have occurred under a system relatively free of government intervention. They conclude that government policies exacerbated the economic impact of the disruption when compared with the probable outcomes of an uncontrolled market response. Furthermore, they conclude that the controls and allocations failed to achieve their stated goals of limiting price increases and directing petroleum products to those experiencing the greatest hardship.

The authors recommend a contingency plan to respond to future disruptions. Their recommendations include a continuously operating options system to buy oil in the strategic petroleum reserve (SPR). Under this plan, responsibility for triggering the actual drawdown of SPR oil would rest with the private sector. Revenue from the sale of SPR oil would be recycled to the states to finance emergency and other essential public services and to alleviate hardship of low-income families. Funding for the purchase of SPR oil would be provided by a two-dollar fee on all imported oil. An accommodating easing of the money supply is also recommended to facilitate the adjustment following an oil supply disruption. The authors find little merit in mandatory measures aimed at restraining demand, including price ceilings combined with coupon rationing, excise taxes or import tariffs imposed during a disruption, or direct demand-reducing regulations, such as minimum or alternate-day gasoline purchases. In addition, they argue that sharing of oil supplies under international agreements is superfluous if carried out at world market prices and is otherwise harmful to the participating countries as a whole.

The book is one in our series of studies conducted under the auspices of the Institute's program in Energy Policy Studies. Under the direction of Dr. Edward Mitchell, the program has conducted studies and conferences on a wide variety of energy issues, including, most recently, the deregulation of natural gas. This study, *Oil Price Shocks, Market Response, and Contingency Planning*, was prepared with the support of the Department of Energy. The opinions, findings, conclusions, and recommendations expressed here, however, are those of the authors and do not necessarily reflect the views of the Department of Energy. Nor can these views be ascribed to the trustees, officers, or other associates of the American Enterprise Institute.

WILLIAM J. BAROODY
President
American Enterprise Institute

# Preface

The writing of this book was stimulated by congressional passage in 1982 of the Energy Emergency Preparedness Act, which directed the secretary of energy to report on the impact of a curtailment in petroleum supplies under free market conditions in the United States. Although the Department of Energy has of course borne the primary responsibility for responding to this request, it was felt that a parallel effort conducted under the auspices of the American Enterprise Institute might be a useful supplement; hence the present monograph.

Chapter 1 introduces two basic scenarios of response to a world oil supply disruption, that of government intervention in the form of price controls and mandatory allocations, delayed drawdown of the strategic petroleum reserve, and a tightening of the monetary growth rate versus the response of the unregulated market, with government involvement limited essentially to facilitating immediate drawdown of the strategic petroleum reserve, implementing a fiscal transfer program to reduce hardship caused by the oil shock, and increasing the growth rate of money.

Chapter 2 develops the free market scenario in some detail, providing theoretical underpinnings, both micro and macro, for the longer-run impact of permanently reduced petroleum inputs in the economy. The process of adjustment leading to the longer-run outcome is also described. Empirical findings drawn from simulations and real world events of the 1970s support the theoretical treatment. Chapter 3 recounts the whole regulatory experience with respect to petroleum during 1973–1981. The regulations and their impact, both on efficiency and on equity, are analyzed theoretically and with reference to the available empirical record.

Chapter 4 considers the role of the strategic petroleum reserve in future oil crises. The topics treated include the justification for the reserve's existence, methods of funding it, and devices for triggering its use. Chapter 5 addresses the establishment of a system for transferring available revenues to consumers undergoing particular hardship during an oil crisis or to those whose public responsibilities, such as the delivery of emergency services, merit special considerations. Chapter 6 examines the possible role of monetary and fiscal policy measures as sources of macro stabilization during disruption periods. This chapter presents empirical research bearing on the subject that has not previously been published.

Assorted policy options touched on briefly, if at all, in the first six chapters are analyzed in chapter 7. These options include the imposition of a tariff on petroleum during a disruption; demand restraint measures, including coupon rationing; the establishment of so-called set-asides of petroleum products for allocation by the states; and participation in the International Energy Agency, particularly its oil-sharing agreement. Chapter 8 summarizes our main conclusions and recommendations.

Throughout the book we freely employ the economist's basic tools of supply and demand in both verbal and diagrammatic form. Both are necessary for the rigor and completeness that our analysis tries to achieve. The reader who feels ill prepared in the technical aspects of economics should nevertheless not feel deterred. First, much, if not most, of the analysis is self-contained; brief explanations of demand as a marginal valuation schedule, of supply as marginal cost, of producers' and consumers' surplus, of resource versus product markets, of aggregate supply and demand, of internationally traded versus nontraded goods, of social versus private benefits and costs, and of risk neutrality versus risk aversion are offered in the passages that introduce these concepts. Second, nontechnical statements and summaries of our essential arguments and findings appear throughout the volume. There are detailed verbal summaries of chapters 2 and 3, the two most technical chapters. Third, most of the book is nontechnical; the reader needs only a general knowledge of how markets work with and without restraints. We offer the lay reader, as well as readers who are more technically adept, a compendium of information that we hope will be useful, covering the whole range of topics relevant to the formulation of effective disruption policies.

Much of the record reported here is empirical, including the remarkable survey data of the New York State Department of Transportation, describing the diverse and unexpected market-based transportation responses to the energy crisis of 1979 (chapter 2); the hypothetical energy savings, based on existing technological coefficients, calculated by the Mellon Institute (chapter 2); the many simulations and econometric studies of the macro impacts of the energy crises (chapter 2); the historical chronicle of the impact of the oil market regulations during 1973–1981 (chapter 3); and the evidence bearing on the existence of oil price drag during 1973–1980 (chapter 6). The last-mentioned material, because it is published here for the first time, includes detailed information on data sources. Although we describe the sources mainly in appendix B, we found it desirable to discuss the basic measurement rationale and procedure openly and in some detail in the text. The reader can, of course, delve into the material in accordance with personal inclination and available time.

We have had the benefit of numerous discussions and of criticisms and findings made by other observers in this rapidly growing area of interest. We especially acknowledge ongoing discussions with our former colleagues in the Office of Oil Policy at the Department of Energy: Daniel Badger, Michael Barron, Jerry Blankenship, Darius Gaskins, Stephen Minihan, Lucian Pugliaresi, Glen Sweetnam, William Taylor, Thomas Teisberg, and Barry Vann. They and their successors in the policy office have provided us with a continuing source of informed opinion, including the unpublished study of contingency planning directed by Michael Barron and containing contributions by a number of department staff members.

Ben Massell of the Office of Emergency Preparedness in the Department of Energy monitored the book throughout its preparation and offered insightful comments. Part or all of the book was also read by Douglas Bohi of Resources for the Future; Arthur Broida and Anne Peck of the American Enterprise Institute; Walter Chilman, Trish Knight, and Inja Paik of the Office of Emergency Preparedness; David Montgomery of the Energy Information Administration; Russell Roberts of the University of Rochester; John Umbeck of Purdue University; and staff members of the American Petroleum Institute, all of whom offered useful comments and suggestions, many of which we incorporated into our text.

The study of oil price drag in chapter 6 was carried out under Department of Energy Contract DEAC-01-79PE-70015, administered by ICF, Inc.; George Horwich was the principal investigator. In the preparation of that material, Nicholas Gal of the American Petroleum Institute was an invaluable source of data and interpretation of the intricacies of oil industry accounting practice. Christine A. Pendzich, also on the institute's staff, provided worksheets from which the cash balance data in table 15 were taken. David Costello, of the Energy Information Administration, supplied numerous worksheets for normally unreported transactions of the companies in the Financial Reporting System. William Curtis, also of the Energy Information Administration, furnished data on industrial energy and labor costs from the Data Resources, Inc. model.

Jerold Levine, of the Amoco Company, was especially helpful in providing an in-depth industry perspective on regulatory experience in the 1970s. Edward Kutler, energy coordinator for the American Enterprise Institute, patiently helped with this project. He sent us a steady flow of reprints, news clippings, energy information, and critical commentary, the bulk of which has been assimilated in the following pages.

Chapter 3 relies heavily on the definitive study of the oil price regulations by Joseph P. Kalt, *The Economics and Politics of Oil Price Regulation.* The authoritative work of William C. Lane, Jr., *The Mandatory Petroleum Price and Allocation Regulations*, was also a valuable reference. We are responsible, of course, for any errors or misinterpretations that remain.

We would like to thank the American Petroleum Institute for permission to reprint tables 18, 19, and 20 from its publication by Nicholas Gal and Christine Pendzich, *Key Financial Data of Leading U.S. Oil Companies, 1968–80*; the MIT Press for permission to reprint data in tables 6, 7, and 11 from Joseph Kalt, *The Economics and Politics of Oil Price Regulation*; David T. Hartgen and *Energy—The International Journal* for permission to reprint table 5 from the paper by Hartgen "New York State's Perspective on Transportation Energy Contingency Planning," in *Energy—The International Journal*, August/September 1983. The material reported by David Hartgen in table 5 and the studies described in chapter 2 do not necessarily reflect the views of the New York State Department of Transportation.

GEORGE HORWICH
Purdue University
West Lafayette, Indiana

DAVID LEO WEIMER
University of Rochester
Rochester, New York

# 1

# Two Scenarios

It is October 1985. The world oil market has been relatively stable for more than two years. A fall in the price of Saudi Arabian marker crude to $28 per barrel, combined with moderate but steady economic growth in the United States, Japan, and Western Europe, has enabled all the major oil-producing countries, except Saudi Arabia and Iraq, to produce at near-capacity levels. The Saudis are producing at only half their 11-million-barrel-per-day capacity in an effort to support the marker price. Although the war between Iran and Iraq has become a stalemate involving border skirmishing, Iraq has been able to maintain its production at only 1 million barrels per day. Thus although there is almost 8 million barrels of productive capacity worldwide above the actual daily production rate of 55 million barrels, most of the excess is located in the Persian Gulf.

Iran, facing growing internal criticism of the war and observing disturbances among the religious groups in Iraq, launches a major attack in an attempt to break the stalemate. Iranian troops achieve a breakthrough on their southern front. Although their northward advance on Baghdad is stopped with heavy losses, they cut off the southern flank of Iraqi troops and drive them first toward, and then across, the Kuwaiti border. As the fighting continues, pipelines and loading facilities are severely damaged, virtually bringing Kuwaiti oil production to a halt. As a warning to the Saudis not to interfere by inviting Egyptian troops into their territory, the Iranians attack several outbound oil tankers. As a consequence, insurance rates for ships and cargoes passing through the Strait of Hormuz skyrocket, discouraging some companies from sending ships into the Persian Gulf. The loss of Kuwaiti production and the reduced loadings at other Persian Gulf terminals reduce the flow of crude oil to the world market by about 3 million barrels per day.

Spot market prices rise sharply, going from $28 to $38 per barrel

1

within a month. Firms that use crude oil and petroleum products, fearing still higher prices, attempt to increase their petroleum stockpiles. Added demand, however, raises spot prices further. Consumers, also anticipating continued price increases, fill their automobile and heating oil tanks to capacity. The temporary jump in demand accelerates the increase in petroleum product prices. Consumption begins to fall, however, as consumers react to the higher prices by driving their cars less and by turning down thermostats. Some firms, unable to pass along their higher production costs immediately, lay off workers. Farmers, truckers, and segments of the vacation industry are particularly hard hit; many must obtain loans to keep operating. Local governments begin to cut back on the services they provide as expenditures for gasoline and fuel oil run ahead of budgeted amounts.

What action does the U.S. government take in an effort to reduce the economic effects of the Persian Gulf crisis? We outline two possible scenarios with very different consequences.

## The Status Quo Scenario

The most effective step the United States can take in response to the oil price shock is to sell oil from the strategic petroleum reserve (SPR). It is assumed that in 1986 the reserve will hold 490 million barrels. It would have held about 540 million barrels if the Reagan administration had not reduced the fill rate from 216,000 barrels per day in fiscal year 1983 to 186,000 barrels per day in fiscal year 1984 and 145,000 barrels per day in fiscal year 1985. An even larger reserve would exist if capacity expansion had not been repeatedly delayed by both the Carter and the Reagan administrations. Still, these issues are now irrelevant. The important question is whether or not the president will order a drawdown of the oil now in the petroleum reserve.

The president receives conflicting advice. On the one hand, most of his economic advisers argue that the costs to the economy of the disruption will be greatest during the initial period of the price shock. The reserve should thus be used immediately to replace a large fraction of the lost supply and to dampen stockpiling by the private sector. They argue that higher prices will bring forth additional supply from outside the Persian Gulf. Accordingly, there is little reason to hesitate in drawing down a large portion of the reserve during the next six months. On the other hand, many of the president's national security advisers urge him not to initiate a drawdown until the full extent of the Persian Gulf crisis is apparent. They worry that the conflict might spread to Saudi Arabia and might result in almost total loss of oil from the Persian Gulf. They also raise the prospect of U.S.

2

military involvement, suggesting that the reserve should be saved for possible military use. In response to this conflicting advice, the president decides to wait for further information about the crisis. He orders oil purchases for the reserve stopped but waits almost two months before initiating a 1-million-barrel-per-day drawdown. Ending additions to the reserve exerts a slight downward pressure on the world price of oil, and the drawdown results in a further noticeable reduction of prices.

In the meantime, public sentiment for governmental action mounts. Congressmen are deluged with complaints about high petroleum prices. Local public officials declare that the high prices threaten their ability to provide essential services. Farmers and truckers who have not been able to raise their prices to cover higher costs begin to demonstrate. As winter unfolds, the media provide a steady stream of stories about poor and elderly persons who face severe hardship from increased heating bills. Accounts of bloated profits in the oil industry also appear.

Some congressmen respond by introducing legislation that would provide federal financial aid to those experiencing hardship. It is difficult to find a consensus for any particular distribution scheme, however, and many observers feel that it will be months before any program can reach the people it is intended to help. Other congressmen call for a return to price controls and allocations. They call for a freeze of domestic well-head crude oil prices at predisruption levels and an entitlements program to equalize the crude oil acquisition cost for all refiners. As in the past, small refiners lobby actively for special treatment. Under the controls, profit margins on product prices would also be regulated and the Department of Energy (DOE) would have the authority to allocate petroleum products to various markets and to particular users. The proposed system is similar to that in effect during much of the 1970s, and Congress enacts it. The president vetoes the legislation, but his veto is overridden. Even before the final vote, the Department of Energy is besieged with pleas for special allocations.

The price controls and allocations greatly increase the costs of the disruption to the U.S. economy. Spot shortages arise because allocations are of necessity based on historical patterns of use that are no longer appropriate. Some firms must shut down for lack of petroleum inputs, and considerable work time is lost because employees must wait in long lines for gasoline. The uncertainty of supply brings intercity recreational automobile travel to a virtual halt. These developments deepen the recession triggered by the increased world price of oil.

3

The price controls also tend to raise the world price. Domestic refiners see an average crude oil price that is below the world level and respond by increasing their petroleum purchases. At the same time, the price controls reduce the incentive for domestic crude oil production. The resulting increased demand gap raises imports and creates a still higher world price. As long as the price of domestic oil is below that of foreign oil, however, it is politically difficult, if not impossible, to remove the price controls.

Meanwhile, the allocation system has led to intensive lobbying by groups seeking a "fair share" of the limited petroleum supplies. Small companies and others experiencing particular hardship are given petroleum expropriated at below market prices from "crude rich" firms. They also receive benefits under the entitlements system, including cash transfers from the major oil companies and exemptions from their own obligations.

The Open Market Committee of the Federal Reserve System, fearing a permanent renewal of inflation, votes to lower the growth rate of the money supply below its previously targeted level. The turnaround in monetary policy causes a further sharp drop in the monthly index of industrial production and a general increase in unemployment.

## An Adequate-Preparation Scenario

In this hypothetical alternative scenario, two important changes were made in the strategic petroleum reserve program in 1984. First, a two-dollar-per-barrel import fee on crude oil and petroleum products was imposed to provide earmarked funding for the reserve. Thereafter, available storage capacity filled at a rapid rate and the expansion of storage capacity accelerated, so that now there are more than 550 million barrels in storage. Second, an options system for drawdowns was implemented. Under this system, options (claims) are sold through weekly auctions for the right to purchase various quantities of reserve oil nine to twelve weeks in the future at a prespecified price.

Prior to the Iranian breakthrough, options for only a few hundred thousand barrels were being purchased at the legal minimum-bid price. As Iranian troops near the Kuwaiti border, but before there is any reduction in world oil supply, options for several million barrels are purchased. When spot market prices begin to rise, owners of options exercise them, initiating a small drawdown of the reserve. Anticipating further oil price increases, refiners increase their purchases of options, raising the price of options above the minimum bid. The drawdown of the reserve and the prospect of a greater drawdown in the near future constrain spot market prices by both raising the supply of oil and reducing the demands for additions to private stocks. Within six weeks, prices stabilize and the sale of options begins to fall. After three months, drawdowns from the exercise of options end. By this time, however, the president has enough confidence about the course of events in the Persian Gulf to order a reserve drawdown for an additional three months.

Although petroleum product prices do not rise as much or as rapidly as they would have without the early use of the petroleum reserve, the higher prices that do result inflict costs on the economy. As consumption patterns change to limit use of petroleum, some firms find demand for their products reduced and must lay off workers. Firms least able to pass along higher costs are particularly hard hit. Many of those suffering economic loss advocate price controls and allocations.

Fortunately, a federal fiscal transfer program was established in 1984 to reduce the hardship caused by petroleum price shocks and to defuse political pressure for government intervention in petroleum markets. Under this program, revenues from the sale of strategic petroleum reserve oil and from the sale of options to purchase reserve oil are immediately divided among the states according to a predetermined formula. The states use their grants in a variety of ways: to assist local governments, including school districts and providers of emergency services; to help low-income consumers pay heating and transportation bills; and to make emergency loans to farmers. By enabling states to deal with the worst cases of hardship, the fiscal transfer program weakens political support for price controls. Although control legislation is introduced, it passes neither house.

Each month the costs of the disruption are reduced as adjustments to the higher oil prices are made throughout the economy. Consumers and producers continually find ways to economize in the use of petroleum products. Oil producers outside the Persian Gulf, including those in the United States, gradually expand their production in response to the higher prices. The output of natural gas, which was fully deregulated in 1984, rises to historic levels. U.S. coal exports also increase, providing a welcome source of foreign exchange. All of these responses lower the world price of oil.

At the very start of the disruption, the Federal Reserve Open Market Committee votes to raise the monetary growth rate two percentage points above the upper targeted boundary for 1986. This higher growth rate is to continue as long as the world price of crude oil is rising and for several months thereafter. The main economic indicators continue to decline, and the increased price of oil and other forms of energy continue to raise the recorded rate of inflation. Later econometric studies of the period, however, attribute the following effects to the more rapid growth rate of money: a diminished rate of decline in the monthly index of industrial production, an increase in the level of real gross national product (GNP), a reduction in the rate of unemployment, and only a minuscule additional increase in the rate of inflation.

The United States has suffered a recession under the scenario, but one that is less severe and of shorter duration than would have occurred under price controls, mandatory allocations, and a tight monetary policy.

## Is There Really Reason to Worry?

The premise upon which our scenarios are based may seem fanciful to some readers. We would agree that an Iranian incursion into Kuwait is unlikely. There are numerous other possibilities, however, that could lead to a disruption of the magnitude described: an Iraqi invasion of Iran, subversion in Saudi Arabia, and civil war in Iran, to name a few. For the foreseeable future, the Persian Gulf will be a major source of supply for the world crude oil market. In light of the political, ethnic, and religious differences that exist in the region, we would be foolish not to anticipate disruptions in the oil supply.

The status quo scenario may strike some readers as unrealistic. Almost all observers who have studied the petroleum price controls and allocations of the 1970s conclude that they were a mistake. A majority of the people who administered the controls would probably agree. Moreover, we presently have a conservative Republican president who is a staunch defender of the market. Still, congressional and popular support for at least standby controls is widespread and growing. As of early 1984, members of both parties of the congressional energy committees are actively drafting new standby control legislation. We should also bear in mind that the president's veto of the Standby Petroleum Allocation Act of 1982 (S. 1503) was almost overridden; that the rival Bradley-Percy bill (S. 1354) of 1981, which advocated a market-oriented response to energy emergencies, received only a handful of votes; that price controls were introduced and strengthened during conservative Republican administrations in the 1970s; and that a future president may, of course, be less committed to the market.

Given our present history and institutions, an essentially free market response to an oil supply disruption can materialize only if it is preceded by a full-scale planning effort. Price controls and allocations will almost certainly be reimposed if the alternative policies have not been carefully articulated and enunciated in legislation supported by both the Congress and the White House.

In the chapters that follow we present detailed arguments as to why the United States should follow the market-oriented second scenario. We begin by describing the impact of oil price shocks on the economy. We next consider the experience with price controls and allocations during the 1970s, as summarized in the first scenario, to show why we should try to avoid them in the future. After discussing desirable changes in the strategic petroleum reserve program, alternative forms of an emergency fiscal transfer, and appropriate monetary and fiscal policies during disruptions, we briefly review other commonly proposed policies.

# 2
# The Costs of Disruption
# under a Free Market

An oil supply reduction raises the relative price of oil and imposes costs on an oil-importing economy. These costs take the form of a loss of social surplus, the traditional measure of economic welfare. We can also show that the loss of surplus has its counterpart in a loss of gross or net national product,[1] which generates the surplus, and in an increased share of U.S. goods and services claimed by foreigners. GNP falls because of a decline in the productive capacity of the economy brought on by the reduced use of oil. The foreign claim to GNP rises because of an increase in U.S. outlays for the postdisruption quantity of imports.

In addition to these direct costs, social surplus and GNP will fall farther while production and consumption are adapting to the higher price of oil and to the changed distribution of income. These costs tend to be temporary, but to the extent that investment declines during the adjustment, there will be a permanently lower stock of capital and, for that reason, reduced GNP and social surplus. We shall describe the costs in more detail by examining the oil and other individual product markets and by summarizing the microeconomic impacts in an aggregate supply and demand framework. Markets are assumed to be free and unregulated.

## The U.S. Crude Oil Market

The U.S. market for crude oil is pictured in figure 1. The U.S. supply, $S_{US}$, and demand, $D_{US}$, have the customary positive and negative slope, respectively, and intersect at a price $p_0$. The market for crude oil, however, is worldwide, and the United States, although a large buyer and producer, does not itself set the price. The world price, at

8

# FIGURE 1

## The U.S. Market for Crude Oil, with Imports Equal to *ab*

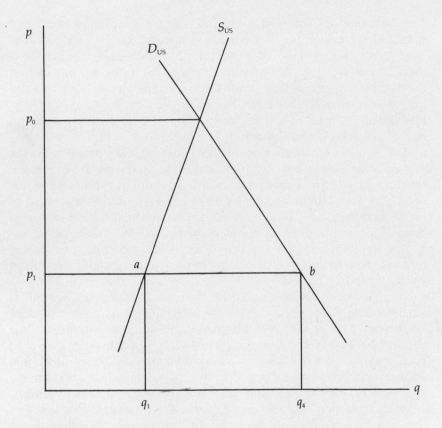

SOURCE: Authors.

which total world supply and demand are equal, is $p_1$. We know that $p_1$ is below $p_0$, since for many years the United States has been a net importer of oil. A country will import oil when, at the world price, its demand quantity exceeds its domestic supply quantity. This case is pictured in figure 1, where, at $p_1$, below $p_0$, the United States demands a quantity, $q_4$, that exceeds domestic output, $q_1$. The excess demand $(q_4 - q_1)$, equal to the horizontal segment *ab*, is equal to crude oil imports.[2]

The economic costs resulting directly from an oil supply disruption are described first with reference to the market pictured in figure 1. Later we will look at the costs as they appear in final product markets. Before proceeding, however, it is necessary to explain in somewhat more detail the meaning of the crude oil demand and supply schedules.

**The Demand for Crude Oil.** Crude oil is a resource that is valued not directly for consumption but rather as an input for the production of final goods and services. The demand for crude oil ($D_{US}$ in figure 1) is thus derived from the relationship between the input of crude oil and the resulting output of final products as valued by consumers. At any given quantity of crude oil, the height of the demand schedule is the additional dollar value of final product that the input of the crude oil makes possible. The demand schedule in figure 1 is thus an economy-wide schedule of resource marginal (additional) value product. Such a schedule serves as a demand function, since at any given price of the resource, it will pay purchasers to buy an amount the use of which results in a net addition to the value of product outputs just equal to the resource price. To buy less of the resource would be to forgo product outputs whose value, as indicated by the height of the resource demand schedule, exceeds the resource cost (price); to buy more of the resource would be to incur costs that exceed the resulting value of product outputs.

The resource demand schedule is downward sloping because (1) successive equal inputs of a resource, while other inputs are constant or increase less, result in successively decreasing additions to final product because of the law of diminishing marginal returns; and (2) final product demands are downward sloping, so that additional quantities of product can be sold in the aggregate only at successively lower prices, thereby reducing the value of additional units of output.

Since the height of the crude oil demand measures the value of the increments to final outputs, the total area under the schedule up to any given quantity is equal to the total value of final outputs, or GNP, attributable to the use of the crude oil.

**The Supply of Crude Oil.** The height of the crude oil supply schedule, $S_{US}$ in figure 1, indicates the marginal (incremental) costs incurred in producing each quantity.[3] Thus, at any given price of crude oil, the amount supplied will be the quantity whose incremental cost, as indicated by the height of the supply schedule, is just equal to the price. Since the supply price measures the additional cost attributable to each successive unit of crude oil output, the total area under the schedule up to any given quantity is equal to the total cost incurred in producing that quantity.

We assume that resources are paid their opportunity cost; that is, the value of products they would otherwise produce in their best alternative use. It follows that the total cost of producing any given quantity of crude oil, equal to the area under the marginal cost curve from the origin to that quantity, is equal to the value of GNP sacrificed as a result of producing the crude oil. This area under the supply (marginal cost) curve, between any given crude oil quantities, contrasts with the corresponding area under the demand curve, which is the GNP gained through use of the crude oil input.

Marginal cost, and hence the supply schedule, rises with increasing outputs of crude oil because of the law of diminishing marginal returns. Equal successive inputs applied to the production of crude oil result in diminishing additional units of oil output. The quantity of inputs required to produce equal additional units of output, and hence the cost of the inputs, rises for each additional unit of crude oil output produced.

### An Oil Supply Disruption: The Direct Costs

We identify the costs of an oil supply disruption with reference to figure 2, which repeats the schedules of figure 1. A permanent reduction in world oil supply is assumed to raise the world price from $p_1$ to $p_2$. (See appendix A for a discussion of the various kinds of crude oil prices.) In response to the higher price, the U.S. demand quantity falls from $q_4$ to $q_3$, the domestic supply quantity rises from $q_1$ to $q_2$, and imports fall from $(q_4 - q_1)$ to $(q_3 - q_2)$. Relevant geometric areas are designated by capital letters. Expressed in terms of these areas, total expenditures on crude oil go from $(H + G + F + E)$ predisruption to $(H + G + F + C + B + A)$ afterward. Expenditures on imports go from $(G + F + E)$ to $(F + C)$.

**Interpretation of Supply-Demand Geometric Areas.** We can see in figure 2 that the reduction in the total consumption of oil from $q_4$ to $q_3$ entails a loss of $(D + E)$ in the total value of final products, or GNP, to which $(q_4 - q_3)$ of crude oil input gives rise. This information, in the form of a downward arrow, is entered in table 1 opposite $D$ and $E$ in column 1, which is labeled "Change in GNP."

The areas $B$ and $G$ are similarly interpreted and are so marked in table 1. $(B + G)$ is the total cost incurred in expanding domestic oil production from $q_1$ to $q_2$, replacing oil that had previously been imported. Granted that resources used in producing oil are paid their

11

FIGURE 2

THE U.S. MARKET FOR CRUDE OIL BEFORE AND AFTER AN OIL SUPPLY
DISRUPTION, WITH DELINEATED AREAS OF WELFARE GAIN AND LOSS

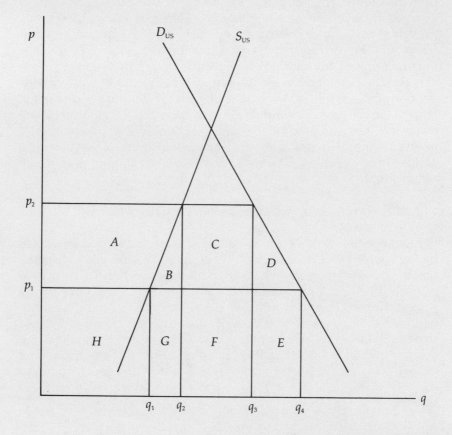

SOURCE: Authors.

opportunity cost $(B + G)$ equals the value of final product sacrificed in
exchange for $(q_2 - q_1)$ in additional domestic oil output. The GNP
made possible by $(q_2 - q_1)$ [which is measured by a vertical extension
of the trapezoid enclosing $(B + G)$ to the height of the $D_{US}$ schedule] is
not, of course, a net increase in GNP; the new domestically produced
oil merely maintains the GNP previously produced by an equivalent
amount of oil imports.

TABLE 1

LOSSES IN GNP AND INCREASED FOREIGN CLAIMS TO GNP FROM AN
OIL SUPPLY DISRUPTION, BY SELECTED GEOMETRIC AREAS

| Area | Change in GNP (1) | Change in Foreign Claim to GNP (2) | Net (3) |
|------|------|------|------|
| A | — | — | — |
| B | ↓ | — | ↓GNP |
| C | — | ↑ | ↑FC |
| D | ↓ | — | ↓GNP |
| E | ↓ | ↓ | — |
| F | — | — | — |
| G | ↓ | ↓ | — |
| H | — | — | — |

NOTE: In summary, the decline in GNP (column 1) is $(B + D + E + G)$; the net rise in foreign claims (column 2) is $(C - E - G)$; total costs (column 3) are $(B + C + D)$. FC = foreign claim to GNP; dashes = no change. See figure 2 for the location of each area relative to the crude oil supply and demand schedules.

SOURCE: Authors.

Although $E$ represents a loss of GNP because of a net reduction in the input of oil, and $G$ represents a loss because of a transfer of resources from the production of final products to the production of oil, both areas also correspond to reduced outlays on oil imports. As such, $E$ and $G$ are subtractions from foreign claims to U.S. GNP and are marked by downward arrows in column 2 of table 1.[4]

The areas $H$ and $F$ are payments made, respectively, to domestic and foreign oil producers both before and after the disruption. Since these expenditure components are unaffected by the disruption, they are shown in table 1 as having no tendency to change the level of GNP or the level of foreign claims to GNP.

Area $A$ is an increase in expenditures on $q_2$ of domestic oil production over and above any costs incurred in producing that quantity. Area $A$ is thus a transfer from domestic consumers to domestic oil producers, for whom it is a pure surplus. Under the usual assumptions of welfare economics, area $A$ is considered a neutral transfer that does not a priori imply that the balance of economic well-being has been altered. Although some readers may object on equity grounds, on efficiency criteria the transfer is an incentive to oil producers to increase oil production in the future. In table 1, area $A$ is shown as having no direct effect on GNP or on the foreign claim to it.

The remaining area of interest is $C$, which is an increased outlay on the postdisruption level of imports. Area $C$ entails no direct effects on the level of GNP but is an increase in foreign producer claims to GNP and is so designated in table 1.

**Summary of the Disruption Costs.** The net costs of the disruption in terms of each area are summarized in column 3 of table 1. Areas $B$ and $D$, which are triangular, are net losses of GNP. The former is an increased real resource cost of producing oil domestically that had previously been imported more cheaply; the latter is simply a loss of final output due to diminished use of oil economywide. The area $C$, a transfer to foreign oil producers, is an increased claim to GNP at the expense of U.S. citizens. The areas $E$ and $G$, although equal to reductions in GNP, also represent reduced imports and hence reduced claims to GNP by foreign producers. The net cost of $E$ and $G$ to the American economy is thus zero, as noted in column 3 of table 1.

The total direct cost of the disruption, in terms of the crude oil market, is the sum of the entries in column 3 $(B + C + D)$. Areas $B$ and $D$ are absolute decreases in GNP, and $C$ is an increased foreign claim to GNP. The separate sum of items in column 1 is the total loss of GNP $(B + D + E + G)$; the items in column 2 sum to the net change in foreign claims to GNP $(C - E - G)$. The sum of columns 1 and 2 is, of course, equal to the sum of column 3.

**The Total Direct Cost as Loss of Social Surplus.** The total direct cost of the disruption $(B + C + D)$, corresponds to an area identified by economists as the net loss of social surplus. Consumers' and producers' surplus, the two components of social surplus, are the gains from trade. Losses of the surplus accordingly measure the true cost of a price increase or other economic disturbance.

To buyers of a good, the consumers' surplus or gain from trade is the excess of the good's value over its cost. The valuation of a good at any quantity is given by the height of the demand schedule, the demand price. In the case of final products, the demand price is equal to the marginal (additional) use value that buyers receive from consumption of the corresponding quantity. In the case of resource goods or inputs, such as crude oil, the demand price (as we have seen) is the addition in the value of final products resulting from use of the oil. The cost of goods to consumers is the price actually paid. As long as a single market price prevails, the consumers' surplus up to any quantity is thus the cross-hatched area pictured in figure 3a: For the quanti-

# FIGURE 3

## ILLUSTRATIONS OF (a) CONSUMERS' SURPLUS AND (b) PRODUCERS' SURPLUS

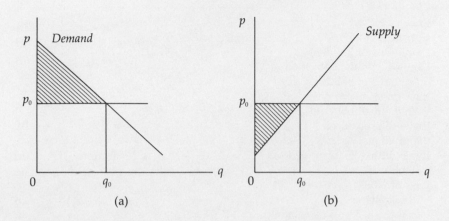

(a)

(b)

SOURCE: Authors.

ties from 0 to $q_0$, the total surplus is the area beneath the demand schedule, above the horizontal price line, and to the right of the vertical axis.

Producers' surplus is the difference between the price received by sellers for a given quantity of a commodity and the additional (marginal) cost—the supply price—incurred in producing that quantity. If we again assume a single market price at which all units are sold, the producers' surplus is the cross-hatched area in figure 3b: For the quantities from 0 to $q_0$, the surplus is the area bounded by the supply schedule, the horizontal price line, and the vertical axis.

In figure 2 the rise in price from $p_1$ to $p_2$ reduces the buyers' surplus by $(A + B + C + D)$ and increases domestic producers' surplus by $A$. The net change in social surplus is thus a reduction of $(B + C + D)$, exactly equal to the disruption costs summarized in table 1.[5]

**A Numerical Illustration.** In order to gain some sense of the magnitude of disruption costs, we estimate the size of the geometric areas by a simple numerical example. The underlying numerical data, before and after an oil supply disruption, are given in table 2 and are

15

## TABLE 2

### SIMULATED NUMERICAL IMPACT OF AN OIL SUPPLY DISRUPTION ON KEY COST COMPONENTS OF THE CRUDE OIL MARKET

|  | Predisruption | Postdisruption |
|---|---|---|
| Price of oil ($/bbl) | 30 | 60 |
| Consumption of oil (millions of bbl/day) | 15.0 | 14.0 |
| Domestic production of oil (millions of bbl/day) | 10.0 | 10.2 |
| Imports of oil (millions of bbl/day) | 5.0 | 3.8 |
| Expenditures on oil ($ billions/yr.) | 164 | 307 |
| Expenditures on imported oil ($ billions/yr.) | 55 | 83 |
| Loss of GNP ($ billions/yr.) | — | 18 |
| Net increase in foreign claims to GNP ($ billions/yr.) | — | 29 |
| Total cost of disruption: loss of social surplus ($ billions/yr.) | — | 47 |

SOURCE: Authors.

applied to the geometric areas of figure 4, a scale rendering of the U.S. crude oil market.

We assume, as indicated in the predisruption column of table 2, that the price of oil is initially thirty dollars per barrel, that U.S. consumption of oil is 15 million barrels per day, that domestic production of oil is 10 million barrels per day, and that imports are 5 million barrels per day. On an annual basis, total expenditures on oil are $164 billion per year, and expenditures on oil imports are $55 billion per year.

The disruption is assumed to raise the price of oil to sixty dollars per barrel. We take the price elasticity of crude oil demand to be $-0.1$, which implies that the quantity of oil demanded falls 1 percent for every 10 percent increase in price. The response of demand is calculated by an equation, $q = cp^{-0.1}$, where $q$ is the quantity of crude oil demanded, $p$ the price of crude oil, $-0.1$ the indicated price elasticity, and $(c>0)$ a fitted constant.[6]

The postdisruption numerical results, including the disruption costs, are entered in the second column of table 2. The predisruption

# FIGURE 4

## THE IMPACT OF A DOUBLING OF CRUDE OIL PRICES ON SOCIAL SURPLUS AND GNP AS REFLECTED IN THE U.S. MARKET FOR CRUDE OIL
### (billions of dollars per year)

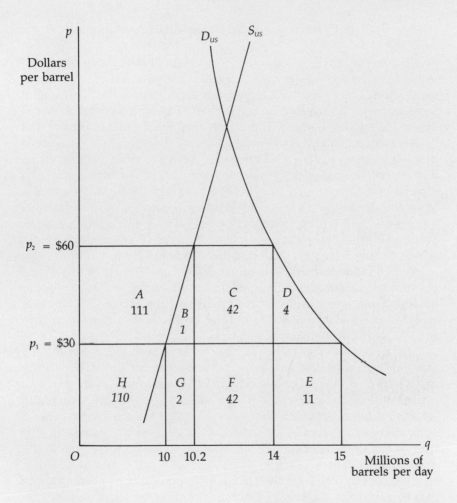

NOTE: Loss of GNP: $B + G + D + E = 1 + 2 + 4 + 11 = 18$. Increase in foreign claims to GNP: $C - E - G = 42 - 11 - 2 = 29$. Loss of social surplus: $B + C + D = 1 + 42 + 4 = 47$.

SOURCE: Authors.

17

and postdisruption data are allocated to the geometric areas of the crude oil market and are entered in figure 4. The decline of GNP at an annual rate is $(B + D + E + G)$, or \$18 billion, and the annual net increase in foreign claims to U.S. GNP is $(C - E - G)$, or \$29 billion. The total direct disruption cost is thus \$18 billion plus \$29 billion, or \$47 billion, which is also equal to the loss of social surplus $(B + C + D)$, or \$47 billion.

## Direct Costs as Reflected in the Product Markets

The increased crude oil costs will appear in the supplies of all the individual final goods and services that employ crude oil in their production. The cost of almost every final product of the GNP will in some measure be affected by the higher cost of petroleum products. These higher costs will take the form of higher transportation fuel costs incurred at all stages in producing and delivering the final product; higher power costs at all stages for final goods and services that rely on oil-driven electricity; and, in many cases, the higher cost of a major raw material, such as petroleum products going to service stations and dealers serving households or to petrochemical industries.

Figure 5 depicts the market of a typical individual final product. To simplify the identification of geometric areas, the product supply schedules are drawn as horizontal lines both before and after the rise in oil prices. This construction removes producers' surplus for suppliers of final products, which would complicate the analysis without enlarging it in any useful way. A horizontal schedule reflects constant marginal costs of production, a not unreasonable assumption regarding long-run product supply behavior.

In figure 5 the rise in the price of crude oil is shown as raising the marginal cost supply schedule of a typical component of GNP—product $X$—from $S_0$ to $S_1$. The product price rises from $p_0^X$ to $p_1^X$, and quantity demanded of the product falls along the given demand schedule from $q_0^X$ to $q_1^X$. The economic cost of the disruption to buyers and sellers of product $X$ is the loss of social surplus, which, in this case, is the loss of consumers' surplus only. The loss is equal to the area designated $(a + c + b + d)$.

The loss in both the value and physical quantity of product $X$ can also be related to the loss of GNP and domestic buyers' surplus described in the crude oil market. If we think of the $(q_0^X - q_1^X)$ loss of product $X$ as occurring incrementally, the loss in the value of $X$, as a component of measured real GNP, is equal to the product of each unit between $q_0^X$ and $q_1^X$ and the corresponding demand prices.[7] The sum of these products is the area $(b + d + e + g)$, which is the share of

# FIGURE 5

## The Impact of a Rise in Crude Oil Prices on the Market for a Representative Final Product, X

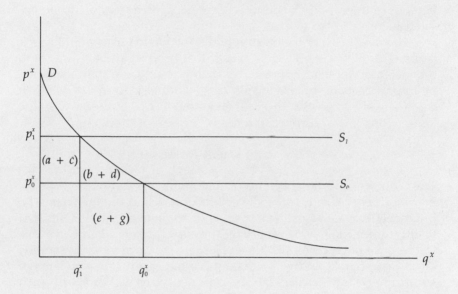

Source: Authors.

product $X$ in the areas $(B + D)$ and $(E + G)$, the total loss in the value of GNP as reflected in the market for crude oil (see figures 2 and 4).

We assume that all resources in the economy remain fully employed. The reduced spending on $(q_0^X - q_1^X)$ of product $X$ is thus equal to reduced expenditures on oil inputs and other resources diverted from $X$ to the production of additional domestic oil. Since the supply schedule of oil imports is horizontal, both reduced consumption of oil and increased domestic oil production result in decreases in oil imports (see figures 2 and 4). The area $(e + g)$, the reduction in the predisruption outlay on $(q_0^X - q_1^X)$ of product $X$, thus corresponds to a reduction in crude oil imports. Like $E$ and $G$ in the crude oil market in figure 2, the loss in the value of product $X$ represented by $(e + g)$ is thus offset by an equal reduction in the foreign claim to the U.S. GNP.

Like $B$ and $D$ in figure 2, however $(b + d)$ in figure 5 is a net loss in the value of product $X$ and, to that extent, in GNP. Relative to the predisruption equilibrium, there are no foreign claims associated with

19

the area $(b + d)$ whose curtailment as a result of the disruption constitutes a welfare gain.

Since the rise in the cost and price of product $X$ is due to the increased price of oil, area $(a + c)$ in figure 5 is the individual final product counterpart to $(A + C)$ in figure 2. Area $(a + c)$ is an increased expenditure on domestic and imported oil in order to maintain product $X$ output level $q_1^X$. The import component, area $c$, is an uncompensated increase in the foreign claim to GNP.

The direct cost of the oil supply disruption in terms of product $X$ is thus $(b + d + e + g)$ in the value of lost product and $(c - e - g)$ in the increased foreign claim to GNP owing to $(c - e - g)$ in increased oil import costs in the production of $X$. The net cost in GNP is $(b + d + e + g + c - e - g) = (b + c + d)$, which is less, by area $a$, than the loss of consumers' surplus suffered by buyers of product $X$.

## The Adjustment Process

The costs we have described occur directly as a result of the increase in the price of oil and ignore any indirect or second-order effects. The indirect effects are adjustment costs and, to some extent, benefits that result from the following aspects of the direct effects: (1) the increase in the price of crude oil will upset the relative price structure among all energy sources and will induce price increases across the energy spectrum; (2) the increases in final product prices will vary with each product's relative use of oil and will induce substitutions of (and thus investments in) products whose prices rise less for others whose prices rise more (for complementary goods, an opposite movement will take place away from products whose prices have risen less to those whose prices have risen more); (3) the added spending on petroleum and petroleum products entails a transfer of income to foreign and domestic producers of oil, altering the pattern of final product demands throughout the economy; (4) the transfer to oil producers not only will alter the pattern of final product demands but also will depress the general level of all nonpetroleum demands if oil producers fail to spend receipts promptly in domestic goods markets.

Each of these indirect effects will be described briefly before being summarized, together with the direct effects, in an aggregate supply-and-demand framework at the close of this chapter.

**Price and Output Response in Oil Substitutes.** There is, of course, a range of alternative energy sources that will reflect, more or less, the rise in the price of oil. The price increases occur as buyers raise their demand for sources whose prices are initially unchanged and are

20

therefore relatively more attractive. This spillover of demand from oil markets will raise both the price and output of alternative fuels. Fuels that are substitutable for oil over a broad range of uses will experience a greater price rise than those that are less substitutable. Given the price increases, the output of each energy source will rise in accordance with its supply elasticity.

The substitution process is illustrated in figure 6, a representation of the aggregate energy market. A single aggregate demand for energy, the schedule $D$, interacts with $S^T$, the horizontal sum of supply

FIGURE 6

THE IMPACT OF (1) AN OIL SUPPLY DISRUPTION ON (1′) THE QUANTITY OF
OIL SUPPLIED, (2) THE AGGREGATE SUPPLY SCHEDULE OF ENERGY,
(2′) THE QUANTITY OF TOTAL ENERGY SUPPLIED, AND
(3) THE QUANTITY SUPPLIED OF ALTERNATIVE ENERGY SOURCES

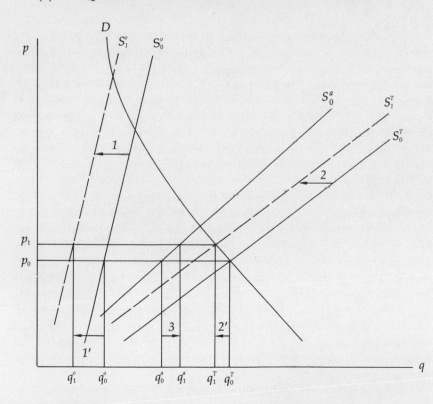

schedules of all individual energy sources. We have pictured only one alternative to oil in order to keep the diagram uncluttered. The alternative, whose supply is $S^a$, is a stand-in for coal, natural gas, wood fuel, hydro and nuclear power, and, to some degree, human labor. The supply of oil is $S^o$. The quantity units are expressed in terms of a common measure, BTUs, and each price on the vertical axis may be regarded as an average of the whole spectrum of energy prices.

The initial price and quantity in the aggregate energy market are $p_0$ and $q_0^T$, respectively, at the intersection of $D$ and the predisruption total energy supply schedule, $S_0^T$. Projecting $p_0$ into the individual markets, the quantity supplied of oil is $q_0^o$ on the initial oil supply schedule $S_0^o$, and the quantity of alternative fuels is $q_0^a$, which lies on $S_0^a$.

The disruption of world oil supply shifts $S_0^o$ leftward to $S_1^o$. The aggregate energy supply moves an equal horizontal distance from $S_0^T$ to $S_1^T$. In the postdisruption equilibrium, the total quantity of energy is lower at $q_1^T$ and the average price is higher at $p_1$. At $p_1$, oil output is down from $q_0^o$ to $q_1^o$ and the output of oil alternatives has increased from $q_0^a$ to $q_1^a$.

This broader view of the impact of the oil supply disruption on all energy markets makes clear that (1) the loss of oil is partially offset by increases in alternative energy supplies; and (2) because of the availability of alternatives, the price of energy overall, including that of oil, rises less than it would if oil were the only energy source. The dampening of the oil price rise is a result of the influence of alternative fuels on the elasticity of the oil demand schedule. The greater the opportunities for substitution of alternatives, the more elastic will the demand for oil be and the less will any leftward shift of oil supply succeed in raising the price of oil in the world market.

At the same time, for any given loss of oil supply, the price of energy in general, in the case of multiple energy sources, will rise less than will the price of oil in the case where oil is the sole energy source. If we assume that the elasticity of total energy demand is the same whether there is one energy source—oil—or many, the demand curve in the case of multiple energy sources will span a greater magnitude and, for any given elasticity, will be flatter than the oil demand over any given interval.[8] A given loss of oil and leftward shift of the oil supply schedule will thus cause a greater increase in the price of oil when traced along the demand-for-oil schedule than it will in the overall price of energy when traced, as in figure 6, along the aggregate demand for energy.

Following a disruption, the spread of the oil price increase to other energy sources will increase the number of final products whose production costs are raised. With the availability of oil substitutes, however, all of the following are less than they would be in the absence of oil alternatives: the absolute and relative loss of energy, the average rise in energy prices, the rise in final product production costs and prices and the reduction in product outputs, and the aggregate loss of social surplus.

**Shifts among Final Products.** In any equilibrium, all product prices and quantities stand in a relationship that is consistent with the products' substitutability and complementarity as perceived by consumers. The rise in energy prices will, of course, affect product costs, and hence prices, differentially and will thereby upset this equilibrium. Goods that are more energy intensive will experience a greater rise in production costs and supply price, raising the product price and reducing quantity demanded more than for goods that are less energy intensive. Consumers will respond by adjusting their purchases so as to restore a pattern consistent with their preferences.

Suppose, for example, that the marginal cost and price of a good rise more than those of a substitute. Consumers will move out of the product whose price has risen more, reducing its price (or, in context, dampening the increase) and output, and into the product whose price has risen less, raising its price and output. This adjustment will continue until consumers are again satisfied with the relative price and consumption levels of the two goods. Goods that, to a degree, are consumer substitutes whose production differs in the input of energy include space heating and sweaters. Since sweaters require relatively less energy to produce, they will rise relatively less in price, becoming more attractive. Over time, we can expect sweaters, and heavier clothing generally, to be substituted for home heating during the colder months.

For goods that are complements, an opposite shift will take place: from the good whose price has risen relatively less to the one whose price has risen more. Take the textbook example of complements, bread and butter, and assume that the baking of bread is more energy intensive than the production of butter. The costs and price of bread will rise, and its output will fall, relatively more than those of butter. To restore balance in consumption, however, consumers will increase their demand for bread and reduce that of butter, bringing the quantities of the two somewhat closer together. This behavior will exacerbate the price increase of bread while lowering the price of butter.

In the aftermath of an oil supply disruption, product shifts, whether between substitutes or complements or simply as the expression of a changed distribution of income (to be described), will tend to

23

reduce GNP and employment. Although these reductions are temporary, pending a reallocation of resources from declining to expanding industries, they can add considerably to the costs of the disruption. The temporary adjustment costs may, in fact, exceed those identified earlier as direct costs occasioned by the reduced supply of oil.

The adjustment costs associated with shifts in demand are illustrated in figure 7. To focus clearly on the costs, two polar market cases that exaggerate the losses associated with short-run adjustment are posited. In figure 7a, which represents the declining market, marginal costs and supply price are completely rigid downward in response to the leftward shift of demand. Thus the market price is constant and output bears the full brunt of the demand loss, falling from $q_0^a$ to $q_1^a$. In figure 7b, to which the demand removed from figure 7a is transferred, supply quantity is completely rigid in the upward direction, and the impact of the increment to demand falls entirely on price, which rises from $p_0^b$ to $p_1^b$.

Since there is no gain of output between the two markets, only a loss, and no decline of price, only an increase, the economy is left

FIGURE 7

THE SHIFT OF DEMAND BETWEEN TWO INDIVIDUAL FINAL
PRODUCT MARKETS, (a) AND (b)

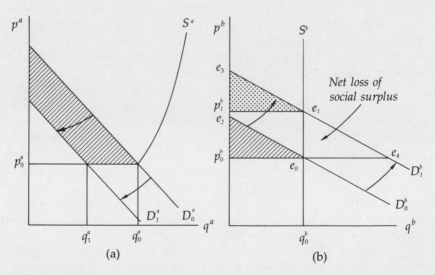

(a)                                         (b)

SOURCE: Authors.

with a net loss of output and a net increase in the price level. Consumers' surplus falls by the cross-hatched trapezoidal area shown in figure 7a and the cross-hatched triangle in 7b and rises by the dotted triangle in 7b. Producers' surplus rises in figure 7b by the rectangle $p_0^b p_1^b e_1 e_0$, leaving a net gain of consumers' surplus plus producers' surplus in figure 7b of $e_2 e_3 e_1 e_0$. How does this latter area compare with the net loss—the trapezoid—in figure 7a? If both markets were characterized by horizontal supply schedules, the reduction of demand and loss of consumers' surplus in figure 7a would, on a first approximation, appear in figure 7b as an equal increase in consumers' surplus of $e_2 e_3 e_4 e_0$. This latter area, then, would be equal to the net loss of surplus in figure 7a and would exceed the net gain in figure 7b by the triangular area $e_0 e_1 e_4$. This net loss of surplus is so designated in figure 7b.

As resources gradually flow into the expanding market in figure 7b, the supply schedule tends to flatten out, restoring GNP and social surplus and reducing prices to their levels preceding the intermarket shift.

**Income Redistributive Effects.** A potential source of considerable demand shifting and resource reallocation is the income transfer from oil purchasers to oil producers. All econometric evidence points to inelastic petroleum demands in the short and intermediate run.[9] The leftward shift of supply along the demand schedule will thus raise petroleum prices relatively more than it will reduce petroleum consumption. As a result, petroleum expenditures and receipts will rise, even (as appears to be the case) after we take into account the influence of simultaneously falling income that shifts demand to the left.

The transfer of income from consumers to producers of petroleum will alter the pattern of product demands throughout the economy, giving rise to the adjustment costs associated with shifting demands, as described in the preceding section. Although the income transfer is not likely to induce as much demand shifting as do the pervasive energy-induced relative price changes, the transfer nevertheless promises to be substantial. In our simple numerical example recorded in table 2, a doubling of crude oil prices from thirty dollars to sixty dollars per barrel, when traced along a demand schedule of elasticity of $-0.1$, reduced consumption from 15 million to 14 million barrels per day and raised annual oil expenditures from \$164 billion to \$307 billion, an increase of \$143 billion.

Small in absolute value, the demand elasticity of $-0.1$, however, is more appropriate to a one- or two-month period immediately following a disruption than to an entire year (and is probably not rele-

25

vant to an increase in oil prices as great as a doubling). As the year progresses, the elasticity is more likely to reach values from −0.2 to −0.3, sharply reducing the price run-up and the magnitude of the transfer. The drawdown of private and public oil stocks will also mute the rise in prices and expenditures—and we have not allowed for the negative income effect that will tend to reduce petroleum demand, constraining both prices and spending during the course of a crisis.

At the same time, several assumptions in table 2 lead to an underestimate of the economic impact of disruptions. The oil loss, 1 million barrels per day, or 6.7 percent of U.S. consumption, is moderate rather than severe. Moreover, we have not incorporated the increased inventory demand that could readily accompany a supply curtailment.

Table 3 provides price and expenditure changes under a broader

TABLE 3

EFFECT OF OIL SHORTFALLS OF 1 MILLION AND 2 MILLION
BARRELS PER DAY ON OIL PRICE AND EXPENDITURES

| | Consumption (millions of bbl/day) | Price ($/bbl) | Expenditures ($ billions/yr.) |
|---|---|---|---|
| Predisruption Levels | 15 | 30 | 164 |
| Loss of 1 million bbl/day | | | |
| $\varepsilon = -0.1$ | | | |
| $\Delta Y = 0$ | −1 | +30 | +143 |
| $\Delta Y = -2\%$ | −1 | +19 | +86 |
| $\varepsilon = -0.3$ | | | |
| $\Delta Y = 0$ | −1 | +8 | +29 |
| $\Delta Y = -2\%$ | −1 | +5 | +16 |
| Loss of 2 million bbl/day | | | |
| $\varepsilon = -0.1$ | | | |
| $\Delta Y = 0$ | −2 | +95 | +431 |
| $\Delta Y = -4\%$ | −2 | +53 | +232 |
| $\varepsilon = -0.3$ | | | |
| $\Delta Y = 0$ | −2 | +18 | +65 |
| $\Delta Y = -4\%$ | −2 | +12 | +36 |

NOTE: $\varepsilon$ = demand price elasticity. $\Delta Y$ = change in income.
SOURCE: Authors.

range of assumptions. The table shows the changes in the price of oil
($p$) and expenditures on oil ($E$) for a 1-million-barrel-per-day loss (the
upper half) and a 2-million-barrel-per-day loss (the lower half), which
is 2/15 or 13.3 percent of U.S. consumption. Under each shortfall, the
price elasticity of petroleum demand ($\varepsilon$) is taken first as $-0.1$ and then
as $-0.3$. For each size of shortfall and elasticity, the simultaneous
change of income ($Y$) is first ignored ($\Delta Y = 0$) and is then, for the
1-million-barrel-per-day shortfall, assumed to be $-2$ percent ($\Delta Y =$
$-2$ percent) and, for the 2-million-barrel-per-day shortfall, $-4$ percent
($\Delta Y = -4$ percent). In all cases that allow for the drop in income, the
income elasticity of petroleum demand is assumed to be 1.[10]

Notice the entry in table 3 under the following categories: a
1-million-barrel-per-day supply loss, a petroleum demand elasticity of
$-0.1$, and the absence of an income effect ($\Delta Y = 0$). The price of oil is
shown as increasing thirty dollars per barrel, and expenditures, $143
billion per year. This case is summarized in table 2. When, for the
same loss of oil and demand elasticity, income is assumed to fall 2
percent, the price of oil rises instead nineteen dollars per barrel, and
expenditures, $86 billion. Similar effects appear in the other columns.
For either loss size and demand elasticity, incorporation of the income
effect on demand dampens the price rise and oil industry receipts.
Raising the absolute demand elasticity produces similar effects. Doubling the loss of oil of course enlarges the price and expenditure
increments.

A more precise summary of the impact of the alternative demand
elasticities, presence or absence of an income effect, and size of shortfall on the price and expenditure data is presented in table 4. The
entries are the ratios of the price and expenditure increases occurring
under alternative assumptions. The first set of entries, for example,
are the ratios of price and expenditure increases under demand elasticity of $-0.3$ to the increases under demand elasticity $-0.1$. The
entry 0.27 is the ratio of the price increase ($+8$ in table 3) occurring
under a 1-million-barrel-per-day shortfall, a zero income effect, and
elasticity of $-0.3$ to the price increase ($+30$ in table 3) occurring under
the same conditions except that elasticity is $-0.1$.

In general, raising the demand elasticity from $-0.1$ to $-0.3$ reduces the price and expenditure increments to as little as 0.15 and as
much as 0.27 of their values under elasticity $-0.1$. Introducing income
effects reduces the price and expenditure increments to a range of 0.53
to 0.63 of their values in the absence of income effects. Finally, doubling the shortfall from 1 million to 2 million barrels per day raises the
increases in price and expenditure by 2.2 to 3.2 times their values
under the 1-million-barrel-per-day disruption. Under elasticity of

# TABLE 4
DIFFERENTIAL EFFECTS OF OIL SUPPLY DISRUPTION ON OIL PRICE AND
EXPENDITURE UNDER ALTERNATIVE ASSUMPTIONS AS TO DEMAND
ELASTICITY, INCOME EFFECT, AND SIZE OF DISRUPTION

| | Price[a] | Expenditure[b] |
|---|---|---|
| | $\varepsilon = -0.3/\varepsilon = -0.1$ | |
| Loss of 1 million bbl/day | | |
| $\Delta Y = 0$ | 0.27 | 0.20 |
| $\Delta Y < 0$ | 0.26 | 0.19 |
| Loss of 2 million bbl/day | | |
| $\Delta Y = 0$ | 0.19 | 0.15 |
| $\Delta Y < 0$ | 0.23 | 0.16 |
| | $\Delta Y < 0/\Delta Y = 0$ | |
| Loss of 1 million bbl/day | | |
| $\varepsilon = -0.1$ | 0.63 | 0.60 |
| $\varepsilon = -0.3$ | 0.62 | 0.55 |
| Loss of 2 million bbl/day | | |
| $\varepsilon = -0.1$ | 0.56 | 0.53 |
| $\varepsilon = -0.3$ | 0.67 | 0.55 |
| | Loss: 2 million bbl per day/ 1 million bbl per day | |
| Elasticity of demand: $\varepsilon = -0.1$ | | |
| $\Delta Y = 0$ | 3.2 | 3.0 |
| $\Delta Y < 0$ | 2.8 | 2.7 |
| Elasticity of demand: $\varepsilon = -0.3$ | | |
| $\Delta Y = 0$ | 2.2 | 2.2 |
| $\Delta Y < 0$ | 2.4 | 2.2 |

NOTE: $\varepsilon$ = demand price elasticity. $\Delta Y$ = change in income.
a. Each entry under this heading is the ratio of oil price increases resulting from the indicated alternative values of demand elasticity, change in income, and size of disruption.
b. As in note a, except that each entry is the ratio of oil expenditure increases.
SOURCE: Authors.

$-0.1$, increasing the shortfall roughly triples the price and expenditure increments; under elasticity of $-0.3$, the enlargement of the shortfall somewhat more than doubles the increases in $p$ and $E$.

One economic response that our simulations have not considered is the buildup or drawdown of oil inventories following the disruption. Drawdown could, of course, offset part or all of the 1- or

2-million-barrel-per-day shortfall. Firms might, however, add to their inventories as a result of their perception of increased uncertainty of future supply. The influence of adding to stockpiles during the crisis, although not treated in table 3, might be gleaned from the entries under the zero income effect. As a rough measure of the impact of stockpiling, these entries could be interpreted as generated by an income effect that is in fact nonzero but is exactly offset by an increased demand for inventories.

**Oil Price Drag.** A question separate from that of the magnitude of the transfer to oil producers in disruptions is the speed with which such transfers are restored to the economy at large. A number of economists, including the Council of Economic Advisers (CEA) during the Iranian crisis, have argued that oil industry delays in spending incremental revenues are considerable.[11] In view of low petroleum demand elasticities, even a moderate supply shortfall could thus create a serious general loss of purchasing power and deflationary adjustment in the nonpetroleum sectors of the economy. As in any such process, the loss of output, employment, and social surplus could be severe.

The temporary draining of funds from nonpetroleum goods markets, commonly called oil price drag, justified, in the opinion of the CEA, controls on oil prices during a disruption in order to limit the size of the transfer. In the *Economic Report of the President* published in January 1980, the CEA estimated that drag had been $53 billion in 1979 and would approach 3 percent of GNP in 1980, an amount equal to $79 billion in light of 1980's GNP of $2,633 billion.[12] Our independent estimates of the drag in 1979 and 1980 are $33 billion and $12 billion, respectively. In these years the U.S. average refinery acquisition cost of crude oil rose sharply—42 percent in 1979 and 58 percent in 1980. During the embargo period, we find drag to have been $11 billion in 1973 and $27 billion in 1974, years in which the crude acquisition cost rose 16 percent and 119 percent, respectively.[13]

These drag estimates, all of which we believe err on the high side, are all-inclusive in that they attempt to capture any tendency to divert funds from final product markets on the part of the domestic oil industry, foreign sellers of oil, and the U.S. government in its disposition of oil industry tax payments. There are several caveats, however, to be observed in interpreting the estimates: (1) More than two-thirds of the funds identified as withdrawn from nonpetroleum goods markets were spent on oil as an intermediate, not a final product (see note 17 below). Accordingly, the relative importance of the magnitudes is properly gauged by comparing them not to GNP but rather to total economic transactions, an amount at least twice the size of the GNP.

(2) The oil price drag estimates are gross figures that make no attempt to net out possible endogenous increases in private domestic spending.[14] (3) The oil price drag estimates do not, in any degree, represent additions to oil industry cash balances; rather the estimates pertain, for the most part, to funds diverted from goods to financial markets. There are three routes by which this diversion occurs: (1) the industry invests oil receipts directly in financial assets or, equivalently, in preexisting fixed assets (as opposed to currently produced goods and services); (2) a portion of domestic oil receipts is spent on oil imports, part of which creates a foreign trade imbalance, raises the exchange rate, and attracts foreign short-term capital; and (3) the industry channels oil receipts into tax payments that reduce government borrowing and release private saving for private investment, which, in the short run, is not wholly realized in expenditures on goods and services.

We provide details regarding the derivation of oil price drag in chapter 6. Chapter 6 will also support the use of monetary ease as an effective and efficient antidote to the adjustment costs, whether they are due to energy-induced relative price changes, to redistributions of income, or to oil price drag. We believe that monetary policy is superior to price controls as a means of lowering these costs. The evidence indicates that monetary authorities in the United States and other countries in the Organization for Economic Cooperation and Development (OECD) have tended to exacerbate the adjustment costs by imposing tight money during the oil disruption episodes.[15]

### The Free Market and Economic Efficiency

The hallmark of the free market is its ability to maximize efficiency: that is, for given levels of output, to minimize cost or, for given costs, to maximize the value of output. The basic mechanism by which the market accomplishes this end is the automatic processing and transmission of information, often on a colossal scale. The transmitting devices are, of course, prices, which reflect the assessments of all potential buyers and sellers. In a market subject to energy disruption, flexible prices are particularly important in signaling the vastly new optimal allocation of resources.

From a policy viewpoint, the essential consideration is that the information cannot be centralized.[16] Indeed, the relevant data are dispersed among millions of participants, any one or group of whom knows only what he, she, or it is directly involved in doing as a single producer or as the consumer of a limited number of products.

**Efficiency as Allocation to Most-Valued Uses.** In terms of our dia-

30

grammatic framework, market efficiency will assure that the uses from which oil is withdrawn are the least-valued ones, represented in figure 8 by the trapezoidal bar inscribed under the demand schedule between the marginal quantities $q_3$ and $q_4$ (which correspond to the same labeled quantities in figure 2). A nonoptimal withdrawal is illustrated by removing an equal but alternative crude oil quantity ($q_6 - q_5$), from its more valued application. The value of final product resulting from the use of ($q_6 - q_5$) is the area of the taller bar inscribed under the demand schedule along that interval. Withdrawal of the ($q_6 - q_5$) segment of crude oil, instead of ($q_4 - q_3$), costs the economy an amount of GNP equal to the difference in the areas of the two bars.

FIGURE 8

THE VALUE, IN TERMS OF FINAL PRODUCT PRODUCED, OF ALTERNATIVE
UNITS OF CRUDE OIL

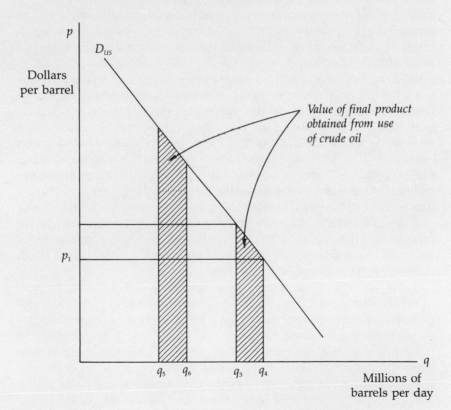

SOURCE: Authors.

31

Corresponding to that net loss of final product is a proportionate loss of social surplus.

Complicating the decision process is the fact that the use represented by the $(q_6 - q_5)$ oil segment not only is more valuable than that of $(q_4 - q_3)$ but is probably a different use than it was prior to the disruption. In view of the pervasive changes in relative energy and final product prices caused by the oil price rise, optimal allocation is likely to require that $(q_6 - q_5)$ be at least partially redirected within the production system.

The market reallocates oil from less valued uses to more valued uses by a bidding process in which those who have the greatest economic stake in the oil offer the highest prices. The highest bidders of petroleum products will tend to be those who drive farthest to their jobs, live in the coldest climates, meet the largest payrolls, or have the least postponable fuel-utilizing tasks, such as farmers who must harvest a seasonal crop. The bids of these individuals will be guided by the market value of their productive efforts, as measured by the height of the trapezoidal bars each generates by use of the oil. The process is one of self-selection, whereby each buyer assesses, as accurately as possible, the highest value that can be obtained from the oil and bids accordingly.

The ability to convert this assessed value into oil-buying power is not a function of the buyer's personal wealth, except where the petroleum is used personally as final product. Personal use is typified by petroleum sales to households for home temperature control and non–work-related driving. Such sales, however, account for less than one-third of total oil purchases.[17] Most petroleum is bought as input for intermediate stages of production. The value placed on these petroleum purchases, as reflected in the height of the trapezoidal bars, is determined by the sum of consumer expenditures on the final non-petroleum products. Any funding gaps between this ultimate source of value and the bidding for oil inputs will be bridged, under competitively supplied information, by the capital markets—that is, through current borrowing against future revenues.

The willingness of suppliers to reallocate petroleum to its new optimal uses springs from the changes in profit margins that accompany the changes in relative prices. The amounts involved need not be great. Even a one cent, or fraction of a cent, per gallon increase in the profit margin will typically attract crude oil to expanding uses or locations without delay. Although the very process of responding to the price and profit signals will eventually eliminate the profit differential, suppliers will not hesitate to seek and receive the greater return as long as it lasts.

**Efficiency as Less Energy-Intensive Methods of Production.** In the process of allocating energy to its most-valued uses, the market will also restructure production so as to employ less oil and less energy-utilizing techniques. The replacement of oil by cheaper alternative fuels and the gradual substitution of less energy-intensive capital will partially reverse the upward shifts of product supply curves (as in figure 5). On the part of both producers and consumers, economizing in the use of fuel will steadily increase the elasticity of the derived energy demand. This will be an ongoing, developing process.

*New York State surveys of transportation response.* The most detailed empirical account of the public reaction to energy disruption comes from a series of surveys of consumers in the 1979 oil shortfall conducted throughout the year by or for the New York State Department of Transportation.[18] In each of the surveys, households in New York State were queried on their transportation responses to gasoline shortages and gasoline price increases of the 1979 crisis. On the basis of the responses, calculations of the resulting gasoline savings were made from known relationships between transportation patterns and fuel use.

The findings, summarized in table 5, revealed a dramatic, diverse, and often unpredictable pattern of energy economizing that varied significantly over time, over demographic and income groups, and, to some extent, over regions of the state. The total saving of gasoline over the first nine and one-half months of 1979 was equal to the shortfall, estimated at almost 6 percent of normal consumption. With reference to table 5, 44 percent of the gasoline conserved was attributed to car-related actions, including reduced driving speeds (2 percent), more frequent tuneups (6 percent), the purchase of more fuel-efficient automobiles (20 percent), and the sale of less fuel-efficient vehicles (16 percent). Work-related responses accounted for 23 percent: the increased use of mass transit (13 percent), carpooling to work (8 percent), and walking and biking to work (2 percent). Of the saving in gasoline, 17 percent was reportedly accomplished by altered shopping patterns: by shopping closer to home (5 percent), by combining shopping with trips for other purposes, including work (6 percent), by shopping less frequently (3 percent), and by switching to mass transit (3 percent). Vacation-related behavior accounted for 13 percent of the decreased gasoline use: cancellation of a vacation trip (4 percent), vacationing closer to home (1 percent), and switching to bus, train, or plane for vacation trips (8 percent). Moves closer to work (1 percent) or taking a job closer to home (3 percent) explained 4 percent of the fuel saving.

33

## TABLE 5
### CONSUMER RESPONSE AND GASOLINE SAVED IN THE 1979 ENERGY CRISIS

| Action | Respondents (percent) | Gasoline Saved | |
|---|---|---|---|
| | | $10^6$ gal. | Percent |
| Work related | | | |
| Bus/subway to work | 12 | 37.0 | 13 |
| Carpool to work | 14 | 22.9 | 8 |
| Walk/bike to work | 8 | 5.5 | 2 |
| Total | | 65.4 | 23 |
| Shopping | | | |
| Shop closer to home | 41 | 13.1 | 5 |
| Combine shopping/other | 47 | 6.9 | 2 |
| Shop on way home from work | 25 | 10.6 | 4 |
| Shop less often | 35 | 7.7 | 3 |
| Bus/subway for nonwork | 15 | 8.2 | 3 |
| Total | | 46.5 | 17 |
| Car | | | |
| Tuneup | 37 | 17.6 | 6 |
| Drive slower | 42 | 5.9 | 2 |
| Buy a more fuel-efficient car | 15 | 57.8 | 20 |
| Sell a car (do not replace) | 8 | 47.3 | 16 |
| Total | | 128.6 | 44 |
| Vacation | | | |
| Cancel a vacation trip | 16 | 10.3 | 4 |
| Change mode for vacation | 16 | 22.5 | 8 |
| Vacation closer to home | 17 | 4.1 | 1 |
| Eliminate RV/boat | 9 | 1.2 | * |
| Total | | 38.1 | 13 |
| Moves | | | |
| Move closer to work | 3 | 3.4 | 1 |
| Job closer to home | 5 | 7.5 | 3 |
| Total | | 10.9 | 4 |
| Total savings | — | 289.5 | 100 |

NOTE: Savings per household was 46.0 gals. RV = recreational vehicle.
* = less than 0.5%.

SOURCE: D. Hartgen, "New York State's Perspective on Transportation Contingency Planning," in G. Horwich, ed., *Energy Use in Transportation Contingency Planning*, p. 605, table 3.

After the first ninety days of the onset of the disruption, reduced travel accounted for 46 percent of the fuel saving; after one year, respondents attributed only 15 percent of the fuel saving to traveling less. Improved fuel efficiency of the automobile fleet appears to have achieved 11 percent of the saving after ninety days and 42 percent after one year. The saving share of all other responses was constant at 43 percent at both points in time.[19]

None of these responses, including the reduction in mobility, is indicative of a free market, since elaborate crude oil and gasoline controls were in force in 1979. Nevertheless, households were responding to higher costs, whether in the form of higher petroleum product prices or nonprice allocation mechanisms. It may be that the sharply reduced mobility of the early months of the disruption could have been avoided by freer price movements in place of nonprice methods, such as early station closings, weekend closings, and queuing, all of which increase the uncertainty of supply and tend to discourage travel outright.

No one anticipated the large role in saving fuel accomplished by turnover of the automobile fleet. The purchase of more fuel-efficient vehicles was, of course, a response characteristic of higher-income households, but it and the sale of old inefficient cars were credited with 36 percent of the reduced gasoline use for the year as a whole.[20] Households earning less than $10,000 per year achieved most of their conservation by other car-related actions not associated with work travel. Altogether, this group accounted for only 10–12 percent of the total fuel saving.

Increased use of mass transit, largely for work-related trips, accounted for 31 percent of New York City's savings. Only 4 percent of fuel saving was effected in this way upstate, where 45 percent of the total state conservation effort took place. Men and women were about equally responsible for fuel saving in all regions, with men concentrating on work travel and women on shopping trips. The elderly neither consumed nor saved much energy. Households with more than two cars are credited with half of the total conservation accomplished in New York State in 1979.

One of the most significant conclusions drawn by the authors of the report summarizing the New York State surveys is that the role of government in achieving energy saving was neither particularly effective nor well targeted:

Perhaps the primary observation from this analysis is the extensiveness and internal rationality of consumer actions to conserve transportation energy. New York residents did respond significantly to the 1979 energy crisis and saved more than 6 percent of the total gasoline used in the first three quarters of 1979 through a variety of actions that cut across all facets of travel. . . .

Contrary to government pressure and exhortations, consumer saving is not accounted for primarily by carpooling, transit, slower driving, or by cuts in discretionary travel. . . .

Most conservation occurred through car-related actions, particularly fuel-efficient car purchasing and car selling. . . .

Consumer actions were generally independent of government directives. . . . government suggestions and efforts to encourage conservation have been narrow and ineffective. . . . the role of government at all levels should be to expand options and make them available to people rather than to constrain and coerce behavior.

Narrow governmental focus solely on transit and ridesharing is unproductive because it encourages actions that in total save little energy and constrain mobility.[21]

More recently, the authors surveyed studies of consumer response in other parts of the country and during the 1973–1974 crisis.[22] There are wide regional differences in the responses to an oil disruption. In the earlier episode, mass transit did not play an important role, even in regions where it was available. A major shift to more fuel-efficient cars did not materialize. Nevertheless, households with high levels of automobile ownership and income do most of the early conserving. In a crisis five years from now, the authors anticipate that the same group will again be poised for a shift to a new generation of more fuel-efficient automobiles and will take the option. In the nearer future, middle- and lower-income households are more likely to improve their fleet efficiency in a disruption.

*Indiana study of energy use in space heating.* A very carefully controlled study of the use of energy for home heating by two rural Indiana communities during the 1973–1974 disruption was conducted by two Purdue University economists.[23] One community was served by natural gas, whose controlled price rose 9 percent during the winter of 1973–1974. The other community, without access to natural gas, relied on liquefied petroleum (LP) gas, whose price rose a net 60 percent during the same period. Allowing for changes in the temperature between the winters of 1972–1973 and 1973–1974, the authors found that the users of LP gas achieved a 14.4 percent increase, and users of natural gas a 5.8 percent increase, in the number of days for which one unit of their respective fuels provided heat.

*The least-cost energy strategy.* Research of the Energy Productivity

Center of the Mellon Institute provides a basis for generalizing to other sectors the kind of energy economizing observed in transportation in New York State.[24] Although the center's findings were concerned with longer-run opportunities for improved energy efficiency, rather than with energy contingency planning, they are relevant to a contingency, since they rely wholly on existing or known technologies. Many of these technologies, like improved automobile fuel efficiency, are developing continuously and can, in many instances, be disseminated at a sharply accelerated rate in response to relative price changes (as was automobile fuel efficiency by turnover of the fleet in New York State in 1979).

Roger Sant, the center's director, outlines a "least-cost energy strategy" that stresses conservation in the delivery of energy services by using less energy rather than by reducing the quantity of services. An example of this strategy is the economizing of fuel in transportation in New York State without loss of mobility. Sant estimates that by restructuring the U.S. fuel delivery system toward cheaper and well-known substitute technologies, the level of energy services seen in the late 1970s could be delivered with 22 percent less energy.[25]

In the household sector, the center refers to established techniques, such as increased use of insulation, often available immediately through relatively simple methods; installation of storm windows; purchase of more energy-efficient appliances; and the replacement of direct electric heating by electric heat pumps, which use 50 percent less electricity, and by gas heat pumps and gas furnaces.

In industry, since 1973, there has been a greater use of high-temperature energy, which can perform a wider range of services—for example, both melting steel and boiling water—than lower-temperature sources; recuperators, which, when attached to steel heat-treating furnaces, recycle otherwise unutilized heat; cogeneration, which recycles hot exhaust fumes and excess steam to increase the production of electricity; more fuel-efficient boilers and furnaces; and variable-speed electric motors.[26]

In transportation, there is little opportunity for substitution of alternative fuels under existing technology, but there exists scope for improved traffic systems, better matching of vehicles to the trip's purpose, attainment of higher load factors for passengers and freight (to a large degree simply through deregulation of regulated sectors), and continued increase of automobile and truck fuel efficiency through weight reduction, power-train improvement, and greater use of diesel engines. The greatest opportunities for energy economizing, in the center's view, lie in the buildings sector, where serious retrofitting of both residential and commercial structures (including the use of co-generation) has only just begun.[27]

The least-cost energy strategy identifies numerous possibilities for energy saving by reallocating the various energy sources among and within sectors. In a hypothetical global blueprint, there would be an increased market share for natural gas and sharply reduced shares for oil and electricity and less direct use of coal.[28]

The center's research goal is not to make any specific proposals for energy use but only to illustrate what it regards as the potential for energy saving within the existing technology and the apparent dictates of relative prices. Only the free market can actually implement least-cost energy use, responding to the signals of an uncontrolled relative price system. The primary task of government thus should be to remove impediments to free pricing, as in natural gas at the well head, at the pipeline, and at the retail distribution level. The center sees potential for the evolution of unregulated utilities, both gas and electric, and of other dealers in energy services beyond the narrow marketing of their specific products:

> The most natural providers of energy services are the public utilities, the fuel oil dealers and, perhaps, even the gasoline stations. If a gas utility, for instance, were allowed to be a seller of all energy services, not just a seller of natural gas, it could compete with the electric utilities or the fuel oil dealers in providing the total energy service requirements for a home. In addition to gas, the utility could provide cost-effective building modifications, efficiency improvements in the furnace and a more efficient water heater. Structural improvements, such as insulation and storm windows, could be provided through subcontractors. The cost of such improvements could then be billed to the customer monthly over their 20-year lifetime, just as gas is now billed. Electric utilities, fuel oil dealers, and independent manufacturers and contractors could provide competition, assuring the availability of least-cost service to the customer. As new technologies develop, such as gas-fired heat pumps or fuel cells, the utility could offer these additional options to the customer. Other segments of the private sector, such as insulation and furnace contractors, or manufacturers of more efficient furnaces, would compete to provide needed repairs or installations to the utility, or compete directly with the utility in providing services to the customer.[29]

From the viewpoint of contingency planning, the important conclusions to be drawn from the Energy Productivity Center's research are several.

1. The market's response to the energy price increases of the 1970s, even though constrained by price ceilings and innumerable regulations, was considerable. Sant observes that U.S. energy use and the growth of output were effectively "decoupled" after the 1973–1974 disruption. In the post–World War II period (1950–1970), total U.S. energy use and real GNP grew at about the same rate, 3.5 percent per year. From 1973 to 1978, energy consumption rose at 0.8 percent per year, less than one-third of the 2.8 percent annual increase of real GNP. For the entire 1973–1980 period, energy consumption rose only 0.2 percent per year, whereas the average annual increase in real GNP was 2.3 percent. The drop in the relative increase of energy use is explained by a 73 percent rise in the index of real energy prices at the end-user level, a price rise that immediately set in motion short-run and longer-run adaptive responses.[30]

2. An uncontrolled market promises to increase the variety of available alternatives for the production, delivery, and use of energy, greatly increasing the range of potential energy-saving responses under emergency conditions. In addition to the findings of the Energy Productivity Center, there is evidence in urban transportation, for example, of emerging market forces entailing new methods of financing, managing, and delivering urban transportation services. Employers, employees, and third parties are experimenting with new systems involving buses, car and van pools, commuter clubs, jitneys, micro or mini automobiles, automobile rental and charter arrangements, vehicle subscription services, and cooperatives centered on homes, neighborhoods, and places of work. These developments are a response to some deregulatory initiatives (in passenger rail, bus, and jitney service) and the simultaneous decline in U.S. urban population density (50 percent since 1950) and in the relative size and importance of publicly owned transit systems.[31]

3. The Energy Productivity Center, like the New York State Department of Transportation, gives low grades to government at all levels in its ability to mandate fuel-efficient conservation standards for the public. Government regulations are simply not based on cost-benefit criteria. No one in fact can determine the cost-beneficial responses independently of prices. With price flexibility, government mandates tend at best to be superfluous and at worst to be counterproductive. In the center's view, government places too much of the conservation burden on transportation; by imposing price controls

and mandatory allocations government also obscures the true opportunity cost of energy and inhibits efficient responses by the private sector—and, one might add, by government itself as an energy user.

## A Macro Synthesis

A final perspective on the oil supply disruption is provided by the aggregate supply-and-demand framework. The aggregate schedules are particularly useful for summarizing the GNP and general price-level effects that have been discussed throughout the chapter.

**Aggregate Supply and Demand.** The schedules appear in figure 9. The real GNP of the economy ($Q$) is measured along the horizontal axis, and the GNP deflator ($P$), an index of all final product prices, along the vertical axis. Aggregate supply ($AS$) and aggregate demand ($AD$) resemble their micro counterparts in that they have the customary upward and downward slope, respectively. They are not, however, obtained by simply taking the horizontal sum of all individual market supplies and demands. The latter, of course, are functions of their individual relative prices, not of the average or general price level. Nevertheless, for many purposes, aggregate supply and demand can be treated as representative prototypical market schedules.

Aggregate supply indicates, at each real GNP produced, the average marginal cost or supply price of that level of output. The schedule takes as given the whole spectrum of nominal resource prices, the size of the capital stock, and the existing technology involved in combining resources. Each of the following changes will cause aggregate supply to shift to the right or, equivalently, to drop vertically: a reduction in average resource prices, an increase in the capital stock, an improvement or increase in technology, and an increase in the mobility of resources.

Aggregate demand relates a little less directly to individual product demands. The schedule is the sum, at each price level, of the major expenditure components, which have already undergone aggregation: consumption, investment, government outlays, and net exports. More precisely, each point on the schedule is the level of real GNP at which, for the given price level, the sum of expenditures is equal to the GNP. Aggregate demand will shift to the right in response to increases in the autonomous component of consumption, investment, government, and net foreign expenditures; decreases in the autonomous component of tax receipts; increases in the quantity or rate of growth of the money supply; and decreases in the demand for money.

## FIGURE 9

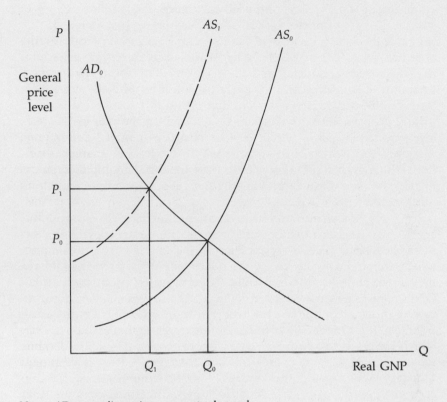

NOTE: $AD_0$ = predisruption aggregate demand.
$AS_0$ = predisruption aggregate supply.
$AS_1$ = immediate postdisruption aggregate supply.

SOURCE: Authors.

The initial pair of schedules drawn in figure 9, $AS_0$ and $AD_0$, intersect at a price level $P_0$ and real GNP $Q_0$.

**The Oil Supply Disruption.** An oil supply disruption, as we have defined it, is an increase in the price of crude oil accompanied by a decrease in the quantity of petroleum demanded. This phenomenon translates into reduced inputs of petroleum products and higher production costs of virtually every final product contained in the GNP. In figure 9, higher marginal costs of production are reflected in higher

41

supply price levels at every output, shown as an upward shift of aggregate supply from $AS_0$ to $AS_1$. The new price level, at the intersection of $AS_1$ and $AD_0$, is higher at $P_1$, and real GNP is lower at $Q_1$.

The rise in the price level may be regarded as resulting from either the upward vertical or the leftward horizontal shift of aggregate supply. The sense of the vertical shift, as we have just stated, is that the price level rises because of the rise in oil prices and final product marginal costs. The sense of the horizontal shift is that the price level rises because of a reduction in both the input of oil and the quantity of final output produced at all price levels while aggregate demand, in the schedule sense, is unchanged. Both interpretations, of course, are valid, and both stress the supply-side source of the rise in the price level and fall in real GNP. The degree to which $AS$ shifts depends on the uses from which oil is withdrawn. If, under free market conditions, the marginal, or least-valued, uses are curtailed and oil remains in or gravitates to its most-valued uses, the leftward shift of $AS$ is minimized.

Aggregate demand and its components will also be reduced, but apart from the complication of oil price drag and reductions in investment because of uncertainty about the composition of future demand, which we shall discuss below, demand falls only in the sense of a movement along the $AD$ schedule. The fall in the production of real GNP, reflected in the leftward shift of $AS$, reduces real income received and thereby the level of real consumption expenditures along $AD$. Real investment falls as the decline in income reduces real saving, which lowers investment by raising interest rates. The fall in income reduces general tax revenues and automatically raises government transfer payments and other outlays. These changes increase the government deficit, raise interest rates, and reduce investment further (although for some combinations of the predisruption deficit and oil price increase, the deficit could be eliminated by the resulting increase in windfall profit and other tax revenues from the oil industry). Although government spending is higher, it is not high enough, under normal parametric values, to prevent the sum of all expenditure categories from falling, as indicated by the downward slope of $AD$.

**The Adjustment Process.** The phases of the adjustment, described earlier, appear in the aggregate supply-and-demand setting as follows:

1. When the rise in the price of oil spreads to substitute energy sources, the price of oil dips (or rises less) and the loss of oil is partially replaced by supplies of alternatives. As we have noted, the substitution entails a compensating dampening in the overall price of

42

energy and a reduction in the absolute and relative loss of energy supply. Hence *AS* shifts to the right, as drawn in figure 10, partially reversing its initial move to the left.

2. The changed relative prices of final product substitutes and complements and the changes in the distribution of income inspire shifts among product demands. The result, as we have seen, is a temporary loss of real GNP and an increase in the average product

FIGURE 10

THE IMPACT ON AGGREGATE SUPPLY AND DEMAND OF (1) THE SPILLOVER OF THE OIL PRICE RISE TO SUBSTITUTE ENERGY SOURCES, (2) DEMAND SHIFTS AMONG PRODUCT MARKETS DUE TO CHANGES IN RELATIVE PRICES AND IN THE DISTRIBUTION OF INCOME, (3) OIL PRICE DRAG AND THE ACCOMPANYING INCREASE IN THE DEMAND FOR MONEY, AND (4) ENERGY SAVING THROUGH MARKET EFFICIENCY ADJUSTMENTS

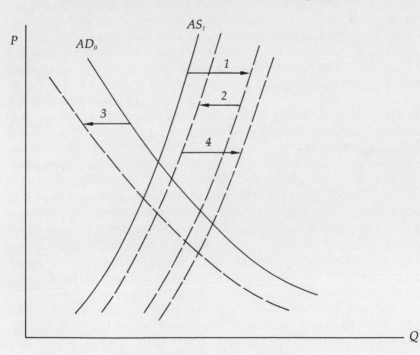

NOTE: $AD_0$ = predisruption aggregate demand.
      $AS_1$ = immediate postdisruption aggregate supply.
SOURCE: Authors.

price, as illustrated in figure 7. Although the changes in GNP and the price level are initiated by individual demand shifts, the demand decrease in one market is offset by a demand increase in an alternative market, and the aggregate demand schedule is assumed unchanged. The price and output changes diagrammed in figure 7 are in fact captured by shifting the aggregate supply schedule to the left. As such a shift makes clear, at any average of product prices (say, $p_0^b$ and $p_0^a$ in figure 7), the combined output is less as a result of the movement between markets. Alternatively, at any given output (say, $q_1^a$ plus $q_0^b$ in figure 7), the average supply price is higher following the shift of demands.

3. Oil price drag, the temporary siphoning of funds from domestic nonpetroleum goods markets, implies that, on average, money is turning over against goods more slowly. In terms of the macro framework, there is an increase in the demand for money accompanied by a decrease in aggregate demand. The slowing down of goods purchases could also result in a decrease in the quantity of money if, as seems likely in the circumstances, bank loans are simultaneously paid off. In either event, $AD$ shifts to the left, as indicated in figure 10.

4. The energy-saving transportation measures taken in 1979, as described by the New York State Department of Transportation, and the actual and potential parallel activity in all sectors over a longer period of time, as outlined by the Energy Productivity Center, increase the elasticity of energy demand. In an unregulated market, this demand response exerts downward pressure on energy prices and reverses some of the initial leftward shift of aggregate supply due to the energy shock. In figure 10, $AS$ is shown shifting to the right.

The net effect on $P$ and $Q$ of these shifts in aggregate supply and demand cannot be anticipated a priori, nor are there empirical estimates of the magnitude of the separate shifts with the exception of that caused by oil price drag, which we derive in chapter 6. Estimates of the combined effect on $P$ and $Q$ of the forces acting on $AS$, however, focusing on the rise in the price of oil and energy in general, are available and are summarized in the following section. All such estimates that are based—properly, in our view—on the supply-side interpretation of the oil shock, confirm a net inflationary and real GNP-depressing impact. Such indeed was the outcome of the 1973–1974 and 1979–1980 disruptions, although they occurred in an energy-regulated and controlled environment. Controls, of course, would tend to increase the initial leftward shift of $AS$ (figure 9) by impeding the removal of oil from least-valued uses, limiting the spillover of oil price increases to alternative sources (particularly controlled natural gas and electricity), reducing the magnitude of the rightward shift 1 of $AS$

(figure 10), and restraining the energy-saving efficiency adjustments summarized in rightward shift 4 of $AS$ (figure 10). The net supply-side effect of controls is thus to exacerbate the increase in $P$ and the decrease in $Q$. If oil price drag is present, however, price controls may succeed in reducing it, thereby curtailing the leftward shift of $AD$ (shift 3 in figure 10) and raising both $P$ and $Q$. The paradox of energy price ceilings is thus that by reducing the total output of the economy or reducing oil price drag, they raise the general price level and, through widespread indexing, the tendency to future inflation.

**Numerical Estimates of GNP, Price Level, and Employment Effects.** Among empirically based estimates of the macro effects of oil supply disruption, the Federal Reserve Bank of St. Louis employs an aggregate supply-and-demand framework compatible with our own.[32] The impact of disruption, however, is measured by a single reduced-form equation in which the overall index of relative energy prices is entered as an independent variable, along with the utilized capital stock and labor force hours of employment. The dependent variable is output of the private business sector. In the two major disruption periods, third quarter 1973 to third quarter 1974 and fourth quarter 1978 to second quarter 1980, in each of which real energy prices rose 40 percent, the resulting fall in business output is estimated to have been 3.7 percent. In the later episode, the capital-labor ratio is estimated as having fallen 5.3 percent as a result of the energy price rise, reducing productivity. The fall in business output implies an elasticity of output with respect to the relative price of energy of $-0.09$.

The estimated price-level elasticity with respect to the relative energy price is 0.09, which implies that three to four percentage points of the rise in the GNP deflator were sparked by the energy price increase. This amount is roughly one-third of the double-digit inflation rates of the two disruption episodes. Energy price increases do not otherwise play a significant causal role with respect to inflation in the 1970s. Thus although energy prices rose on other occasions during the decade, the increases appear to have been an effect, not a cause, of general inflationary forces.

The adjustment to the higher relative price of energy takes six quarters. In the new equilibrium, real GNP is 3 percent lower and the price level is 3 percent higher than they would have otherwise been. These are the permanent changes. In the first two quarters of the transition following the energy shock, GNP falls less than 3 percent, then falls at a greater rate and, in the sixth quarter, rises rather sharply to the level of its permanent decline. During the transition, the price level tends to be affected less than its permanent change. The unemployment rate attributable to the energy price increase in 1974–1975 is, first, a reduction of 0.5 percentage points, followed by a rise of 1.7 percentage points. In 1979–1980 the unemployment rate is lowered 0.3 percentage points in the first year and is raised 0.3 percentage points in the second year. This pattern of alternating unemployment rates reflects a substitution (and increased employment) of labor for energy-intensive capital in the early stages, followed by a decline in all factor inputs as the GNP downturn accelerates and dominates employment decisions.

These estimates are based on the actual events of the 1970s, including, of course, the regulated energy environment. Several attempts have been made to measure the effect of controls. A team led by David Couts in 1978, employing a theoretical framework consistent with that of aggregate supply and demand, estimated that a 4-million-barrel-per-day petroleum shortfall (22 percent of U.S. consumption) lasting one year would, in the absence of price and allocation controls, reduce real GNP 4.4 percent and, with controls in place, between 5.5 and 15.8 percent (depending on the design and enforcement of the controls).[33]

A 1979 simulation study by George Schink for the Department of Energy found the GNP losses of a net 3.95-million-barrel-per-day oil shortfall to be 7.7 percent without controls and 8.6 percent with them.[34] Schink's estimate is consistent with a 1980 study by the Congressional Budget Office, which projects, for petroleum shortfalls of 1 million, 2 million, 3 million, 4 million, and 5 million barrels per day, each lasting for one year in a decontrolled environment, simultaneous losses of real GNP of 1.6 percent, 3.6 percent, 5.5 percent, 7.5 percent, and 9.4 percent, respectively.[35]

Knut Mork, using an improved version of a model developed earlier by Hall and Mork,[36] simulates the effects of a 10-million-barrel-per-day worldwide disruption lasting one year.[37] The supply of oil is gradually restored over a four-year period; the loss to the United States is about one-third of the world shortfall. The oil market is completely decontrolled. The percentage drops in U.S. real GNP in the year of the disruption and the following two years are −7.9, −4.1, and −2.8, respectively. The price level changes 5.7, 0.0, and −0.3 percentage points in successive years. Unemployment rises by 3.0, 0.7, and 0.2 percentage points. Nominal energy prices rise 35.3, 16.9, and 5.1 percent.

In 1982 prices, the losses of real GNP in successive years are $251 billion, $133 billion, and $94 billion. The percentage decline in real investment is −28.2, −14.6, and −10.4, or in 1982 prices, $206 billion,

$116 billion, and $90 billion. Real consumption falls −1.6 percent each year; in 1982 dollars, by $31 billion, $31 billion, and $32 billion. The total economic cost of the disruption to the United States, in terms of the present value of lost consumption during the current year and all future years, is, in 1982 prices, $539 billion. Mork attributes about three-fourths of the losses in real GNP and its components to adjustment costs and the remainder to reduced productive capacity of the economy.

Gilbert and Mork describe circumstances under which oil price controls could both lower the inflation rate and raise real GNP by shifting aggregate supply to the right.[38] Both the domestic oil supply and the supply of oil imports must be absolutely inelastic. In that event, a ceiling price below the market-clearing price of oil would have no effect on the quantity of oil supplied and would serve to reduce production costs and to lower the *AS* curve. There are two profound difficulties, however, with this outcome, of which Gilbert and Mork are aware: (1) Since the price of oil is held below market clearing, the resulting shortage (excess demand) requires that the supply be allocated by mandatory rules or by ad hoc and impromptu procedures. In neither case is the oil likely to find its most-valued uses. The resulting allocational inefficiencies could easily reverse the downward shift of *AS* created by the artificially lower price of oil. (2) Although import supply could be quite inelastic in the several weeks during which a disruption is actually occurring, this condition will not last. The highly competitive and efficient world tanker market will rapidly restore the normal state of affairs: highly elastic supply at the world price, whatever its level, to individual buyers almost anywhere in the world. A price ceiling on both domestic and imported oil will thus cause not only the usual attrition of domestic supply over time but, in an even shorter run, the complete loss of imports.[39]

**Policy Implications.** The macro perspective on oil supply disruptions directly indicates a number of policy prescriptions:

1. Since the disruption is essentially a supply-side disturbance, causing aggregate supply to shift to the left, the most efficient policy measures are those that tend to shift *AS* back to the right. Such measures would raise real GNP while lowering the price level. Policies aimed at raising aggregate demand above its predisturbance level would, at best, raise the price level further while raising real GNP. In fact, net upward movements of demand, designed to offset the loss of oil, are likely to encounter a relatively steep *AS* path owing to the dislocation and numerous adjustments imposed on markets by the oil

shock. The major impact of an increase in aggregate demand is thus likely to be to raise the price level with very little positive effect on output.

2. The most efficient responses to the disruption are those that lower the price of oil by replacing the lost oil with additional supplies. Replacement can be accomplished effectively in the short run by the use of public and private stockpiles of oil and other fuels. We believe that the most promising approach in this regard is the development of a large publicly sponsored strategic petroleum reserve, the subject of chapter 4. Stockpiles of other fuels such as natural gas, however, can also play a role as a reserve energy source. We have noted that additional supplies of any energy source will, to some degree, substitute for oil and shift AS back to the right.

3. Attempts to prevent the price of oil from rising by imposing ceilings are, as we have seen, counterproductive in that they prevent oil from finding its most-valued uses, thereby shifting AS farther to the left. Ceilings, by creating excess demand for oil, will also increase the price rise of alternatives to oil, among both energy and nonenergy goods.

4. In principle, the oil-induced leftward shift of AS can be offset by reducing nonoil marginal costs of production, the largest of which are labor. Mork, alone and with Hall and Gilbert, has stressed the importance of reducing payroll taxes early in a disruption as a very efficient way to counter the rise in energy costs.[40] The effect would be to maintain the employment level by accelerating the substitution of labor for energy. Our preliminary assessment of this policy option in chapter 6 leads us to doubt that it would be well targeted; that is, the benefit of payroll tax reductions would frequently go to firms whose energy costs are an extremely small percentage of their total costs. For such firms, a temporary reduction in labor costs, conferred by the tax cut, would appear unlikely to justify an expansion of the work force in disruption circumstances. The reduction in payroll taxes would simply yield a temporary windfall of no net social value. The Mork-Hall-Gilbert model, we believe, is not adequately sectored between more and less energy- and labor-intensive firms to detect the lack of targeting.

5. We believe an easing of monetary policy can greatly facilitate the adjustment to an oil supply disruption. If there is oil price drag, which is manifested in an overall increase in the demand for money (or, as suggested above, in a decrease in the quantity of money), an increase in the supply of money is the most direct and flexible antidote. This response is not to be confused with policies aimed at creating a net increase in aggregate demand, which are generally inappro-

priate in a supply disruption. In the context of oil price drag, monetary expansion is designed to offset a possible downward shift of aggregate demand; that is, to stabilize the $AD$ schedule. This subject will be discussed in greater detail in chapter 6. We shall also argue there that monetary ease, shifting $AD$ on net somewhat to the right, can be justified as an offset to the loss of output caused by the shift of demand between individual product markets (and manifested, as noted above, in a leftward shift of the $AS$ schedule). In this case, a slight rise in the inflation rate helps relative prices adjust in the face of nominal price rigidity, such as downwardly sticky nominal wages for labor.

## Summary

The costs imposed by an oil supply disruption are identified in the market for crude oil, a factor of production, as a loss of real GNP produced and an increase in foreign claims to GNP. This GNP loss includes the traditional social surplus measure of economic loss: the loss of the excess of consumers' valuation (demand price) over market price plus the excess of market price over producers' cost (supply price). All three components—the loss of final product, the increase of foreign claims to final product, and the loss of social surplus—are identified in the market for a representative final product.

In addition to these direct costs of the oil supply disruption, there are indirect or adjustment costs incurred in moving from the predisruption equilibrium to the postdisruption equilibrium. The first response is actually a reduction of costs, which occurs when the higher price of oil spreads to alternative energy sources. The effect is to reduce the absolute and relative loss of energy as a whole and to moderate the increase in the price of oil.

The rise in energy prices increases the prices of all final products in accordance with their relative use of energy and their demand elasticities. This restructuring of final product relative prices upsets the relationships among commodities and induces a broadly based shift of demands among product markets as consumers reestablish compatible relative prices and quantities among substitutes and complements. In the short run, output falls in contracting markets, with little fall in price; price rises in expanding markets, with little rise in output. On net, total product output is down, the average of product prices is up, and social surplus is lower.

Further shifts among product demands result from the transfer of income from consumers to oil producers. Another cost in this transfer arises if there are significant delays in restoring oil industry receipts to the economy at large. Such delays could impose a temporary but serious loss of purchasing power in nonpetroleum product markets. Our estimates of this so-called oil price drag for the disruption period 1979–1980 are considerably less than those of the Council of Economic Advisers during that episode. The derivation of our estimates for the entire decade is presented in chapter 6, along with a defense of monetary ease as the appropriate antidote to oil price drag. The CEA had proposed oil price ceilings as a way of containing the drag.

A free market in oil, in disrupted or nondisrupted periods, offers the best opportunity for achieving economic efficiency. The market, operating through relative prices, allows decisions to be made by buyers and sellers who are intimately involved in consumption and production and possess the most detailed and comprehensive information about oil's most-valued uses.

Following a disruption, the market will restructure the delivery of energy services in the direction of less energy-utilizing techniques. Surveys conducted by and for the New York State Department of Transportation in 1979 reveal that 44 percent of reduced gasoline use was accomplished by car-related actions (involving the maintenance, driving speed, and fuel efficiency of cars). The most significant such action was, surprisingly, the purchase of new, more fuel-efficient automobiles and the sale of old, less efficient ones. Households owning more than two cars were responsible for half of the state's total conservation effort. Reduced travel accounted for almost half of the fuel saving in the first ninety days but only 15 percent after one year. A study of rural Indiana households during 1973–1974 showed an efficiency response in the use of heating fuels that varied directly with the rise in each fuel's price.

The least-cost energy strategy, drawn up by the Energy Productivity Center of the Mellon Institute, indicates that the level of energy services economywide in the late 1970s could be delivered using 22 percent less energy, under known techniques. The relevance of this study for contingency planning is that it suggests for all sectors the broad range of price-directed market options, involving energy use, that are available and can often be tapped on relatively short notice.

In an aggregate supply-and-demand macro framework, the loss of oil and its higher price cause a leftward shift of the supply schedule. Free market responses, including the increase in alternative energy prices and outputs and the emergence of energy-saving technologies, shift aggregate supply back to the right. The changed structure of relative product prices and the changed distribution of income cause a shift of demands among product markets and a temporary leftward shift of aggregate supply. Oil price drag appears as a leftward shift of aggregate demand. The most plausible simulations of the macro impacts of oil supply disruptions suggest a greater loss of real GNP under controls than in an uncontrolled energy environment.

The most efficient policy responses to an oil disruption are those that act to reverse the leftward shift of aggregate supply. Drawdown of public and private oil stockpiles will have such an effect. Reduction of payroll taxes, although acting positively on aggregate supply, does not appear to be well targeted with respect to the distribution of energy costs among firms. A moderate expansion of the monetary growth rate is proposed as the most promising countermeasure to oil price drag and to leftward shifts of aggregate supply due to intermarket shifts of product demand.

# Notes

1. The appropriate measure of total product is net national product. In the context of the present analysis, however, net and gross national product will change equally, and we shall use the terms interchangeably.

2. The world price, at which total world supply and demand are equal, is also a price at which a positive U.S. excess demand $(q_4 - q_1)$ is matched by an equal excess supply in the rest of the world. Algebraically, where ROW denotes the rest of the world, we write the equality of world supply and demand:

$$S_{ROW} + S_{US} = D_{ROW} + D_{US}$$

Rearranging terms yields

$$S_{ROW} - D_{ROW} = D_{US} - S_{US}$$

3. The relevant costs are not only those involved in extracting oil from the ground but also the revenue in future periods forgone as a result of producing oil—from finite pools—in the current period. The latter, called user cost, is the present value of the forgone future revenues and is not, unlike extraction costs, reflected in current outlays on factors of any kind.

4. Although U.S. oil imports give rise, in the first instance, to additional receipts of foreign oil producers, the exchange rate will shift so as to create a generalized claim on U.S. goods and services that any foreigner, not just oil producers, can exercise.

5. The use of consumers' and producers' surplus is well grounded in microeconomic theory. Its practical application is somewhat clouded, for example, because of changes in income and the distribution of income, which, following disturbances, tend to shift the demand schedule. This tendency creates before and after geometric areas neither of which clearly measures the change in surplus. For a discussion of these issues and others and a defense of social surplus as a good first approximation to welfare, see A. C. Harberger, "Three Basic Postulates for Applied Welfare," *Journal of Economic Literature*, vol.

9, no. 3 (September 1971), pp. 785–97. For the possible relationship between social surplus and welfare in terms of revealed preference, see Robert D. Willig, "Consumer's Surplus without Apology," *American Economic Review*, vol. 65, no. 4 (September 1976), pp. 589–97.

6. At the initial values of $q = 15 \times 10^6$ and $p = 30$, $c = 21.0767 \times 10^6$.

7. The assumption that there are incremental additions to output, each valued by the corresponding price on the final product demand schedule, in fact underlies the derivation of the crude oil demand schedule. See the discussion involving the schedule $D_{US}$ in figure 1.

8. Elasticity is equal to $(\partial q/\partial p)$ $(p/q)$, where the derivative is the slope of a schedule with respect to the vertical $(p)$ axis at a given price $(p)$ and quantity $(q)$. The derivative can also be written as $\partial p/\partial q)^{-1}$, which is the reciprocal of the slope relative to the horizontal $(q)$ axis. For any given level of elasticity, the greater is $q$, as in the case of multiple energy sources, the greater is the absolute slope with respect to the vertical axis and the less is the slope relative to the horizontal axis.

9. See Douglas R. Bohi, *Analyzing Demand Behavior: A Study of Energy Elasticities* (Baltimore: Johns Hopkins University Press, 1981), chap. 5 and p. 159 (summary table), for the range of price elasticities for petroleum products.

10. See ibid., chap. 5.

11. Edward R. Fried and Charles L. Schultze, "Overview," in Fried and Schultze, eds., *Higher Oil Prices and the World Economy* (Washington, D.C.: Brookings Institution, 1975), pp. 3–5; Council of Economic Advisers, *Economic Report of the President* (Washington, D.C., January 1980), pp. 29, 51, 64–65, and 163–64. See also the discussion in George Horwich, "Government Contingency Planning for Petroleum-Supply Interruptions: A Macroperspective," in G. Horwich and E. J. Mitchell, eds., *Policies for Coping with Oil-Supply Disruptions* (Washington, D.C.: American Enterprise Institute, 1982), pp. 33–65.

12. Council of Economic Advisers, *Economic Report of the President*, pp. 64–65. The CEA places the drag for 1980 at $24 billion but adds that it will rise to 3 percent of the GNP by the end of the year. There is no indication, however, that these drag estimates anticipated, or could have been based upon, the very substantial oil price increases that in fact occurred throughout 1980. The CEA's estimates of the drag would apparently have been much higher if the price increases had been known and taken into account.

13. Although the price increase in 1973 was relatively small, the possibility for drag lies in the fact that U.S. consumption of oil rose in 1973 by 5.4 percent, reflecting a net increase in demand. In contrast, consumption fell in the supply-disrupted years: −4.3 percent in 1974, −2.3 percent in 1979, and −8.8 percent in 1980.

14. See George Horwich, "Government Contingency Planning for Petroleum-Supply Interruptions," p. 42.

15. For a summary of monetary growth rates during the disruption periods, see R. W. Hafer, "The Impact of Energy Prices and Money Growth on Five Industrial Countries," *Federal Reserve Bank of St. Louis Review*, March 1981, pp. 19–26. For references to the nonaccommodating posture of monetary

policy in 1973–1974, see R. M. Solow, "What to Do (Macroeconomically) When OPEC Comes," in S. Fischer, ed., *Rational Expectations and Economic Policy* (Chicago: University of Chicago Press, 1980), p. 263; and E. S. Phelps, "Commodity-Supply Shock and Full-Employment Monetary Policy," *Journal of Money, Credit, and Banking,* vol. 10, no. 2 (May 1978), p. 215.

16. That this generalization extends beyond the narrow economic realm is apparent from the voluminous studies of social response to natural disasters by Russell Dynes and associates. See Dynes, "Problems in Emergency Planning," in G. Horwich, ed., *Energy Use in Transportation Contingency Planning,* special issue of *Energy—The International Journal,* August-September 1983, pp. 653–60 and the references cited on p. 660. Dynes argues that the household and community response to disturbances tends to be far more efficient than the response pattern imposed by centralized decision makers. The efforts of command and control central planners are almost invariably counterproductive relative to the "emergent human resources" behavior that arises spontaneously from emergency situations.

17. Data on household petroleum use were provided by the Energy Information Administration of the Department of Energy. Calculations were based on tables in the EIA publications, *Residential Energy Consumption Survey: Consumption and Expenditures: April 1980 through March 1981,* pt. 1, National Data (Washington, D.C., September 1982), p. 21, and *Residential Energy Consumption Survey: Consumption Patterns of Household Vehicles, Supplement: January 1981 to September 1981* (Washington, D.C., February 1983), p. 11. The EIA provided unpublished estimates of the residential sector's share of oil-generated electricity. The residential sector's petroleum consumption (mainly for heating and cooling) for the survey period was 2.17 quadrillion BTUs ("quads"); household vehicle use of petroleum in 1981 was 9.37 quads. The total, 11.54 quads, is 35 percent of the average of the total U.S. petroleum consumption in 1980–1981 of 34.20 quads (taken from recent issues of DOE's *Monthly Energy Review*). Household vehicle use includes both work and non–work-related travel.

18. See David T. Hartgen and Alfred J. Neveu, "The 1979 Energy Crisis: Who Conserved How Much?" in *Considerations in Transportation Energy Contingency Planning,* Special Report 191, Transportation Research Board, National Research Council, National Academy of Sciences (Washington, D.C., 1980), pp. 157–65; David T. Hartgen, "New York State's Perspective on Transportation Energy Contingency Planning," in G. Horwich, ed., *Energy Use in Transportation Contingency Planning,* special issue of *Energy—The International Journal,* August-September 1983, pp. 603–08; and David T. Hartgen, Joanna M. Brunso, and Alfred J. Neveu, "Initial and Subsequent Consumer Response to Gasoline Shortages," paper presented at the Transportation Research Board Conference on Energy Contingency Planning in Urban Areas, Houston, Tex., April 7–9, 1983 (forthcoming in the published conference proceedings).

19. The results reported in this paragraph are taken from Hartgen, "New York State's Perspective on Transportation Energy Contingency Planning," p. 606 (figure 1).

20. The data reported in the remainder of this paragraph and in the following paragraph are from Hartgen and Neveu, "The 1979 Energy Crisis," pp. 159–61.

21. Ibid., pp. 161–62.

22. Hartgen, Brunso, and Neveu, "Initial and Subsequent Consumer Response to Gasoline Shortages."

23. A. E. Peck and O. C. Doering III, "Voluntarism and Price Response: Consumer Reaction to the Energy Shortage," *Bell Journal of Economics*, vol. 7, no. 1 (Spring 1976), pp. 287–92.

24. Roger W. Sant, *The Least-Cost Energy Strategy: Minimizing Consumer Costs through Competition* (Washington, D.C.: Carnegie-Mellon University Press, 1979). An update of the information and elaboration of the argument are contained in Roger W. Sant and Steven C. Carhart with Dennis W. Bakke and Shirish S. Mulherkar, *Eight Great Energy Myths: The Least-Cost Energy Strategy—1978–2000* (Washington, D.C.: Carnegie-Mellon University Press, 1981).

25. Sant, *The Least-Cost Energy Strategy*, pp. 35–36.

26. Ibid., p. 23.

27. Ibid.

28. Ibid., pp. 27–35.

29. Ibid., pp. 43–44.

30. Ibid., pp. 22–23. The energy consumption data given above were taken from the *BP Statistical Review of the World Oil Industry* (London: British Petroleum), various annual issues. The energy price data are from the *OECD Economic Outlook* (Brussels: Organization for Economic Cooperation and Development, December 1980).

31. The data on urban population density are taken from table 18 of the *Statistical Abstract of the United States* (Washington, D.C.: U.S. Bureau of the Census), various issues (see also chap. 3, n. 40). For an account of developments in urban transit, see Milton Pikarsky and Christine M. Johnson, "Transportation in Transition," and George Horwich, "Energy Use in Transportation Contingency Planning: Introduction and Summary," in G. Horwich, ed., *Energy Use in Transportation Contingency Planning*, special issue of *Energy— The International Journal*, August-September 1983, pp. 589–99 and 569–74, respectively.

32. John A. Tatom, "Energy Prices and Short-Run Economic Performance," *Federal Reserve Bank of St. Louis Review*, January 1981, pp. 3–17. For a more detailed treatment, see Robert H. Rasche and John A. Tatom, "Energy Price Shocks, Aggregate Supply, and Monetary Policy: The Theory and the International Evidence," in K. Brunner and A. H. Meltzer, eds., *Supply Shocks, Incentives, and National Wealth*, vol. 14 (Rochester: Carnegie-Rochester Conference Series on Public Policy, 1981), pp. 9–107. See also the earlier studies by Robert S. Pindyck, "Energy Price Increases and Macroeconomic Policy," *Energy Journal*, vol. 1, no. 4 (October 1980), pp. 1–20; Robert H. Rasche and John A. Tatom, "The Effects of the New Energy Regime on Economic Capacity, Production, and Prices," *Federal Reserve Bank of St. Louis Review*, May 1977, pp. 2–

12; "Energy Price Shocks" and "Energy Resources and Potential GNP," *Federal Reserve Bank of St. Louis Review*, June 1977, pp. 10–24.

33. D. Couts, Y. Mansoor, E. Novicky, and J. Schneider, *Economic Analysis of Petroleum Supply Interruption Contingency Actions*, Science Applications, Inc., DOE Contract CR-1360885 (Washington, D.C., September 1978), vol. 1, pp. 1–26. For a similar outcome in a more recent simulation, see R. G. Hubbard and R. C. Fry, Jr., "The Macroeconomic Impacts of Oil Supply Disruptions," Discussion Paper Series, E-81-07, Energy and Environmental Policy Center, John F. Kennedy School of Government, Harvard University, Cambridge, Mass., June 1982, esp. pp. 40–47.

34. George R. Schink, *Simulation Study of Eight Petroleum Supply Scenarios* (Washington, D.C.: U.S. Department of Energy, April 1979), pp. 98 and 103 (table 1).

35. U.S. Congress, House, Subcommittee on Energy and Power, Committee on Interstate and Foreign Commerce, *An Evaluation of the Strategic Petroleum Reserve* (Washington, D.C., June 1980). A more recent enriched set of simulations for DOE has been published by ICF, Inc., and employs a wide range of alternative assumptions regarding U.S. vulnerability and responsiveness. Vulnerability is lower for low levels of U.S. oil consumption, imports of oil, and the price of oil and for greater spare capacity of the Organization of Petroleum Exporting Countries (OPEC). Responsiveness is lower for low levels of supply and demand elasticities and drawdown of private inventories. See Joseph M. Anderson, Stephen Garbacz, and John Peterson, *Estimates of the Macroeconomic Effects of Oil Supply Disruptions* (Washington, D.C.: ICF, December 14, 1982).

36. The earlier studies are Knut A. Mork, "Energy Prices and Inflation," in *Petroleum and Natural Gas in Illinois: Proceedings of the Seventh Annual Illinois Energy Conference*, October 9–11, 1979, pp. 189–97; K. A. Mork and R. E. Hall, "Energy Prices and the U.S. Economy in 1979–81," *Energy Journal*, vol. 1, no. 2 (April 1980), pp. 41–53; and Mork and Hall, "Energy Prices, Inflation, and Recession, 1974–75," *Energy Journal*, vol. 1, no. 3 (July 1980), pp. 31–63.

37. Knut A. Mork, "The Economic Cost of Oil Supply Disruptions," chap. 5, and "Macroeconomic Modeling of Oil Supply Disruptions," app. C, in J. Plummer, ed., *Energy Vulnerability* (Cambridge, Mass.: Ballinger, 1982), pp. 83–112 and 375–90, respectively. This model, like that of the St. Louis Federal Reserve Bank, is cast in the mold of aggregate supply and demand. Aggregate output is a function of labor, of which there is a single variety with wages that are rigid, capital, and a single composite energy good. Consumption is a function of permanent income, investment is the rate of change of a capital stock equation, and government expenditures and net exports are exogenously given. A single money-market equation relates the price level to the quantity of money and the rate of interest. See also the useful survey of recent macro simulations in *The Domestic Impact of Reliance on Market Forces during a Substantial Petroleum Supply Disruption* (Washington, D.C.: U.S. Department of Energy, August 1983), chap. V.

38. Richard J. Gilbert and Knut A. Mork, "Coping with Oil Supply Disrup-

tions," in J. Plummer, ed., *Energy Vulnerability* (Cambridge, Mass.: Ballinger, 1982), pp. 169–78; and "Managing Oil Supply Disruptions," Massachusetts Institute of Technology, Energy Laboratory Working Paper MIT EL 81-048WP, October 1981, pp. 43–50.

39. Dramatic examples of the effects of price controls on petroleum supplies, most of which are imported, occurred in Italy and Sweden during the 1979 crisis. Whole categories of petroleum products virtually disappeared, impelling each of the two countries, whose losses far exceeded those of other European countries, to appeal to the International Energy Agency under its sharing agreement. In both instances, the IEA refused to implement sharing and recommended removal of the price controls. Each country did so, and petroleum imports rose dramatically thereafter. See also chap. 7, n. 13.

40. See Mork, "Energy Prices and Inflation," pp. 194–97; Mork and Hall, "Energy Prices and the U.S. Economy, 1979–1981," pp. 47–48; and Gilbert and Mork, "Coping with Oil Supply Disruptions," in J. Plummer, ed., *Energy Vulnerability* (Cambridge, Mass.: Ballinger, 1982), pp. 150–58.

# 3

# The Impact of Petroleum Market Regulations, 1973–1981

The world oil market began experiencing turbulence in the fall of 1972. In September, the Rotterdam spot price of oil stood at approximately $3 per barrel and the Saudi light contract price at about $2.50. By October 1, 1973, the spot price had soared to $10, whereas the contract price had risen to $3.01. In the next three months, during and after the outbreak of hostilities in the Middle East, the spot price rose to $19 and beyond, whereas by January 1, 1974, the Saudi price was $11.65.

Accompanying these price movements was a sudden cessation in the growth of production by the Organization of Petroleum Exporting Countries. After a compound annual increase of almost 11 percent since 1970, OPEC production dropped 10.5 percent in the last three months of 1973. It was this drop, and not the widely proclaimed embargo of shipments to the United States and the Netherlands (which was in any case ineffective), that caused the price rise.

**The Rationale for Government Interventions in 1973–1974.** The oil supply disruption coincided with phases III and IV of the general wage and price controls that had been imposed in the United States in August 1971. The controls were designed as an anti-inflation measure. It was therefore consistent, as well as procedurally simple, to retain official price ceilings on oil and petroleum products, modifying them only as the special circumstances of the period seemed to justify. The containment of inflation, however, was only one of a number of reasons for the decision to control oil prices.

The national consensus was that although little could be done to prevent OPEC from rigging the price of oil by cartel or other illegal actions, there was no reason why domestic oil companies should be permitted to raise prices equally and share in the ill-gotten gains. Not only would uncontrolled price increases enrich the companies unjustly, but higher prices would impose severe hardships on lower-income families and on all middle Americans, whose dependence on low heating costs and low automobile fuel costs was an economic and political fact of life.

In addition to these equity arguments, there was a widespread feeling that the free market was not capable of distributing petroleum products to their most-valued uses in emergency conditions. Government allocation was seen as absolutely essential to ensure that petroleum went to those whose need was greatest, such as farmers, people residing in cold climates, providers of emergency services, and companies within the oil industry—typically, smaller ones—whose supplies were unusually low or whose access to oil was considered unduly restricted. Allocation rules were also believed necessary to prevent hoarding by the public and withholding of supplies by the oil companies, who would otherwise attempt to raise prices to stratospheric levels.

In the months that followed the embargo period, another reason was frequently cited in support of government intervention in the petroleum markets. In the absence of oil price ceilings, the run-up of oil prices along highly inelastic demand schedules would cause a massive transfer of purchasing power from consumers to oil producers. The oil industry would be unable to spend its receipts without significant delay, imposing a severe deflationary adjustment on the rest of the economy. This argument refers to the oil price drag phenomenon discussed in chapter 2. In the wake of an increase in oil prices, the free market was thus a likely source of both inflationary and deflationary tendencies.

**The Proper Economic Role of Government.** The general goal of economic policy in responding to oil supply disruptions should be to minimize the loss of social surplus and GNP. In order to do so, government must act where private markets act insufficiently or not at all because the benefits are external to the individual participants. Our analysis of free market efficiency indicates, and the macro simulations reported in chapter 2 illustrate, that government will rarely, if ever, have the information to justify direct intervention in individual buying and selling decisions. The comparative advantage of government will lie where there are broad externalities—for example in oil stockpiling and in the imposition of import fees, which enable government to internalize the nation's monopsony power and national security interests and compensate for government's own deterrent effect on private stockpiling; in monetary and other macro stabilization policies, from which private individuals cannot internalize a return; in the dissemination of information regarding diplomatic and political influences acting on energy markets that only government is likely to possess; and in the distribution of resources to low-income households, local governments, and providers of emergency services whose budgetary constraints tend to be inflexible and whose protection against higher energy costs is deemed to be in the public interest.

In all of these cases, government is likely to make a net contribution to minimization of the disruption costs only if it employs market-compatible measures, such as redistributing income by cash transfers, rather than direct allocations of oil, and letting the market allocate the petroleum reserve and share in the drawdown decision.[1] Acting in this way in response to clear externalities, government will moderate the early costs of disruption and will smooth the path to a new energy-constrained equilibrium in the event that the disruption is a permanent loss of supply.

**The Impact of Controls.** The evidence indicates that instead of facilitating the adjustment, government price ceilings and allocations tended to inhibit and prolong it and raise the ultimate costs of reaching the new equilibrium. Although these government policies appeared superficially to reduce costs and to enhance equity, they blunted incentives for the domestic production of crude oil, increased the level of petroleum imports, increased total petroleum consumption, sharply reduced the efficiency of the petroleum distribution system, inhibited precrisis stockpiling, lowered the relative costs of (and hence encouraged) stockpiling during crises, prevented refineries from adjusting smoothly and rapidly to changing grades of crude oil in the world market and to changing demands for petroleum products (such as unleaded gasoline) in the domestic market, exacerbated inflation by reducing the aggregate supply of output, and redistributed oil (and, indirectly, income) generally from larger companies to smaller ones and from "crude rich" to "crude poor" firms on the basis of criteria that were at least questionable with respect to equity and unquestionably counterproductive from the standpoint of efficiency. We turn now to the specific controls on crude oil and petroleum products and analyze them in light of the claims of both equity and efficiency made on their behalf.

### Price Controls and Allocations in the Crude Oil Market

Authority to regulate petroleum prices under phase IV controls and to determine allocations of petroleum in all stages of production and distribution was formalized in late November 1973 with passage of the

59

Emergency Petroleum Allocation Act of 1973 (EPAA). We begin with discussion of the crude oil price regulations.

**Price Controls.** A two-tiered price ceiling on U.S. crude oil, prescribed under EPAA, emerged in the fall of 1973 and was in force, with modifications, for the rest of the decade.[2] *New oil* was defined to mean the production of wells developed after 1972 and that portion of production from existing wells that exceeded the level of the corresponding month of 1972. Such oil sold at the world price. Oil from wells that produced less then ten barrels a day, so-called stripper wells, was also exempted from controls. All other oil, designated *old oil*, was limited to its May 1973 price plus $0.35 per barrel. In December the ceiling was raised an additional $1.00, bringing the average price on old oil to $5.03. The world price continued to rise, however, and at year's end the price of new and stripper oil was more than twice that of old oil. In 1974 and 1975 the old oil price remained $5.03, whereas in those two years the world price averaged $10.13 and $12.03, and the average U.S. prices for the two years were $6.87 and $7.67, respectively.

In December 1975 all crude oil was brought under price control by the Energy Policy and Conservation Act (EPCA). The price of new and stripper oil, renamed *upper-tier* oil, was lowered to its September 1975 level less $1.32. Thereafter the prices on old, or lower-tier, and upper-tier oil were to increase by the inflation rate plus an incentive amount. The two together were not to raise the overall domestic price by more than 10 percent per year. In September 1976 the maximum overall increase was placed at 10 percent, independently of component adjustments. At the same time, stripper oil was again exempted from controls, creating a third price tier equal to the world level.

The price adjustments under EPCA established an average lower-tier price in 1976 of $5.14, an upper-tier price of $11.57, and an overall domestic average of $8.14.[3] These compared with pre-EPCA prices in January 1976 of $5.03 (old), $12.99 (new), and $8.63 (domestic average). In 1977 the prices were $5.19 (lower tier), $11.22 (upper tier), $13.59 (stripper and world price), and $8.57 (domestic average). The 1978 prices were $5.46 (lower tier), $12.15 (upper tier), $13.95 (stripper), and $9.00 (domestic average). In May 1979, just before the thirty-month decontrol of all prices began under presidential authority granted by EPCA, the prices were $5.91 (lower tier), $13.02 (upper tier), $17.53 (stripper), and $10.71 (domestic average). Throughout the control period, the average U.S. crude oil price was thus three dollars to seven dollars below the world price.[4]

The existence of price controls meant that U.S. refiners with access to domestic controlled oil captured the windfall—the difference between ceiling and world prices times existing output levels—that would otherwise have gone to the crude oil producers. This was a sizable sum, as table 6 indicates. The windfall, or rent, is based on the difference between the average refiner acquisition cost of domestic crude oil (column 1) and imported crude oil (column 2), as reported in column 4 of the table. The estimates in column 5, based on the quantities of each separate category of controlled domestic oil, were made by Joseph Kalt. In 1980 prices, the rent averaged $24.5 billion throughout the control period.

*Entitlements.* A year before passage of EPCA, the Federal Energy Administration (FEA) created an important modification to the price controls known as the *entitlements* system. Entitlements were salable claims designed to give all U.S. refiners a proportionate share of the lower-priced old oil and the rent associated with it. Starting in December 1974, U.S. refiners were required to transfer funds so that they could more or less equalize their crude oil acquisition costs. Refiners who had bought disproportionately more of the old oil in each preceding month were required to buy entitlements from those who had bought disproportionately more oil at world prices or at prices above the average of all crude oil sold in the United States. In 1974 the prices of new, stripper, and imported oil were at the world level; after EPCA, only the latter two were, but the upper-tier price was still above the national average, and buyers of all three categories received full or partial entitlements that had a resale value equal to the difference between the uncontrolled and lower-tier price.

Table 7 indicates the size of the transfers under the entitlements program. Column 1, the difference between the average cost at the refinery of imported oil and all crude oil, domestic and foreign, is computed from columns 2 and 3 of table 6. This difference indicates the maximum subsidy, through the purchase of entitlements, that could be paid by buyers of old oil for each barrel of oil bought at the world price. Fractional parts of entitlements would go to buyers of upper-tier oil, whose price, beginning in 1976, was somewhat below the world level. Several earmarked subsidies of entitlements, however, prevented full equalization of refiner acquisition costs. These special subsidies included, most significantly, disproportionately large numbers of entitlements that were granted to small refiners (those with capacity under 175,000 barrels per day) under the so-called Small Refiner Bias; partial entitlements that were given, from time to time, to importers of certain refined products; numerous exemptions from the purchase of entitlements granted to refiners on a monthly basis under the exceptions and appeals procedure; and the

TABLE 6

COSTS OF CRUDE OIL TO U.S. REFINERS AND RENT ON CONTROLLED CRUDE OIL, 1974–1980

|  | *Refiner Acquisition Costs* | | | | |
|  | Domestic Oil[a] (1) | Imported Oil (2) | Composite Costs (3) | Imported Oil Minus Domestic Oil (4) | Rent (5) |
| --- | --- | --- | --- | --- | --- |
| 1974 | 7.18 | 12.52 | 9.07 | 5.34 | 23.8 |
| 1975 | 8.39 | 13.93 | 10.38 | 5.54 | 23.1 |
| 1976 | 8.84 | 13.48 | 10.89 | 4.64 | 17.9 |
| 1977 | 9.55 | 14.53 | 11.96 | 4.98 | 17.5 |
| 1978 | 10.61 | 14.57 | 12.46 | 3.96 | 13.6 |
| 1979 | 14.27 | 21.67 | 17.72 | 7.40 | 30.7 |
| 1980 | 24.23 | 33.89 | 28.07 | 9.66 | 45.0[b] |

NOTE: All oil prices (costs) are in current dollars per barrel; rent is in billions of 1980 dollars per year.
a. The prices in column 1 (as in column 2) include the cost of transporting oil to the refinery and thus are greater than the average domestic wellhead prices cited in the text.
b. Estimate for first quarter 1980.

SOURCE: Columns 1–4: Energy Information Administration, *1981 Annual Report to Congress*, vol. 2 (Washington, D.C.: U.S. Department of Energy, 1982), pp. 51, 91. Column 5: Joseph Kalt, *The Economics and Politics of Oil Price Regulation*, p. 47 (table 2.2). Kalt's estimates are based on data in the *Monthly Energy Review*.

## TABLE 7
### POTENTIAL AND ACTUAL SUBSIDIES AND MAXIMUM CASH TRANSFERS FOR CRUDE OIL COST EQUALIZATION UNDER THE ENTITLEMENTS PROGRAM, 1974–1980

| | Imported Price Minus Composite Price[a] (1) | Actual Subsidy per Barrel[a] (2) | Total Subsidy[b] (3) | Share of Lower-Tier Production $(q_L/q_4)$ (4) | Maximum Transfer $[1 - col.\ 4] \times col.\ 3^c$ (5) |
|---|---|---|---|---|---|
| 1974 (Nov.–Dec.) | 3.33 | 2.03 | — | 0.46 | — |
| 1975 | 3.55 | 2.85 | 18,165.4 | 0.42 | 10.5 |
| 1976 | 2.59 | 2.51 | 16,676.6 | 0.33 | 11.2 |
| 1977 | 2.57 | 2.27 | 15,449.5 | 0.26 | 11.4 |
| 1978 | 2.11 | 1.60 | 10,270.9 | 0.22 | 8.0 |
| 1979 | 3.95 | 3.08 | 17,771.6 | 0.17 | 14.8 |
| 1980 (Jan.–Mar.) | 10.88 | 5.16 | 27,483.1 | 0.13 | 23.9 |

a. Current dollars per barrel.
b. Millions of 1980 dollars per year.
c. Billions of 1980 dollars per year.

SOURCE: Column 1: Table 6. Column 2: Kalt, *The Economics and Politics of Oil Price Regulation*, p. 58, table 2.3. Column 3: Kalt, ibid., p. 191, table 5.1. Column 4: *Monthly Energy Review*, various issues.

granting of entitlements to the federal government itself to fund a part of its purchases for the strategic petroleum reserve.

Column 2, calculated by Kalt, is the per barrel subsidy actually paid to recipients under the entitlements program to equalize refiner crude oil costs. The remainder of the total available amount was allocated to the special programs mentioned above. Column 3 is Kalt's estimate of the total dollar subsidy, in 1980 prices, paid under entitlements by producers of lower-tier crude oil to refiners for price equalization. With reference to figure 12 below, the entries in column 3 are $(p_W - p_A)q_4$, where $p_W$ is the world price, $p_A$ is the average price of oil produced in the United States, and $q_4$ is total U.S. consumption of crude oil. Column 3 thus includes the difference between $p_W$ and $p_A$ that purchasers of lower-tier oil were permitted to retain as their share of the subsidy. Kalt estimates that 10–20 percent of the cost of imported oil was paid for through entitlements.

Data on the actual cash transfers carried out under the entitlements program are not available. Column 5, however, is our estimate of the maximum possible cash transfer from purchasers of lower-tier oil to purchasers of upper-tier and uncontrolled oil, including imports. The maximum transfer occurs when all the old oil is bought by purchasers who buy it exclusively and must therefore purchase the maximum number of entitlements from all other buyers, who have purchased only upper-tier and uncontrolled oil. The maximum cash transfer is $(p_A - p_L)q_L$, where $p_L$ is the lower-tier price and $q_L$ is the lower-tier quantity produced. We estimate the transfer in table 7 by taking $[1 - (q_L/q_4)]$ times the entries in column 3. By this procedure, an average maximum of \$13.3 billion in 1980 dollars was transferable each year from buyers of lower-tier oil to all other domestic buyers of crude oil under the cost-equalization program. The actual transfers of course involved less money, since buyers typically obtain a mix of lower-tier, upper-tier, and uncontrolled oil and purchase entitlements only for the amount of lower-tier oil exceeding their proportionate share.

*Small Refiner Bias.* Estimates by Kalt of benefits under the Small Refiner Bias for 1978 and May 1980 are presented in table 8. The smallest refiners, those with capacity under 10,000 barrels per day, each received extra entitlements valued at as much as \$6.9 million per year in 1978 and \$22.9 million in 1980. The largest subsidies went to refiners in the 30,000-barrel-per-day class, \$9.4 million per year in 1978 and \$31.2 million in 1980. The relative importance of these subsidies can be assessed by referring to the investment in refineries of this size: \$2,500 per barrel of capacity, at 1973 prices.[5] For a 10,000-barrel-

TABLE 8

SUBSIDIES PAID TO SMALL REFINERS UNDER THE SMALL REFINER BIAS
PROGRAM, 1978 AND MAY 1980

| Refiner Size (thousands of barrels per day) | | | Value of Bias per Refiner (millions of dollars per year) | | | | | |
| --- | --- | --- | --- | --- | --- | --- | --- | --- |
| | | | 1978 | | | May 1980 | | |
| 0 | to | 10 | 0 | to | 6.9 | 0 | to | 22.9 |
| 10+ | to | 30 | 6.9 | to | 9.4 | 22.9 | to | 31.2 |
| 30+ | to | 50 | 9.4 | to | 6.3 | 31.2 | to | 20.9 |
| 50+ | to | 100 | 6.3 | to | 3.8 | 20.9 | to | 12.6 |
| 100+ | to | 175 | 3.8 | to | 0 | 12.6 | to | 0 |

SOURCE: J. P. Kalt, *The Economics and Politics of Oil Price Regulation*, p. 59, table 2.4 (1978 data); J. P. Kalt, "The Creation, Growth, and Entrenchment of Special Interests in Oil Price Policy," in R. G. Noll and B. M. Owen, *The Political Economy of Deregulation* (Washington, D.C.: American Enterprise Institute, 1983), p. 111 (table 6.1; May 1980 data).

per-day unit, the investment was $25 million, or approximately $36 million in 1978 prices and $42 million in 1980 prices. The subsidy, continuing year in and year out, was thus 6.9/36, or 19 percent of the initial investment in 1978 and 22.9/42, or 55 percent, in 1980.

A general-purpose refining plant not specializing in exotic products or products for limited regional use reaches its optimal size at 200,000 barrels per day. The Small Refiner Bias led to a proliferation of small units in the 10,000–50,000-barrel class that would otherwise never have been built. About fifty such refineries, producing about 6 percent of domestic refined output, came on stream beginning in 1975. These refineries typically were minimally equipped and produced the heavier residual fuel as opposed to the lighter, more widely demanded petroleum products such as gasoline. By January 1982, almost sixty refineries, mainly in the under-50,000-barrel-per-day class, had shut down following the onset of decontrol and the phasing out of entitlements in 1979.[6]

The bias was widely held to be justifiable on the grounds that small refiners could not compete unaided with the integrated companies (the *majors*) and with the large independent refineries and therefore should be subsidized on equity grounds. Support of the small companies was further said to increase the competitiveness of the industry and to assure lower prices for consumers of petroleum products. When decontrol was being seriously debated in 1979 and

1980, protection of small refiners was also sought on national security grounds: Allowing domestic refining capacity to return to preentitlement levels would increase imports of petroleum products, making the United States more vulnerable to supply disruptions.

The equity argument for subsidizing small refiners hinged on their lack of access to contract crude oil and their dependence on higher-priced spot market supplies in times of disruption. The question of access, however, can also be interpreted in terms of efficiency rather than equity: In nondisrupted periods the small refiners preferred to rely on lower-priced spot market oil, forgoing longer-term and more expensive contract supplies. If this view is correct, subsidizing small refiners in the face of their failure to provide for the future is less an adjustment for equity than a reward for inefficiency.[7]

Competition is not, of course, enhanced by firms of uneconomic size that owe their existence wholly to government subsidies. Indeed, the bias, together with ceilings on prices and profit margins and mandatory allocations, limited entry and exit for the industry as a whole and severely constrained its competitive responses. In particular, the industry failed to adapt to changing grades of oil in the world market and to meet changes in the desired product slate, such as the increase in demand for unleaded gasoline.

The national security argument for the bias or for some other form of protection for the small refiners was equally tenuous.[8] As controls and entitlements were being phased out, the small independent refiners lobbied for a tariff on petroleum product imports, which promised to displace domestic refining capacity. The imports of refined products that would be shut out by a tariff, however, would be replaced by almost equal imports of crude oil needed as inputs to the small refineries. Imports of petroleum products and crude oil are thus, under the circumstances, substitutes. Furthermore, although all supply disruptions, whether of crude or product supplies, tend sooner or later to affect all consumers proportionately, there is surely a greater likelihood of disruption in crude supplies than in product and a corresponding initial advantage in minimizing crude rather than product imports.

Any national security benefits of a refined product tariff must, of course, be weighed against the costs. The Department of Energy study cited in note 8 estimated that a tariff that would prevent the failure of most of the small "bias" refiners would cost (in 1980 prices) $500 million per year and would entail a transfer of $12–14 billion per year from consumers to government and to the industry. A destruction of refining capacity in Canada, the Caribbean, or Western Europe might conceivably justify such an expenditure in support of small

U.S. refiners. The probability of such a destruction, however, is so low that less costly, more direct security measures, including military strategies, would surely dominate support of otherwise inefficient refineries as the optimal policy.

**Consumption and Welfare Effects of Price Controls.** We turn now to the impact of the multitiered system of price ceilings on domestic production, consumption, and economic welfare, using our basic diagram of the crude oil market. Figures 11 and 12 repeat the U.S. supply

FIGURE 11

THE U.S. MARKET FOR CRUDE OIL WITH CONTROLLED DOMESTIC PRICES
($p_D$) BELOW THE WORLD PRICE ($p_W$), NO ENTITLEMENTS

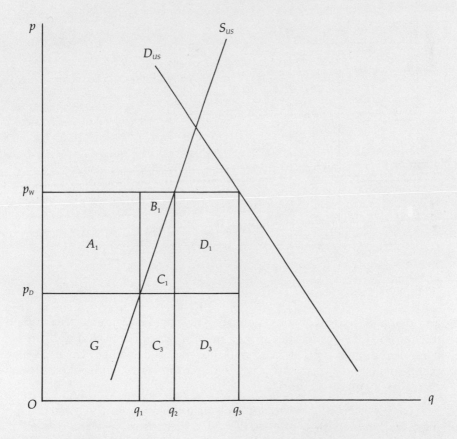

SOURCE: Authors.

FIGURE 12

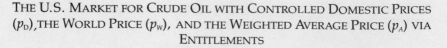

THE U.S. MARKET FOR CRUDE OIL WITH CONTROLLED DOMESTIC PRICES
($p_D$), THE WORLD PRICE ($p_W$), AND THE WEIGHTED AVERAGE PRICE ($p_A$) VIA
ENTITLEMENTS

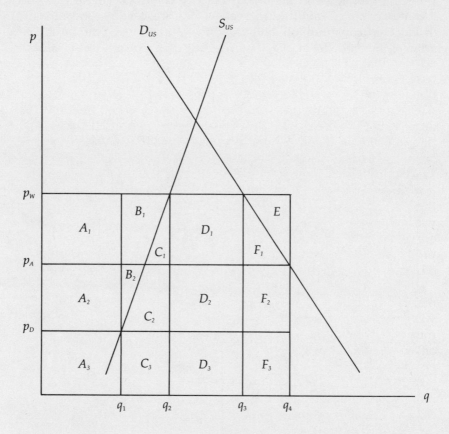

SOURCE: Authors.

and demand schedules for crude oil. The postdisruption world and
uncontrolled domestic price is $p_W$, the average of controlled and uncontrolled domestic prices is $p_D$, and the weighted average, via entitlements, of $p_W$ and $p_D$ is $p_A$. We analyze the controls first without entitlements, referring to figure 11.

*Controls without entitlements.* To isolate the effect of the price ceilings, we begin with a free market in which the U.S. price for all
categories of oil is $p_W$, the world price. At $p_W$, U.S. production of crude

oil is $q_2$, consumption is $q_3$, and imports are $(q_3 - q_2)$. Total outlays on imports are equal to the area represented by $(D_1 + D_3)$. (The labeling of areas is designed for consistency with later use of the graph in figure 12).

Next we impose ceilings below $p_W$ on various categories of oil produced in the United States, yielding the average domestic price $p_D$. The controlled categories include old, or lower-tier, oil and, after December 1975, controlled upper-tier oil. The uncontrolled categories include, before December 1975, new oil and, for most of the decade, stripper oil. For the moment, there are no entitlements to equalize the cost of imported and domestic crude oil. At $p_D$, U.S. crude oil production falls from $q_2$ to $q_1$. Consumption beyond $q_1$ can only be accommodated in the world market at $p_W$, for which the total demand quantity is $q_3$, as before. With lower U.S. production, however, a greater portion of consumption $(q_3 - q_1)$, is supplied by imports. Expenditures on imports are now equal to the area $(B_1 + C_1 + C_3 + D_1 + D_3)$.

Since $p_W$ is the effective market price of crude oil—the price on the last units purchased—buyers of domestic oil receive a windfall on their $q_1$ purchases equal to the area $A_1$. The effect of domestic ceilings without entitlements is thus to reduce U.S. production, to grant buyers of controlled domestic oil a windfall at the expense of domestic producers, to raise imports, and to leave total consumption of crude oil unchanged.

The GNP and social welfare impact of the price ceilings is summarized in table 9. The area $A_1$, for which no GNP changes are involved, is the refiners' windfall at the expense of domestic oil producers. In column 3, labeled "Change in Social Surplus," equal offsetting changes in domestic producers' surplus (PS) and refiner buyers' surplus (RS) are entered, leaving a zero net change in column 4.

The area $B_1$ is a component of the increased expenditures on imports resulting from the domestic price ceilings. It is thus shown in column 2 as an increase in the foreign claim on GNP. Area $B_1$ is also a loss of domestic producers' surplus. The simultaneous loss of surplus by domestic producers and gain by foreign claimants are entered in column 4.

The areas $C_1$ and $C_3$ are also components of the added expenditures on imports and are shown in column 2 as increasing the foreign claim. At the same time, however, $C_1$ and $C_3$ are the reduction in resource costs associated with reducing domestic crude oil output from $q_2$ and $q_1$. Resources equal in value to $C_1$ and $C_3$ are thus released for producing additional output elsewhere in the economy in the new postcontrol equilibrium. An upward arrow in column 1, "Change in GNP," reflects this fact. Since no changes in social surplus are in-

## TABLE 9
EFFECT ON GNP AND SOCIAL SURPLUS OF PRICE CEILINGS ON DOMESTIC CRUDE OIL WITHOUT ENTITLEMENTS, BY SELECTED GEOMETRIC AREAS

| Area | Change in GNP (1) | Change in Foreign Claim to GNP (2) | Change in Social Surplus (3) | Net (4) |
|---|---|---|---|---|
| $A_1$ | — | — | ↑PS, ↓RS | — |
| $B_1$ | — | ↑ | ↓PS | ↑FC = ↓PS |
| $C_1, C_3$ | ↑ | ↑ | — | — |
| $D_1, D_3$ | — | — | — | — |
| $G$ | — | — | — | — |

NOTE: In summary, the rise in GNP (column 1) is $(C_1 + C_3)$; the net rise in foreign claims (column 2) is $(B_1 + C_1 + C_3)$; the net change in social surplus (column 3) is ↓PS = $B_1$; total costs (column 4) are $B_1$. FC = foreign claim to GNP; PS = domestic producers' surplus; RS = refiner buyers' surplus; dashes = no change. See figure 11.
SOURCE: Authors.

volved here, the offsetting effects in columns 1 and 2 leave a zero net change in column 4.

Areas $D_1$ and $D_3$ are expenditures on imports, unchanged from the precontrol period. They are therefore not associated with further GNP or social welfare effects. Area $G$, a combination of producers' surplus and real resource cost, is also unaffected by the controls and is similarly shown as without effect in table 9. Thus $B_1$, a loss of domestic producers' surplus to foreigners, remains the only net change resulting from the imposition of crude oil price ceilings without entitlements.

The paradox of the controls is that they increase GNP by releasing resources from crude oil production. Americans do not gain from the GNP, however, since it is claimed entirely by foreigners. At the same time, foreigners also receive revenues that, prior to the controls, had been going to the oil industry as producers' surplus. Thus where $(q_2 - q_1)$ in crude oil had been produced in the free market using real resources of $(C_1 + C_3)$, the controls exact a cost of $(B_1 + C_1 + C_3)$.

Finally, since the ceilings, relative to a free market, reduce U.S. crude oil output (by an amount equal to the additional imports), world supply is correspondingly less and the world price higher. Assuming that the domestic price is unaffected by this circumstance, or, in the spirit of the controls, rises less than the world price, the welfare

# TABLE 10
## Effect on GNP and Social Surplus of Price Ceilings on Domestic Crude Oil with Entitlements, by Selected Geometric Areas

| Area | Change in GNP (1) | Change in Foreign Claim to GNP (2) | Change in Social Surplus (3) | Net (4) |
|---|---|---|---|---|
| $A_1, A_2$ | — | — | ↓PS, ↑RS | — |
| $B_1, B_2$ | — | ↑ | ↓PS | ↑FC = ↓PS |
| $C_1, C_2, C_3$ | ↑ | ↑ | — | — |
| $D_1, D_2, D_3$ | — | — | — | — |
| $E$ | — | ↑ | ↓RS | ↑FC = ↓RS |
| $F_1, F_2, F_3$ | ↑ | ↑ | — | — |
| $G$ | — | — | — | — |

NOTE: In summary, the rise in GNP (column 1) is $(C_{1,2,3} + F_{1,2,3})$; the rise in foreign claims (column 2) is $(B_{1,2} + C_{1,2,3} + E + F_{1,2,3})$; the net change in social surplus (column 3) is $\downarrow PS = B_1 + B_2$, $\downarrow RS = E$; total costs (column 4) are $(B_1 + B_2 + E)$. FC = foreign claim to GNP; PS = domestic producers' surplus; RS = refiner buyers' surplus; dashes = no change. See figure 12.

SOURCE: Authors.

loss $(B_1)$ due to the controls is greater than in the absence of the price rise.

*Controls with entitlements.* The case in which there are ceilings on domestic crude oil prices with entitlements is diagrammed in figure 12. The weighted average price of $p_W$ and $p_D$, $p_A$, created by the entitlements system, is assumed to be the effective purchase price of all crude oil, domestic and foreign. The effect of entitlements is thus to raise crude oil purchases from $q_3$ to $q_4$. Since $p_D$, the average of domestic prices, most of which are controlled, remains the price received by domestic producers, domestic output is still $q_1$. The $q_4$ demand quantity can thus only be met by imports of $(q_4 - q_1)$ at the world price $p_W$.

Table 10 summarizes the GNP and welfare effects. As in figure 11, without entitlements, the area in figure 12 between $p_W$ and $p_D$ for the $q_1$ quantity of domestically produced oil constitutes rents captured via the price ceilings. The area is designated by two components, $A_1$ and $A_2$, though together they are equivalent to $A_1$ in figure 11. Both $A_1$ and $A_2$ are a loss of producers' surplus and a gain of surplus, through entitlements, by buyers of imported, upper-tier, stripper, and other released domestic oil.

Area $B_2$, like $B_1$, is a component of the increase in the expenditure on imports due to the price ceilings. It simultaneously raises the foreign claim on GNP and lowers producers' surplus. Area $C_2$, like $C_1$ and $C_3$, is an increase in the expenditure on imports and the foreign claim to GNP offset by the release of oil industry resources for use elsewhere in the domestic economy. Area $D_2$, like $D_1$ and $D_3$, is a component of the precontrol outlay on imports and so does not change any of the dependent variables in table 10.

The differential net effect of the entitlements appears in the additional outlays on imports that they stimulate. In this connection, the area $E$ not only raises the foreign claim to GNP but is a deduction from refiners' surplus, since it is an expenditure that lies above the benefits area whose upper boundary is the demand schedule. Phrased differently, $E$ is a purchase of imports the cost of which exceeds the benefits they yield. This characteristic is a consequence of the distortion that entitlements cause in the price of imports, lowering it by subsidy below the level at which purchases in the world market are actually made.

The areas $F_1$, $F_2$, and $F_3$ are additional outlays on imports that give rise to corresponding increases in GNP and offsetting foreign claims to it.[9] The area $G$, as in the preentitlements case, is unaffected by the controls and therefore has no incremental effects on the variables of table 10.

The net effect of the controls is thus a loss of $B_1$ and $B_2$ in domestic producers' surplus, due to the price ceilings, and $E$ in consumers' surplus, due to the entitlements. They are efficiency losses that result in equal gains by foreign producers. Once again, the welfare losses, measured on the assumption of a given world price, are in fact greater as a result of a higher price caused by increased U.S. imports.

*Numerical estimates.* Estimates by Kalt of the efficiency loss by producers (areas $B_1$ and $B_2$) and consumers (area $E$) and the additional quantity of and expenditure on imports due to each are presented in table 11. Kalt assumes a price elasticity of supply from existing oil properties of 0.1, a price elasticity of supply from new sources of 0.5, and a price elasticity of demand of $-0.5$. These are intermediate-run estimates, covering a three- to five-year time span. Increasing the (absolute) elasticities will increase the efficiency losses in approximately the same proportion.

The mean of column 1 indicates that, on average, $1.8 billion in 1980 dollars was funneled each year from domestic producers' surplus to OPEC; the mean of column 4, that $0.8 billion was spent on imports above their value to consumers. In column 7, the mean of the

## TABLE 11

### ESTIMATED EFFICIENCY LOSSES AND EFFECT ON IMPORTS DUE TO DOMESTIC CRUDE OIL PRICE CEILINGS WITH ENTITLEMENTS, 1975–1980

| | Producer Efficiency Loss[a] ($B_1 + B_2$) (1) | Additional Crude Oil Imports Due to Col. 1[b] (2) | Expenditure on Additional Imports in Col. 2[a] (3) | Consumer Efficiency Loss[a] (E) (4) | Additional Crude Oil Imports Due to Col. 4[b] (5) |
|---|---|---|---|---|---|
| 1975 | 963.0 | 99.4 | 1,947.9 | 1,037.2 | 490.9 |
| 1976 | 1,045.5 | 344.4 | 6,288.3 | 851.8 | 477.3 |
| 1977 | 1,213.3 | 454.6 | 8,443.7 | 654.2 | 433.0 |
| 1978 | 815.7 | 347.6 | 6,034.1 | 299.5 | 304.8 |
| 1979 | 1,851.5 | 331.2 | 8,443.9 | 627.4 | 360.9 |
| 1980 (Jan.-Mar.) | 4,615.9 | 529.5 | 20,214.3 | 1,037.8 | 373.4 |
| Mean | 1,750.8 | 351.1 | 8,562.0 | 751.3 | 406.7 |

a. Millions of 1980 dollars per year.
b. Millions of barrels per year.

(Table continues)

## TABLE 11 (continued)

| | Expenditure on Additional Imports in Col. 5 [a] (6) | Total Efficiency Loss (Col. 1 + Col. 4) [a] ($B_1 + B_2 + E$) (7) | Total Increase in Imports (Col. 2 + Col. 5) [b] (8) | Total Expenditure on Additional Imports (Col. 3 + Col. 6) [a] (9) |
|---|---|---|---|---|
| 1975 | 9,601.6 | 2,000.2 | 590.3 | 11,549.5 |
| 1976 | 8,764.2 | 1,897.3 | 821.7 | 15,052.5 |
| 1977 | 8,051.9 | 1,867.5 | 887.6 | 16,495.6 |
| 1978 | 5,285.2 | 1,115.2 | 652.4 | 11,319.3 |
| 1979 | 9,199.6 | 2,478.9 | 692.1 | 17,643.5 |
| 1980 (Jan.-Mar.) | 14,260.5 | 5,653.7 | 902.9 | 34,474.8 |
| Mean | 9,193.8 | 2,502.1 | 757.8 | 17,755.9 |

a. Millions of 1980 dollars per year.
b. Millions of barrels per year.
SOURCE: Kalt, *The Economics and Politics of Oil Price Regulation*, p. 191 (table 5.1; cols. 4–6); p. 201 (table 5.2; cols. 1–3).

total efficiency loss is thus $2.5 billion per year in 1980 dollars, although in the first quarter of 1980, the last full year of controls, the total loss rose above $5 billion. The ceiling on domestic crude oil prices reduced domestic output and raised imports an average of 351 million barrels a year, whereas the entitlements program raised crude oil consumption and imports 407 million barrels a year. The total increase in imports due to controls averaged 758 million barrels annually and 2.08 million barrels daily.

Economists generally argue that the world price of oil does not completely reflect the cost to the United States of dependence on unstable foreign sources of oil. Kalt suggests that we add a premium of perhaps two to five dollars per barrel to make this cost explicit. Doing so will raise the average efficiency loss due to controls from $2.5 billion to $4.0–6.4 billion per year.

**Impact in Petroleum Product Markets.** Given that rents on crude oil, net of efficiency losses, have been captured through entitlements by refiner purchasers, to what degree are these rents passed on to the consumers of petroleum products? Whether consumers experience any benefits or not depends on whether the products are internationally traded. If the products are so traded, their prices, like that of crude oil, will be set in the international market. U.S. controls would then tend to have no direct effect on petroleum product prices and the quantity consumed; as petroleum product supply schedules shifted to the right in response to lower crude costs, product imports would simply be replaced by additional domestic output. On the other hand, if the products were not so traded, the lower domestic crude prices would lead to lower product prices and to increased product consumption.

We shall examine the two polar possibilities with regard to the "pass-through" of crude oil price and quantity changes to the petroleum product markets. Figure 13 depicts the case of a petroleum product that the United States imports at a price set in the world market. The U.S. demand for the product is the schedule $D_{US}$. Prior to the imposition of crude oil controls, the domestic supply of the product is $S_{US}$, based on the world crude oil price $p_W^c$. The given internationally determined product price is $p_W^p$, at which domestic production is $q_1$, total quantity demanded is $q_3$, and imports of the product are $(q_3 - q_1)$.

Price ceilings with entitlements are now introduced into the U.S. crude oil market, reducing the average refiner acquisition cost of crude oil from $p_W^c$ to $p_A^c$. The lower cost of crude oil input shifts $S_{US}$ in figure 13 to the right, as indicated, raising domestic production to $q_2$

FIGURE 13

THE IMPACT OF CRUDE OIL PRICE CONTROLS ON INTERNATIONALLY
TRADED PETROLEUM PRODUCTS (ZERO PASS-THROUGH)

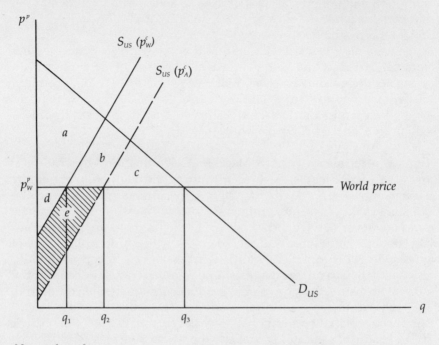

NOTE: $p_A^c < p_W^c$.
SOURCE: Authors.

and lowering imports to $(q_3 - q_2)$. Total U.S. consumption, at the constant product price $p_W^p$, is unchanged at $q_3$.

The net welfare effect in the petroleum product market is shown by the cross-hatched area, $e$, a gain in producers' surplus. Since the price is constant, consumers' surplus, the sum of $a$, $b$, and $c$, is unaffected by the shift of supply; $d$, a component of producers' surplus, is also invariant under the shift.

The case of a petroleum product that is not internationally traded and whose price is domestically determined is shown in figure 14. The product price is initially $p_0^p$ and the quantity supplied and demanded, $q_0$. Producers' surplus plus consumers' surplus is the area $(a + b + c)$. The supply curve again shifts to the right as refiner crude oil acquisition costs fall from $p_W^c$ to $p_A^c$. This time, however, the product

FIGURE 14

THE IMPACT OF CRUDE OIL PRICE CONTROLS ON NONINTERNATIONALLY
TRADED PETROLEUM PRODUCTS (COMPLETE PASS-THROUGH)

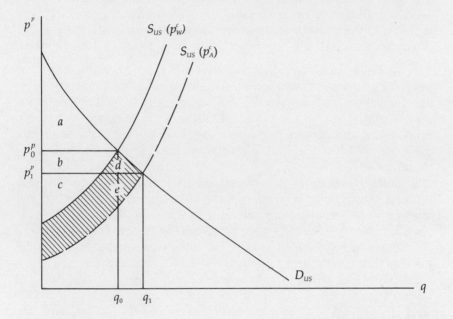

NOTE: $p_A^c < p_W^c$.
SOURCE: Authors.

price falls to $p_1^p$ and the total quantity demanded and supplied rises to $q_1$. The net gains in social surplus, equal to the cross-hatched areas, are $d$ to consumers and $e$ to producers. The surplus areas $a$ and $c$ are unaffected by the shift; $b$ is a simultaneous gain to consumers and a loss to producers and hence a "wash."

Exhaustive empirical analysis by Kalt confirms the findings by DOE and others that roughly half of the rent captured by buyers of controlled crude oil through entitlements was passed on in the form of lower prices, increased consumption, and additional surplus to buyers of petroleum products. Some products, such as residual fuel, are widely traded internationally and conform to the model pictured in figure 13. Others, including gasoline and middle distillates, are best interpreted as nontraded goods. Overall, Kalt estimates a conservative average pass-through of 40 percent of the crude oil entitlements subsidy in the form of lower refined product prices.[10]

**Direct Crude Oil Allocations.** The entitlements program was by far the most elaborate and comprehensive allocation system for distributing crude oil among refiners. Entitlements affected allocation, however, by influencing the price paid for crude oil by various classes of refiners. At the same time, a number of programs in force in the 1970s directly determined the physical movement of crude oil among users.

1. The most pervasive direct allocation principle was the supplier/purchaser freeze, initiated during the embargo period and formalized as a published regulation by the Federal Energy Office (FEO) on January 15, 1974. The freeze required all sellers of crude oil and petroleum products, except at retail,[11] to continue selling the same percentage of their supplies to each buyer that they sold in the corresponding month of 1972.

2. The buy/sell program required the fifteen largest refiners, whose ratios of crude oil to refining capacity exceeded that of the national average, to sell crude oil to small refiners whose ratios were below the national average. (During the embargo period, the program applied to all refiners, regardless of size.) The sales were to be made at the average purchase price of oil during the previous quarter.

3. Exceptions relief, initially under FEA's Office of Exceptions and Appeals and later under DOE's Office of Hearings and Appeals (OHA), resulted in numerous reallocations of oil outside the established regulatory provisions. The allocations took the form of individual modifications of the entitlements program or of mandated direct transfers of oil to petitioning parties.

Like the entitlements program, the direct crude oil allocations were the government's response to widespread criticism of market allocation following the imposition of price controls. The supplier/purchaser freeze was intended as a broad equitable approach to the extensive shortfalls and shortages that appeared in petroleum markets prior to and during the embargo period. The buy/sell program was a specific response to the inability of smaller refiners and rural and agricultural users to secure customary petroleum supplies. This group appears to have been particularly affected by the imposition of Special Rule 1 in March 1973 under phase III of the general wage and price controls. The rule imposed price ceilings on the sale of crude oil and petroleum products by firms whose annual sales exceeded $250 million.[12] These firms, of which there were twenty-three, tended to be primary suppliers to the small refiners and other inland users. The

78

inability of the largest firms to pass on the rising costs of petroleum products and crude oil, much of which they imported, while other firms were less tightly controlled, thus caused customers of the larger companies to experience disproportionate reductions of petroleum supply.

*The supplier/purchaser freeze.* The freezing of supplier/purchaser relationships could be an optimal economic response only in completely static circumstances. Even in nondisrupted periods, allocation of any good is constantly changing in response to the entry and exit of buyers and sellers, to shifting geographical patterns, and to a myriad of continuous changes in industrial processes, structure, and consumer tastes. Following a supply disruption, the optimal crude oil allocation is, of course, drastically altered. Significant shifts occur in the uses of petroleum products, and hence crude oil; for example, shifts between heating (or cooling), travel, power, and petrochemical production and within each of these categories as well. We saw in chapter 2 that the travel pattern undergoes a radical postdisruption transformation, shifting between vacation and work and various modes, including between public and private conveyances. These changes vary among individuals with respect to income, demographic characteristics, urban and rural location, regions of the country, age of the vehicle, and—above all, from the standpoint of the freeze—over time. Thus, in slightly more than a year, as between the embargo period 1973–1974 and any corresponding month in 1972 (the base period), there were widely disparate rates of growth among the states. Regional distributors of crude oil, locked into the freeze, were unable to prevent severe shortfalls in expanding states such as Florida and California, whereas much of the frost belt, both in 1973–1974 and in 1979, experienced less severe reductions and even local surpluses.

In the interval between disruptions, 1974–1978, buyers adhered to the supplier/purchaser freeze more or less rigidly as they sought and sometimes found alternative sources of supply. The freeze caused damage in the long run, however, in that it raised the costs of such alternatives, giving buyers an incentive to remain with historical suppliers and, with an eye to a future updating of the base period, to buy oil in an amount beyond that which would otherwise be optimal. At the same time, since base-period quantities were zero, existing suppliers were unable to enter new markets, and new suppliers were unable to enter any market, except with case-by-case bureaucratic authorization. All suppliers were discouraged from accepting new customers, since an otherwise casual transaction could, in a later updating of the base period, be converted into a long-term commitment.

The base period was in fact unchanged at 1972 when the 1979 disruption struck in the spring of that year. The base was quickly and hastily moved to the corresponding month of 1978 but included a provision raising allocations in response to "unusual growth" occurring in the October 1978–February 1979 period. This provision ignored the seasonal pattern in petroleum use and resulted in severe shortfalls in vacation and resort areas in the summer of 1979.[13]

*The buy/sell program.* The ability to buy crude oil in weakening world markets between 1974 and 1978 rendered the buy/sell program more or less inoperative. During the disruptions, when crude oil prices rose continuously, the program forced the large refiners to surrender oil at prices generally below acquisition cost and invariably below current marginal cost. Unless we regard bigness as routinely meriting penalties and ignore the inefficiencies of nonmarginal cost pricing, buy/sell was thus neither equitable nor efficient. The program also distorted incentives, discouraging precrisis stockpiling by the large companies and rewarding small refiners who failed to stockpile and, through contracts or other means, to make provision for emergency periods. Although the buy/sell program was directed at crude oil allocation, it tended to exacerbate shortages in gasoline and other "lighter" refinery output, since these products were generally outside the productive capability of the small recipient refineries.[14]

*Exceptions relief.* The allocations under exceptions relief were even more doubtful than those under buy/sell, from both an equity and an efficiency standpoint. Beginning under the FEO in January 1974, special allocations of either crude or product supplies were made to firms suffering "serious hardship" or "gross inequity" under the regulations. In particular, firms whose very solvency was threatened under the regulatory framework were to be given special consideration for relief.[15]

As recounted in *Federal Energy Administration Regulation: Report of the Presidential Task Force*, exceptions relief quickly mushroomed into a broadly based, free-wheeling quasi-judicial process. Rulings in individual cases not only determined the direct transfer of oil between firms but also resulted in exceptions to the crude oil price ceilings and in special grants of entitlements to purchasers of crude oil. The original requirement that qualifying firms be experiencing gross hardship or inequity under the rules was liberalized. Relief was granted to induce firms to produce more oil rather than undertake alternative investments or to help a firm achieve its historic rate of return or simply to avoid a serious loss of revenue. Under these general criteria, the exceptions procedure was almost unrestrained in its ability to contravene market outcomes without regard to efficiency and to transfer income between firms—almost invariably from larger to smaller and from successful to less successful companies.[16]

A perusal of DOE Decision and Order releases reveals something of the character and scope of OHA intervention. The Ashland Oil Company sold its domestic and foreign crude oil–producing properties in 1978 and quickly contracted for imports from Iran. When the president embargoed Iranian imports after the seizure of the American embassy in November 1979, Ashland appealed to OHA and was granted $218 million in oil from nine of the largest majors at prices below market. Ashland was permitted to buy this oil during December 1979 through February 1980 at the average price it paid for crude oil in November and December 1979. Contract prices were rising rapidly in this period from near twenty dollars per barrel to nearer thirty dollars. Upon learning later that Ashland had overstated its Iranian imports, OHA ordered the company to repay $5.7 million to the majors, equal approximately to half of the majors' forgone profits on the mandated sale to Ashland.[17]

Measures to maintain a historical rate of return on investment are analogous to the rate-of-return regulation applied to public utilities. The hazard of such regulation is, of course, the tendency to mandate prices sufficient to cover cost increases, whether the costs are economically justified or not (something that may in fact be unknowable even to the firm, to say nothing of the regulator). Given its goal of maintaining rate of return, such regulation is thus effectively unable to mandate a price decrease, a decrease in the rate of return, and eventual liquidation of the firm's assets, even though such measures might be the socially efficient response to a firm's ineptitude or to declining market demand in a given region or nationwide.

After the regulatory principle in the Delta and Beacon refinery cases had been embraced,[18] it was inevitable that exceptions relief would soon provide a lifeline in the form of crude oil allocations and special grants of entitlements (or exemptions from purchasing entitlements) to firms far and wide. The sheer magnitude of the applications for relief—as many as several thousand per week in mid-1979—made it impossible for the appeals office to employ standards of investigation and verification that measured up even to the less-than-satisfactory performance of established regulatory agencies. OHA had little choice but to proceed on what it characterized as the "assumed accuracy" of unaudited company-provided information.[19]

An example of the pitfalls in this approach to rate-of-return regulation is the case of the Southland Oil Company, a collection of three small refineries in Jackson, Mississippi, with a total capacity of 21,000 barrels per day. Southland had included a life insurance subsidiary in its investment base and had transferred funds greater than its after-tax profits to its parent company, Vermont Gas Systems, Inc., which had the effect of reducing Southland's apparent profitability. Upon learning of these practices in 1981, OHA asked Southland to return about half of the $25 million in entitlements received free of charge from 1975 to 1977. There were no other sanctions.[20]

The Little America Refining Company (LARCO) received subsidies of approximately $200 million above those received as part of the Small Refiner Bias program. LARCO had the initial advantage of being permitted to maintain its two refinery units as separate entities, thereby qualifying for greater subsidies (see table 8). In the late 1970s, LARCO invested heavily in its refinery capacity, pipelines, terminals, and marketing facilities and in hotels, including the Sun Valley Ski Resort. The investment base upon which rate of return was to be calculated was thus expanded to include oil and nonoil properties, not all of which, as it turned out, were profitable. OHA eventually took a dim view of this practice but applied no sanctions and granted LARCO a final $30 million in an effort to restore its deteriorating cash flow.[21]

OHA was only following the logic of rate-of-return regulation, providing support only to ailing firms, when it denied relief to the Indiana Farm Bureau, an agricultural cooperative operating a 21,200-barrel-per-day refinery in Mt. Vernon, Indiana. Indiana Farm claimed that exceptions relief to a local competitor, Energy Cooperative, Inc. (ECI), had placed Indiana Farm at a competitive disadvantage. OHA observed, however, that Indiana Farm was profitable and showed no evidence of "irreparable injury" as a result of paying higher prices than its competitors did for crude oil.[22]

The ECI refinery had been purchased from Arco by a group of nine farm cooperatives. It was in poor physical condition with outmoded equipment and required steady infusions of cash and low-priced crude oil to keep operating. In December 1980, ECI requested almost $100 million to remain solvent. OHA provided only $10 million, however, following the receipt of which ECI indeed went bankrupt.[23]

**The Relation of Crude Oil Controls and Allocations to Supply and Demand.** None of the price controls and mandatory allocations that we have discussed created shortages in the crude oil market in any economic sense. The economic definition of shortage is, of course, an excess of demand quantity over supply quantity at the going market price. In this context, demand and supply are voluntary, effective,

82

cost- or budget-constrained behavioral aggregates. In these economic terms, there were no crude oil shortages during the control period; the excess demand in the domestic crude oil market simply spilled over into the foreign market, where, except possibly during the initial stages of disruption, it was fully met by oil imports (see figures 11 and 12 above).

The government intervened in the market by transferring supply among demanders outside the price-determined market allocation. Government implemented a political redistribution, partly by the cash transfers of the entitlements system, partly by the mandated supplier/ purchaser freeze and buy/sell programs, and partly by the expropriations and transfers of supply under exceptions relief. This action affected supply and demand by imposing disincentives on supply and forcing demanders to move to different markets, including the overseas market, depending on their share of the redistributed supplies. There were no shortages and accompanying queues in the economic sense, only in the political sense. The queues were in Congress, in the Department of Energy, and wherever extramarket demand received a sympathetic hearing.

## Price Controls and Allocations in Petroleum Product Markets

We will discuss the impact of controls on petroleum product prices in general and then with particular attention to the retail market for gasoline. A brief survey of the mandatory allocations in the nonretail product markets will be followed by an evaluation of the claims made on behalf of the regulatory system.

**Price Controls in General.** Although the price ceilings on petroleum products were in some sense less rigid than those on crude oil, there was not, in the case of most products, an effectively unlimited supply of imports to absorb the unsatisfied domestic demand. This circumstance, together with mandatory allocations, left the petroleum product markets in a state of shortage or malfunction throughout the control period. In the short run, retail product markets were characterized by queuing and other search activity; in the long run, all markets exhibited deteriorating service and unresponsiveness of supply.

The initial impulse of the regulatory authorities during the embargo period was to peg petroleum product prices, along with domestic crude oil, at May 1973 levels. Mounting pressure from refiners and resellers of refined products to raise their prices to cover rising crude oil costs led to numerous exceptions to the ceilings. Finally, in November 1973, the passage of EPAA established the principle that crude oil costs, or *product* costs, as they were called, could be fully passed on to the price of petroleum products at all stages of production and distribution.[24]

Operating costs, or *nonproduct* costs, could also be passed through to price, but capital and interest costs could not be. Moreover, the nonproduct costs were subject to stipulations as to how much could be passed through in any time period and how such costs were to be allocated among the individual components of a refinery's product slate. Any eligible costs, product or nonproduct, that sellers could not or did not choose to add to price could be held in abeyance, or *banked*, as the basis for future price increases.[25]

Maximum allowable profit margins for sellers of refined products at all stages of production and distribution were also prescribed. The margins were initially frozen at their May 15, 1973, levels but were gradually increased during the decade for various classes of product and of sellers and resellers. Inflation, however, rose more rapidly and, during the decade, reduced the real value of the profit margins.

Nonproduct costs were to be allocated among a refiner's product slate in proportion to each product's volume except that after 1978 a disproportionate amount could be charged to gasoline. This provision was designed to encourage gasoline output while continuing to limit the revenues from gasoline sales. Until 1979, however, the regulations treated gasoline as an undifferentiated homogeneous product. As the demand for the unleaded variety grew, the regulations did not permit the pass-through of investment costs necessary to produce unleaded gasoline in the desired amount.[26]

The price ceilings on all major petroleum products except gasoline, propane, and jet fuel were removed in 1976. Jet fuel was decontrolled early in 1979.[27] Gasoline and propane remained subject to the DOE ceilings (with cost pass-through) until the final decontrol in January 1981. Gasoline, of course, is the single largest petroleum product, accounting for 35–40 percent of refined output. Even the officially decontrolled products, however, became subject to the so-called voluntary price guidelines administered by the Council on Wage and Price Stability (COWPS) beginning in November 1978. These guidelines placed limits directly on the increase in prices in any period or, if the firm chose, indirectly, by limiting the increase in profit margins. In any year, a firm's prices could increase by 0.5 percent less than its average price increases in 1976–1977. If raw material cost increases made this option unpalatable, price increases could create a gross profit margin that equaled the average of those in two of the past three years but was not more than 6.5 percent greater than the margin of the previous year. Because of crude oil price increases, the oil industry generally abided by the gross margin rule.[28]

The COWPS price restrictions were widely publicized and were taken quite seriously by the oil companies. Initially, violators were prohibited from bidding on federal oil leases. Thus, in a real sense, all petroleum product prices remained under some degree of control until 1981.[29]

**Price Controls in the Retail Market for Gasoline.** We turn now to a detailed analysis of the impact of price ceilings on petroleum product consumer markets, taking retail gasoline as the prototypical case.[30] Figure 15 represents the national gasoline market before and after a crude oil supply interruption. The gasoline supply and demand are purely domestic, as in figure 14. International trade in gasoline is negligible, involving mainly imports from a few offshore Caribbean refineries. Like the crude oil schedules in figure 1, the supply and demand for gasoline are marginal cost and marginal valuation functions, respectively. Crude oil itself is, of course, an input in the production of gasoline through the refining process and the various stages of marketing and distribution.

Prior to the disruption, the demand for gasoline $D_0$ intersects the supply $S_0$ at a price $p_0$ and quantity $q_0$. A reduction in the world supply of crude oil raises its price and shifts the domestic supply of gasoline upward and leftward to $S_1$. The equilibrium, or market-clearing, price of gasoline rises to $p_1$ and quantity falls to $q_1$.

Both supply schedules are drawn with flat portions extending from the vertical axis, followed, in the case of $S_1$, by a steeply rising segment. The flat portion of supply reflects the rigidity of short-run marginal costs in downward movements along the schedule; in $S_0$, it also reflects constant long-run marginal costs in the production of gasoline. The nearly vertical segment of $S_1$ reflects the inability of supply quantity to increase substantially in the short run. This upper limit on supply is certainly characteristic of a disruption and its immediate aftermath, but any short-run upward movement along any supply schedule is likely to be restrained.[31]

The pass-through of product and eligible nonproduct costs creates a ceiling price of $p_2$ greater than $p_0$ by the amount of those costs but less than $p_1$, the market-clearing price. At $p_2$, the quantity demanded is $q_2^D$, which is greater than the quantity supplied, $q_2^S$. The difference, or excess demand quantity, is ($q_2^D - q_2^S$), a shortage in the economic sense.

The difference between $p_2$ and $p_1$ is an increase in the profit margin, which, under EPAA, was not permitted. In the absence of

85

FIGURE 15

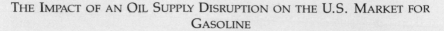

THE IMPACT OF AN OIL SUPPLY DISRUPTION ON THE U.S. MARKET FOR
GASOLINE

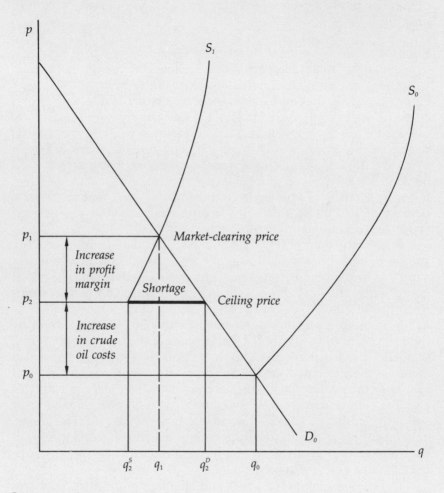

SOURCE: Authors.

market clearing (and even under market clearing, as we shall see), allocation within industry was governed by mandatory rules, such as the supplier/purchaser freeze, state set-asides, a designated system of priority uses and users, and exceptions relief. We shall discuss these devices shortly. At the retail level, however, there were no mandatory allocations, only natural market forces characteristic of shortage situations. We describe these in the following section.

*Nonprice allocation and the shadow prices.* Impromptu allocative methods typical of shortage markets quickly sprang up in retail gasoline distribution following the disruptions. Queues formed. Station owners resorted to limiting the number of gallons sold to each buyer, preference for established customers, and early closings as the limited supplies rapidly disappeared. Several states and regions mandated alternate-day eligibility for gasoline purchases, which day depending on whether the last digit of the license number was odd or even. In general, consumers resorted to search activity, which was costly, because of both the time and the transportation, including the use of fuel, involved in seeking out the available supplies.

The extent to which search costs are incurred can be determined from the supply-and-demand picture of the controlled gasoline market. Figure 16 reproduces the postdisruption portion of figure 15. We saw that at $p_2$, which is the ceiling and actually prevailing price, the quantity $q_2^S$ was supplied and $q_2^D$ demanded. Since $q_2^S$ is the total quantity that consumers in fact receive, however, the value they place on it is given by the height of the demand schedule segment (drawn in bold) over the range of quantities from 0 to $q_2^S$. Thus the first unit supplied is valued by a buyer at a maximum of $p_n$ dollars per gallon. The second available unit is worth a maximum of $p_{n-1}$ to someone, and so on down to $p_3$, which is the market's valuation of the last unit supplied, the $q_2^S th$.

These valuations ($p_n$, $p_{n-1}$, . . . , $p_3$) are known as *shadow prices*, which are values consumers place on a commodity that, for institutional reasons, are not reflected in observable market prices. The shadow prices have no direct bearing on consumer behavior in a free market, where there is a single market-clearing price and supply and demand are in balance. (The difference between the shadow prices and the market-clearing price is, of course, the source of consumers' surplus.) In a price-controlled market, however, with unsatisfied demand, the shadow prices associated with the de facto available supply quantity measure the total cost consumers are willing to incur and will seek to incur to acquire that quantity. Since the law prohibits a market price above $p_2$, consumers will attempt to spend the difference between their shadow prices and the legal ceiling price in nonmonetary ways.

Each individual buyer will tend to incur search and other nonmonetary costs until the cost of each unit of the available gasoline is $p_3$, of which $p_2$ is paid in the form of a direct cash outlay and the

FIGURE 16

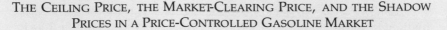

THE CEILING PRICE, THE MARKET-CLEARING PRICE, AND THE SHADOW
PRICES IN A PRICE-CONTROLLED GASOLINE MARKET

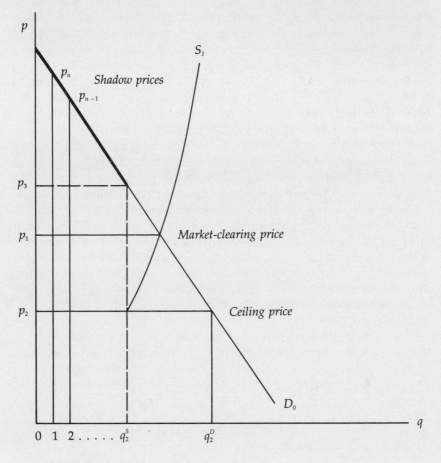

SOURCE: Authors.

difference $(p_3 - p_2)$, takes the form of valuable time and fuel spent in searching for gasoline, waiting in line for it, and creating special relationships with the people who sell it. Individual buyers have shadow prices above $p_3$ and would be willing to search and wait in queues longer than those that yield a cost of $(p_3 - p_2)$. Competitive searching among buyers, however, tends to equalize the length of queues and other search activity until all yield a cost equal to $(p_3 - p_2)$.

During the 1979 crisis, economists at DOE estimated that motorists were spending an average of thirty to fifty cents per gallon *above* the legal ceiling prices of $0.90 to $1.10 per gallon in the form of time spent and gasoline used in the search effort and while waiting in line. Time was valued modestly at $4.00 per hour, which was less than half the average of $10.10 per hour of total compensation being earned in the U.S. private sector. These economists further claimed that the shadow price of about $1.50 per gallon exceeded the free market price by at least fifteen or twenty cents, as implied by an intersection of supply and demand in figure 16 at a price *below* the lowest shadow price.[32]

The social welfare effect of the ceiling price in combination with the influence of the shadow price is shown in figure 17. In a completely free market, with price $p_1$, consumers' surplus is the area ($A$ + $B$ + $C$) and producers' surplus is ($D$ + $E$). The imposition of ceiling price $p_2$, without consideration of the shadow price and the behavior it provokes, leaves consumers' surplus at ($A$ + $B$ + $E$) and producers' surplus at zero. The ceiling price transfers surplus of $E$ from producers to consumers and simply eliminates $C$ and $D$ from consumers' and producers' surplus, respectively ($C$ and $D$ are "dead-weight" losses attributable to the price ceiling). Now, however, as consumers, guided by the shadow price, incur costs of ($p_3 - p_2$) in searching for each gallon of gasoline ($B$ + $E$) tends to be converted from surplus to cost, eroding consumers' surplus. Producers, meanwhile, gain no surplus from consumer search behavior. Queuing, driving about looking for open service stations, and the like are costly activities in which, relative to a free market, there are no gainers, only losers.

*Nonprice allocation and reduction in product quality.* Markets always clear—by prices or by other devices. We have seen that if prices are controlled below market-clearing levels, then initially supply and demand are brought together by search and queuing activity. As time passes, however, more adaptive behavior emerges to eliminate the excess demand: (1) Under controls, suppliers will typically reduce the quality of the product and its cost of production. This reaction tends to shift the supply schedule down and to the right. (2) Demanders will respond to the reduced quality by reducing their demand, which appears as a leftward shift of the schedule. (3) Demanders will eventually transfer any remaining excess demand to other markets. We shall deal with this last response shortly.

In the early stages of oil supply disruption, the reduced quality and range of services with which gasoline was delivered were simply a means of allocating a virtually fixed supply in a price-controlled market. Stations were open for shorter intervals, closing earlier on

# FIGURE 17

### Areas of Consumers' Surplus and Producers' Surplus in a Free Market, in a Price-Controlled Market, and under the Influence of the Shadow Price

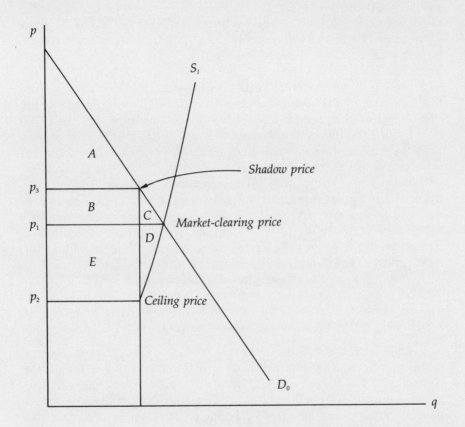

Source: Authors.

weekdays and entirely on weekends. Services, including the pumping of gas, cleaning of windshields, and checking under the hood, were curtailed. The octane rating of gasoline fell. As the disruption episodes passed, however, these reductions in the "quality" of delivered gasoline tended to become permanent.

In a longer time frame in which the supply again became more or less variable, the quality reductions were a way of lowering the cost of supplying any given quantity of gasoline. The cost reductions offset nonproduct costs that could not be passed through or, where permitted, raised profit margins or otherwise prevented margins from falling. The deterrence to quality and cost cutting that would have come from competitive forces, including the contrary preferences of consumers, was absent since, under the mandatory allocations described below, firm entry and exit were tightly controlled. Meanwhile, the appearance of a cheaper and lower-quality, but more plentiful, version of a price-controlled product provided consumers with a viable alternative to search and other welfare-destroying activity.

The quality reductions were, to some degree, imposed on suppliers by outside forces. The decline of average octane rating was partly a result of regulations discouraging refinery investment and retrofitting in the face of changing grades of crude oil in the world market. The general sluggishness of the fuel distribution system was partly attributable to the mandatory allocations, especially to the supplier/purchaser freeze, which limited entry and exit and made responsive, competitive supply a thing of the past. The reduction of services, although initially a take-it-or-leave-it phenomenon, evolved later in the decade into a consumer choice option, self-service.

Nevertheless, by initiating or acquiescing to these changes and by taking other labor and capital cost-reducing actions, the gasoline distribution system shifted its supply curve to the right (or offset any tendency of the curve to shift to the left), as shown in figure 18. This closed part of the excess demand gap ($q^D - q^S$), at the ceiling price, $p_C$.

At the same time, the value of gasoline to motorists who could no longer count on finding gasoline of given quality at almost any time of the day or week, accompanied by the usual services, was also reduced. The lower valuation would be reflected in lower prices offered by demanders at each quantity. The demand curve thus dropped or, equivalently, shifted to the left, as shown in figure 18. The operation of the tendency toward quality deterioration can thus be expected to cause both supply and demand to shift downward until they meet at a common, intermediate quantity at the ceiling price, as pictured.

The process just described, whether allocating a fixed or a variable supply, replaces the search, queuing, and general scramble spurred by high shadow prices that hang over controlled gasoline markets in the aftermath of supply disruptions. Since search and queuing tend to reduce consumers' surplus sharply, the market clearing pictured in figure 18 though not involving the product attributes consumers most prefer, nevertheless yields positive surplus to both producers and consumers and is thus likely to represent a higher level of welfare.

91

## FIGURE 18

### Market Clearing Achieved through Product Quality Deterioration in a Price-Controlled Gasoline Market

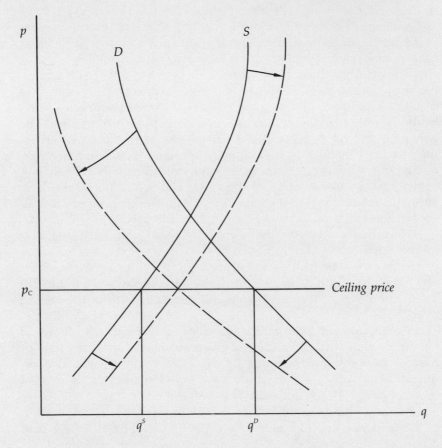

SOURCE: Authors.

*Nonprice allocation and transfer of the unsatisfied demand.* No matter how nonprice allocation is carried out—whether by mandatory rules, by ad hoc search and queuing governed by the shadow prices, or by market clearing through product quality deterioration, part or all of the original demand at the ceiling price remains unsatisfied. It is unlikely, however, that the inability to purchase gasoline in desired amounts and quality would lead to a permanent reduction in the total level of consumer expenditures. Consumers will eventually transfer the unrealized gasoline expenditures to more or less related markets.[33]

92

## FIGURE 19

### The Transfer of Unsatisfied Demand from (a) a Price-Controlled Market to (b) an Uncontrolled Substitute Market

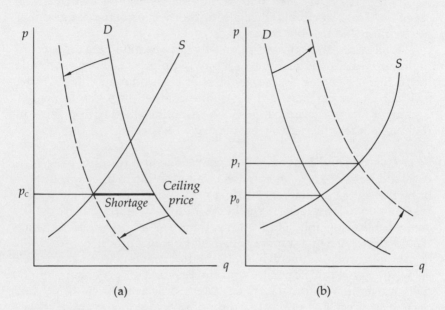

(a)                                                    (b)

SOURCE: Authors.

An example of the transfer is shown in figure 19a, which depicts the market for a product whose price is controlled at a ceiling, $p_c$, below the market-clearing level. The excess demand is equal to the bold horizontal segment. The funds underlying that excess demand are transferred to an uncontrolled substitute product. This transfer is shown in the controlled market as shifting the entire demand schedule to the left. Once the unspent funds intended for purchase of the commodity at $p_c$ are removed from the market, these funds are also unavailable for expenditure on the commodity at any other price. The net effect is a reduced ability to buy the quantity previously demanded at all prices.

In figure 19b, which pictures the market for an uncontrolled substitute commodity, the transfer of unsatisfied demand from the controlled market is shown as shifting demand to the right over the entire range of prices. This rightward shift raises both the market price and the quantity of the substitute commodity.

In the case of gasoline for automobile use, there are no close substitutes in the short run, but part of the excess demand was transferred to alternative transportation modes—air, train, and bus.[34] To some extent automobile travel was replaced by nontravel activities, such as a vacation in a person's home area rather than at a distant resort. In such cases a portion of the excess gasoline demand was spent on local restaurants, theaters, and other recreational items that were obtainable without travel.

In all cases, the spillover of unsatisfied gasoline demand created higher prices elsewhere in the economy. The price ceilings were thus ineffective in keeping the *average* level of prices down. Although the residual excess demand in the gasoline market gave rise to neither consumers' or producers' surplus, however, it created both of these in the markets to which it was transferred.

**Price Controls and Economic Efficiency.** The end result of price controls and nonprice allocation in the retail gasoline market was thus to bring the ceiling and market-clearing prices together. The ceiling price rose initially in response to eligible product and nonproduct cost increases following the supply disruption. In time, the ceiling price would rise somewhat more as other eligible nonproduct costs could be passed through. Meanwhile, the higher market-clearing price fell as product quality deteriorated and the residual excess demand gradually moved to other markets. The market-clearing price would also decline as the rising portion of the supply schedule eventually flattened out in response to increasing supply and easing prices in the world oil market.

The same process could be expected to occur in other sectors of the petroleum product market. At the refining and other intermediate levels, the allocation rules (to be discussed) would obviate the intensive search and queuing of the early stages of a disruption. The tendency to reduction of product quality, however, and the transfer of excess demand to other markets would be present.

The equalizing of ceiling and market-clearing prices does not imply that prices are determined by market forces. The reason is that the ceiling price, which is always the prevailing price, can never fully adapt to shifts of supply and demand. When supply fell, as in figure 15, the eligible cost pass-through did not include a rise in the profit margin, which accounted for most of the difference between the ceiling and market-clearing price. An increase in demand would affect the market similarly. As firms attempted to expand output, costs, some of them eligible for pass-through, would increase. The greater part of the immediate rise in the market-clearing price, which would

94

be ineligible for inclusion in the ceiling price, would again be an increase in the profit margin.

The failure of the regulations to allow profit margins to rise under changing supply and demand and the requirement that cost increases precede price increases negated the market allocation mechanism.[35] Although the flow of resources—for example, into markets where price and margins have risen—soon restores the margins to their pre-disturbance level, the temporary movement of profit margins is the fundamental driving force of the allocative process.

The regulations mandated occasional increases in the margins of all firms in order to prevent widespread business failures or to keep pace with inflation. These across-the-board increases, however, did not in any sense provide the spontaneous margin adjustments, varying with respect to firm, particular product, and region, that would have enabled the market to exercise its normal allocative function.

**Price Controls and Inflation.** The analysis of the retail gasoline market indicates that, in general, price ceilings on individual products tend to raise, rather than to lower, the overall price level. In the retail market, where there were no mandatory allocations, the initial impact of the ceilings was to create search and queuing costs. These costs are not included in the common measures of inflation, the consumer and other price indexes, but the costs are nonetheless real. Moreover, the search and queuing costs tend to be carried to the level of the shadow prices, which exceed the market-clearing price.

At the retail or any other level, we saw that the ceilings also promote product quality deterioration, which again represents higher costs to buyers that are not captured by price indexes but could be massive. We also observed that eventually the remaining excess demand in any controlled market moves to uncontrolled markets, where prices are directly increased.

Finally, as noted in chapter 2, in the preceding section, and in our discussion below of mandatory allocation, price ceilings combined with mandatory allocations prevent petroleum products from finding their most-valued uses. This tendency will reduce the aggregate supply of output and will raise the general price level as measured by the price indexes.

**Mandatory Allocation of Refined Products.** Petroleum products, except at retail, were subject to the same mandatory distribution according to historical use that applied to crude oil and were equally the object of redistribution by directive of the Office of Hearings and

Appeals. In addition, petroleum products were allocated to broad classes of users by a priority schedule; there was also a special set-aside to state governments. The product allocation programs were thus:

1. The supplier/purchaser freeze, as described above in connection with crude oil allocations.

2. The requirement, as specified by the federal government, that suppliers set aside a given percentage of sales of each product in each state for allocation by the state in dealing with hardship cases and emergency functions; 4 percent of middle distillates and 3 percent of other products were so specified. In the spring of 1979, there was an across-the-board increase to 5 percent.[36]

3. After subtraction of the state set-aside, and layered over the freeze, was a schedule of six priority categories that allocated, at the highest priority, 100 percent of "current requirements" (as defined by the user). Users in five other priority groups received a designated quantity multiplied by an allocation fraction, which was the seller's available supply in any month relative to the 1972 base period. The designated quantities were 100 percent of current requirements and, in order, 110 percent, 100 percent, 95 percent, and 90 percent of the buyer's base-period use. Defense and agricultural production were assigned the highest priority for all petroleum products; that is, they were to receive their "current requirements." Emergency services, telecommunications, sanitation services, passenger transportation, medical and nursing buildings, and several other activities and facilities were permitted their current requirement multiplied by the supplier's allocation fraction. Space heating received 110 percent of base-period use times the allocation fraction. Nonpassenger transportation, industrial, commercial, and non–defense-related governmental uses received 100 percent of the base-period level times the allocation fraction. Other uses received 95 percent or 90 percent of the base-period amount multiplied by the allocation fraction.[37]

4. Exceptions relief, as described under point 3 of the crude oil allocations and in the subsequent discussion under that topic, required orders for specific allocations.

Accompanying these general allocative programs were literally thousands of written and oral interpretations, adjustments, and rule changes to meet unanticipated individual circumstances. During the 1979 crisis, there were twenty-seven rule changes governing the allocation of gasoline and middle distillates, frequently made on an ad hoc basis without systematic analysis and prior public comment. The regulatory amendments concerning the base period for gasoline allocation were, on several occasions, effective on issuance without advance notification. Almost 200 changes—two a month—in the price ceilings on various refinery products were made during the eight-year duration of EPAA. In DOE's own evaluation of these procedures, "refiners, suppliers, and consumers were so barraged by these constantly changing requirements, that planning and compliance were a virtual impossibility."[38]

**Mandatory Allocation and Economic Efficiency.** The supplier/purchaser freeze of petroleum product use had no more a priori claim to efficiency than that of crude oil. By the very nature of a disruption and the relative price changes that result, the optimal allocation of fuel is inevitably different from any past distribution, including that which immediately preceded the disruption.

*Priority classification.* The designation of priority classes was at best an intuitive ordering of claims that also could not possibly meet efficiency criteria. In the absence of free market prices, no one has any way of determining the economic amount of fuel in any particular use. To compound the difficulty, we have seen that artificially suppressed prices generate shadow prices that exaggerate (grossly if demand is inelastic) the value of a commodity relative to its postdisruption market-clearing price. Under these circumstances—ignorance of the uncontrolled market price and intimate knowledge of the higher shadow prices—an optimal allocation, which maximizes postdisruption GNP and employment, is effectively unattainable.

Even without the distorted information structure, the grant to any sector (defense, agriculture, or any other) of 100 percent of self-defined requirements invites—indeed, begs for—abuse. It should come as no surprise that many farmers were observed reselling diesel fuel during the spring and summer of 1979.

There is no more economic standing, however, in the lesser allocations: 110 percent of base-period use times the allocation fraction to space heating and lesser amounts to commercial and industrial use (100 percent) and retail gasoline purchasers (no priority listing). Space heating by oil may appear crucial, as indeed it is in some sectors at some minimal level. Household automobile travel would seem to be readily reducible. Empirically derived demand price elasticities, however, do not support this ranking. Among the three use categories, space heating tends to exhibit the greatest elasticity in response to price increases—the largest percentage of voluntary reduction—and motor gasoline demand the least.[39] This tendency implies that there are greater perceived opportunities and willingness in the economy as a whole to reduce petroleum use in heating, by substituting nonpetroleum fuels or by turning down thermostats, wearing heavier clothing, and shutting off heat in selected rooms. Motor gasoline and diesel fuel users are less able and less willing to conserve. In short, at the margin, the uses of gasoline and diesel fuel are economically more valued than those of heating oil.

The common public policy of placing the greater burden of an oil disruption on automobile use is thus inconsistent both with the efficient use of energy and consequently with the maintenance of GNP. The disproportionate curtailment of driving caused severe distress in tourism and related industries, in which many Americans earn their living. More fundamentally, the automobile in America is at least as much a factor of production as it is a consumer good. The United States is a country with extraordinarily low population density and with GNP heavily dependent on fast and flexible transportation, which only the automobile provides.[40] It should also be noted that air travel, which soared during the crises as a result of the limitation on driving, is more energy intensive on a per passenger basis than are the least fuel-efficient automobiles.

The allocation ratios used in determining priority suffered from geographical rigidity. They were based on the product supplies available to each seller on a local or regional level. No attempt was made to assess the available supply of each product nationally, taking into account opportunities for geographical redistribution, nor was any effort in the priority classification system directed toward preventing nonpriority uses of fuel by priority users. It is doubtful that the necessary surveillance could, in any case, have been successfully mounted.[41]

The general problems of mandatory allocation were not peculiar to Washington. Citing the Cabot report, William Lane describes the states as "unprepared to administer the set-aside."[42] Referring to the 1979 crisis, Lane writes:

> Each state apportioned the set-aside supplies differently. At the beginning of the shortage, many states provided additional supplies to tourist areas, where demand was already down and supplies were more than adequate. . . . The fact that, by July, most states were directing set-aside supplies back to [urban] retailers demonstrates that the set-aside program acted as an administrative bottleneck and delayed the distribution of supplies to areas where they were most needed. The Department of Justice study points out that the set-aside program had "the effect of forcing the industry to

withhold 5 percent of available supplies for most of each month. During periods of tight supplies, this additional 5 percent can be the difference between relative calm and long lines at the service stations." [pp. 83–84]

*Other problems of centralized allocation.* A centralized authority tends to rely on convenient administrative rules (the supplier/purchaser freeze), moral judgments as to desirable and undesirable uses of energy in an emergency (space heating is preferred to automobile travel; small companies and an occasional unsuccessful large company are more deserving than large companies in general), and political pressures—the United States is, after all, a democracy.

When allocation enters the political realm, groups that are highly organized (for example, farmers) and well financed (for example, small refiners) play a major role. Although amply financed individuals also do well in the free market, their influence there is constrained by competitive forces. In the political arena, they effectively acquire monopoly power—the ability to arrange for government-mandated noncompetitive prices and wealth transfers.

In May 1979, farmers in the Midwest felt threatened by the lack of diesel fuel in order to carry out their spring planting. Special Rule 9 granted agricultural production its self-determined "current need" of middle distillates. No fuel provision for trucks that carry agricultural produce, however, was made until truckers went on strike, as they had six years earlier. A June 1 amendment to Special Rule 9 granted truckers of perishable commodities who were bulk purchasers their current fuel needs but ignored nonbulk truck purchasers and railroads (which carried fertilizer and equipment to the farms and grain from the farms to the market).[43]

Under centralized allocation, rules tend to be changed not frequently enough or too frequently. On the one hand, bureaucratic decisions must be cleared through many channels and, in a democracy, through open forums, including political ones. This statement was true of the six-year effort to allow refineries to distinguish between leaded and unleaded gasoline and to allocate costs to each variety realistically; it was also true of the delays that innumerable individuals faced, from a school district that wanted to replace a fraudulent fuel supplier (four months from the initial request, a year from the date of the supplier's conviction) to an automobile manufacturer that needed gasoline to conduct mandatory emissions tests for the Environmental Protection Agency, without which the entire automobile industry would have been legally required to shut down (five months, just five days before the shutdown order would have become effective).[44]

On the other hand, the hopeless task of identifying all individuals or groups who might qualify for allocations led, as we have seen, to daily rule changes and amendments that could not claim to reach more than a tiny fraction of the eligible population. Individuals who are likely to be overlooked and yet who might readily qualify under most-valued-use criteria include migrant workers, who must travel to survive; busy suburban housewives, who may be able or willing to curtail some, but not all, of their driving chores without incurring unacceptable costs; and vacationers, who may be planning a once-a-year trip. In contrast, identification in an unregulated market is accomplished by self-selection in a process highly responsive to daily, even hourly, changes in underlying economic conditions, as revealed by price.

**Controls and Stockpiling.** Mandatory allocations were regarded as necessary to prevent "hoarding" of supplies in a period of shortfall. It is, of course, impossible to judge whether a given addition to inventories ("hoards") is a socially desirable transfer of goods from present to future consumption based on still higher expected future prices or whether it is a hoarding action not justified by a cool, rational evaluation of future availability. Still, the very existence of price controls with the attendant search, inconvenience, and pervasive uncertainty of supply is an incentive to "topping" of gasoline tanks and other attempts to increase inventories. In a controlled market, hoarding is likely to be a cheaper, more efficient alternative to the search and queuing it replaces. In the absence of controls, the higher price would raise the cost of holding inventories and would tend to lower, not to raise, such holdings.

Price controls served not only to encourage stockpiling during shortfalls but, together with mandatory allocations, to inhibit precrisis stockpiling. The anticipation of price ceilings and of possible expropriation or receipt of supplies, as the case may be, under mandatory allocations deterred provision of supplies for future use. DOE itself describes the case of propane:

> DOE's regulations actually penalized those who did attempt to engage in prudent planning. For example, DOE's special use limitation on propane prohibited companies from acquiring or accepting propane from their suppliers if inventories were above certain levels, whether propane was in short supply or not. Companies were also prohibited from consuming

100

more propane for industrial and other uses than was used during the base period, even from their own supplies. This prevented some companies from fully utilizing propane they had stockpiled for a shortage, and almost certainly discouraged others from building inventories for future shortages. Moreover, the regulations provided little incentive for emergency planning. Refiners, dealers, and larger wholesale consumers were hesitant to build emergency stockpiles, which, under the regulations, could be redirected away from them by DOE during a shortage. On the other hand, priority users, many of whom consumed large amounts of petroleum products, had little incentive to make emergency plans or to conserve because they were entitled to their full requirements in a shortage.[45]

### Controls and Equity

Was equity served by the oil price controls and allocations? The central consideration from the viewpoint of the general public is that the regulations caused markets to malfunction and created allocative inefficiencies in petroleum and in numerous other goods and services. There was a loss of consumer satisfaction in individual products, a higher level of inflation, and greater unemployment. Lower-income families and individuals were almost certainly affected disproportionately by these outcomes, which most people would regard as highly inequitable.

The common measure of the impacts of the regulations on income classes is the resulting reduction in expenditures on petroleum products as a fraction of income. This very superficial measure does not begin to capture the full costs of controls—the high shadow prices, the deterioration of product quality, the spillover effects from petroleum into other markets, and the widespread allocative inefficiencies and heightened adjustment costs, not the least of which is the additional loss of jobs.

Let us turn now to the equity aspects of the specific regulatory programs, most of which were directed in the first instance at the business sector:

1. The price ceilings on domestic crude oil were designed to limit windfall gains to the owners of these properties and indeed did so. The exemption of stripper-well prices was perceived as a benefit for small owners, as to a large extent it was, though many of these small wells were owned by the majors and by very wealthy independent families.

101

2. The entitlements system was designed to equalize the price of crude oil for all refineries. Apart from the Small Refiner Bias, exceptions relief, and other special measures, entitlements succeeded more or less in transferring the rents on domestic crude oil proportionately to all purchasers (see tables 6 and 7), but at the enormous cost of subsidizing imports.

3. The Small Refiner Bias was designed to keep small refiners afloat. It doubtless did so but simultaneously brought into existence forty or fifty new refineries, some of whose annual subsidies were one-fifth to more than one-half of their initial investment (see table 8). Many of their owners became instant millionaires. Such rewards were almost certainly not intended by most of the congressional supporters of the bias legislation.

4. The exceptions relief was a massive transfer of wealth essentially from majors to other segments of the oil industry—for the most part, to smaller firms. The transfers could also be characterized as going from haves to have-nots, the former including small firms that had anticipated the shortfalls and the latter including an occasional large company that had not. Like the Small Refiner Bias, these transfers went well beyond the initial "relief of hardship" goal of the program. Exceptions relief created its own constituency, funneling millions, tens of millions, and hundreds of millions of dollars into the hands of individuals, many of whom were new and ephemeral investors in the oil industry and whose firms tended to be small, badly managed, and well represented by legal counsel or had all of these characteristics. As we have indicated, the funds often found their way into nonpetroleum industries. The program was unbelievably lax in its failure to verify claims, in its acceptance of prospective damages—anticipated but not yet experienced—as a basis for relief, and in its failure to apply appropriate sanctions in cases where recipient firms had blatantly violated OHA's standards and procedures.

5. The supplier/purchaser freeze was seen partly as an equity measure, an attempt to protect relationships established in calmer times from the ravages of supply-disrupted markets. Like the Small Refiner Bias and exceptions relief, the freeze was also regarded as meeting efficiency goals—preserving competition and preventing hoarding and alleged price-ratcheting schemes by large companies. The priority categories, however, were viewed as more an efficiency than an equity corrective.

6. The buy/sell crude oil allocations were akin to the Small Refiner Bias and exceptions relief in serving primarily perceived equity goals.

7. Among the most important equity measures were the price

ceilings on petroleum products. One goal of the ceilings was to limit the profits of oil companies by fixing profit margins. In spite of the controls, the oil industry experienced historically high profits during the disruption episodes. The profits were partly from uncontrolled foreign operations and from windfalls on foreign and domestically held inventories. To some extent, established companies gained from the entry restrictions and reduced competition engendered by the mandatory allocations. Another goal of the price ceilings was to keep petroleum products affordable to the majority of Americans and particularly to those with low incomes. It is doubtful, however, that the ceilings significantly lowered the consumers' cost of petroleum products. It is true that noninternationally traded products (such as gasoline) were priced 10–15 percent below their foreign counterparts. It may be argued, however, that the U.S. regulatory system, although holding down petroleum product prices directly, raised them indirectly by raising the world price of crude oil. The U.S. controls contributed to a higher crude price by discouraging output of domestic crude oil and natural gas while stimulating domestic petroleum consumption through the entitlements.[46] Finally, it is highly unlikely that during the crises, ceilings in the retail markets, combined with search and queuing, served the interests of low-income Americans more than, or even as much as, those of Americans in general. Although the poor have a lower opportunity cost of time and can better afford queuing, the rich often employ surrogates (for example, their teenage children) to conduct the search while in addition wielding influence and personal connections that the poor do not have but that are very important under nonprice allocation.

The best that can be said of the ceilings and allocations as equity measures is that they were not carefully evaluated in advance and were poorly targeted and controlled in their implementation. The ceilings on crude oil clearly limited the rent on producing properties, but then, through the entitlements and Small Refiner Bias, transferred the rent to companies large and small, "deserving" and otherwise. Transfers under buy/sell and exceptions relief were equitable only on the assumption that large or successful companies have an obligation to share the wealth as mandated by these programs. The equity of the supplier/purchaser freeze can lie only in a preference for older, established noneconomic relationships over contemporary, sometimes radically altered economic ones. The price ceilings on products, assuming they in fact created lower prices, benefited, at best, rich and poor alike.

The record is spotty, viewed from most equity standpoints. Weighed against the efficiency losses that all of the regulations entailed, they are hard to defend. Arrow and Kalt found that the efficiency gains of deregulation were more than enough to compensate low-income consumers for the rise in product prices.[47] The authors took the gains as the increase in producers' and consumers' surplus due only to removal of the crude oil ceilings and entitlements. They took no account of the benefits of reversing the distortions created by all the other control programs throughout the decade.

## Summary

After the sharp increase in the world price of oil in the fall of 1973, the U.S. government imposed a system of price ceilings and mandatory allocations on the domestic oil market. Codified through two major legislative acts, the controls remained in force until January 1981. The goal of the controls was to limit the general inflationary impact of the price increases, to limit the profits of the U.S. oil industry, to keep petroleum product prices affordable to the majority of Americans, to assure that petroleum products were directed to those whose need was greatest, to discourage hoarding of supplies by the public and the companies during crises, and to prevent a massive shift of purchasing power from consumers to the oil industry, which would cause a deflationary adjustment in the nonoil sectors of the economy.

A three-tier system of crude oil price ceilings evolved through the 1970s: the May 1973 price (plus minor adjustments) on oil produced before that date; a price that averaged three to seven dollars less than the world price on oil produced after May 1973; and the world price on oil from stripper wells (wells that produced fewer than ten barrels per day).

Accompanying the crude oil ceilings was a system of "entitlements" which, apart from special programs, transferred cash among all refiners so as to equalize their crude oil acquisition costs. Since the average domestic price was less than the world price, the averaging of all prices through entitlements constituted a subsidy to imports.

The Small Refiner Bias program allotted extra entitlements to small refiners, particularly those in the 10,000–50,000-barrel-per-day size range. In 1978 the bulk of subsidies to each refiner extended from just under $4 million to more than $9 million per year. In 1980, the annual grants ranged from almost $13 million to $31 million per refiner. For the small 10,000-barrel units in 1978, the yearly subsidy was almost one-fifth of the initial investment in the refinery; in 1980 it was more than one-half.

The market impact of the crude oil controls without entitlements is a reduction of domestic oil output and an increase in crude oil imports. The welfare effect is a net loss of domestic producers' surplus. Entitlements raise both total petroleum consumption and imports by lowering the perceived price of crude oil. In addition to the loss of producers' surplus due to the ceilings, there is a decrease due to the entitlements in consumers' surplus owing to an expenditure on imports that exceeds the benefits received.

Kalt estimates that the entitlements system lowered the effective price of imports 10–20 percent and created annual average losses in producers' surplus of $1.8 billion in 1980 dollars and in consumers' surplus of $0.8 billion. If we assume that the cost of dependence on unstable foreign oil was two to five dollars per barrel, the total average efficiency loss of the crude oil price controls with entitlements was $4.0–$6.4 billion per year (in 1980 dollars). Kalt also estimates that 40 percent of the rent captured by refiners from price-controlled domestic crude oil was passed on to consumers of domestic petroleum products in the form of lower prices.

The mandatory allocations of crude oil included a supplier/purchaser freeze, the buy/sell program, and exceptions relief. The freeze required that each seller, except at retail, continue to provide a given base-period percentage of supplies to each purchaser. The requirement was ipso facto nonoptimal following supply disruptions and tended to discourage buyers from seeking alternative sources of supply and to discourage sellers from accepting new customers. Changes in the base period were implemented tardily and clumsily.

The buy/sell program was a mandatory redistribution of crude oil from the largest refiners to small ones at the average price of the preceding quarter. It discouraged precrisis stockpiling by all refiners and exacerbated shortfalls of gasoline, which the small crude oil recipient refiners were generally unable to produce. Exceptions relief, designed to assist companies suffering "serious hardship" under the regulations, evolved into a massive redistribution of wealth generally from large or successful oil companies to small or unsuccessful ones.

The price ceilings on petroleum products permitted crude oil costs to be passed through to price, along with a majority of other costs, but froze profit margins. Since changes in profit margins are the fundamental allocating device of unregulated markets, the controls effectively precluded market allocation of petroleum products. In the retail product markets, in which there were no mandatory allocations, supply disruptions led to search and queuing. The costs of this activity were limited by shadow prices that exceeded both the ceiling price and the market-clearing price. In time, the market-clearing price in both retail and wholesale refined product markets fell to the level of the ceiling price by reductions in the quality of the product, which shifted both supply and demand curves downward, and by transfer of remaining excess demand to other markets.

The product price controls were ineffective in limiting general inflation. Excess demand in controlled markets was transferred to uncontrolled markets, where it raised prices. Search and queuing costs and reduction in quality of controlled products raised their effective, if not their recorded, price. Failure under the regulations to allocate petroleum to its most-valued uses reduced aggregate supply and raised the recorded general price level.

Mandatory allocation of petroleum products (at other than the retail level) was carried out by the supplier/purchaser freeze, a product set-aside by suppliers for each state government, a schedule of six priority categories, and exceptions relief. Numerous adjustments and continuing rule changes accompanied the basic programs.

The priority classification included a user category that determined its own fuel requirements. During the 1979 crisis, this category included defense and agriculture. Abuse of the system was inevitable. The allocations generally were inconsistent with empirically measured demand price elasticities, which record the ability of groups to reduce petroleum use voluntarily in response to price increases. The priority allocations particularly underestimated the ability to reduce the use of petroleum in space heating and overestimated the ability to curtail, and the economic desirability of curtailing, automobile use.

The administration of the state set-asides showed no greater preparedness, flexibility, or ability to deliver petroleum products to areas where they were most valued than did the federal programs. Centralized allocation, in general, tends to sacrifice economic efficiency for convenient rules (the supplier/purchaser freeze), for moral judgments as to desirable and undesirable uses of energy (the preference for space heating over automobile travel or for allocation to small companies rather than to large ones) and, inevitably in a democracy, to political pressures. Bureaucratic allocation tends to make rule changes too frequently or not frequently enough and cannot hope to identify all groups or individuals that would qualify for allocations.

The whole regulatory system inhibited precrisis stockpiling by virtue of the price ceilings, allocations to companies with low supplies, and expropriations from companies with more plentiful supplies. During crises, the regulations encouraged stockpiling by reducing its cost relative to search and other nonprice allocative methods.

As equity measures, the controls probably imposed an unequal share of the disruption costs on lower-income groups, who were affected disproportionately by the resulting malfunctioning of markets, allocative inefficiencies, and increased inflation and unemployment.

106

The regulatory programs directed at the oil industry were poorly targeted, partly because of their presumption that *small* and *poor*, or *small* and *deserving*, were like categories. Both the Small Refiner Bias and exceptions relief carried out massive transfers that appeared to go well beyond the original intention of these programs. The subsidy to small refiners demonstrably reduced the efficiency of resource allocation in refining. Exceptions relief, effectively a tax on large companies that were almost certainly more efficient as a group than recipient companies, also thereby achieved equity at the expense of efficiency.

It is questionable whether the controls overall succeeded in lowering petroleum product prices for Americans in general or for poor Americans in particular. Although the major U.S. refined products were priced lower than products overseas, the regulations simultaneously raised the world price of crude oil by discouraging U.S. production of both crude oil and natural gas and by raising U.S. demand for crude oil via the entitlements.

# Notes

1. The use of market-compatible measures, however, such as distributing cash instead of product, is not sufficient justification for a government program. The entitlements system, which equalized the crude oil acquisition costs of refiners by cash transfers, is shown below to be welfare reducing on net.

2. The price data and other regulatory information in this section are taken from Joseph P. Kalt, *The Economics and Politics of Oil Price Regulation* (Cambridge, Mass.: MIT Press, 1981), chap. 1.

3. These prices are the average of those during February-December 1976. See Kalt, *The Economics and Politics of Oil Price Regulation*, p. 18.

4. Production of old, or lower-tier, oil fell steadily from an average of almost two-thirds of U.S. crude oil output in 1974 to one-third in June 1979 when decontrol began. New, or upper-tier, oil rose from 15 percent of total production in 1974 to one-third in June 1979. Stripper oil was 12 percent of output in 1974 and 16 percent in 1979.

5. James H. Gary and Glenn E. Handwerk, *Petroleum Refining—Technology and Economics* (New York: Marcel Dekker, 1975), p. 20.

6. "Cost Squeeze on Oil Refiners," *New York Times*, March 18, 1982.

7. See the statement espousing this viewpoint by Edward J. Mitchell in "Protection for Petroleum Refiners?" *Regulation*, July-August 1981, pp. 37–42.

8. See the letter written in response to Mitchell's article by G.Horwich, in *Regulation*, November-December 1981, p. 55, and the larger study by G. Horwich, W.B. Taylor, B. Vann, et al., *Costs and Benefits of a Protective Tariff on Refined Petroleum Products under Crude Oil Decontrol*, DOE/PE0028 (Washington, D.C.: U.S. Department of Energy, April 1981).

9. The crude oil expenditures, $F_1$, $F_2$, and $F_3$, may not in fact give rise to additional GNP if the petroleum products thereby produced simply displaced an equal amount of imported petroleum products. The displacement would occur for something like residual fuel, whose price is set in the world market, as is that of crude oil. In that case, the shift to the right of the petroleum product supply schedule in response to the lower average price of crude oil would not reduce the price of the petroleum product or raise its consumption and thereby the GNP. Instead the effect would be, as indicated, to shut out an equal amount of, say, residual fuel imports. The reduction in these imports would increase the domestic claim to GNP, however, with the same welfare effects that would be caused by an increase in GNP.

10. Kalt, *The Economics and Politics of Oil Price Regulation*, p. 184.

11. End users who were bulk purchasers in the base period were, however, covered by the freeze.

12. See the history and rationale of Rule 1 in William C. Lane, Jr., *The Mandatory Petroleum Price and Allocation Regulations: A History and Analysis* (Washington, D.C.: American Petroleum Institute, 1981), pp. 14–17 and 24. Lane notes that the rule was imposed in the belief that the largest firms were the price setters at every level of oil industry activity and that restraining their prices would contain oil prices generally.

13. See the discussion in Lane, *The Mandatory Petroleum Price and Allocation Regulations*, p. 80.

14. Ibid., pp. 69–71.

15. See Paul W. MacAvoy, ed., *Federal Energy Administration Regulation: Report of the Presidential Task Force* (Washington, D.C.: American Enterprise Institute, 1977), pp. 108–09.

16. Ibid., pp. 110–22.

17. *Federal Energy Guidelines*, Ashland Oil Company, 9 Dept. of Energy Par 81,058 (Chicago: Commerce Clearing House, 1982).

18. *Federal Energy Guidelines*, Southland Oil Company, 7 Dept. of Energy Par 82,608 (Chicago: Commerce Clearing House, 1981).

19. See, for example, the statement to this effect at the conclusion of Department of Energy, Decision and Order, July 19, 1982, p. 61.

20. Department of Energy, Decision and Order, February 23, 1981, case DEX-0058.

21. *Federal Energy Guidelines*, Little America Refining Company, 6 Dept. of Energy Par 81,001 (Chicago: Commerce Clearing House, 1980).

22. *Federal Energy Guidelines*, Indiana Farm Bureau, 7 Dept. of Energy Par 81,269 (Chicago: Commerce Clearing House, 1981).

23. *Federal Energy Guidelines*, Energy Cooperative, Inc., 10 Dept. of Energy Par 81,017 (Chicago: Commerce Clearing House, 1983).

24. Lane, *The Mandatory Petroleum Price and Allocation Regulations*, pp. 20–23.

25. Kalt, *The Economics and Politics of Oil Price Regulation*, p. 135; and David Couts and George Horwich, "Government Contingency Planning for Petroleum-Supply Interruptions: A History and a Market Perspective," in G.

Horwich and E. J. Mitchell, eds., *Policies for Coping with Oil-Supply Disruptions* (Washington, D.C.: American Enterprise Institute, 1982), p. 149.

26. Couts and Horwich, "Government Contingency Planning," pp. 156–58; Lane, *The Mandatory Petroleum Price and Allocation Regulations*, p. 87.

27. Kalt, *The Economics and Politics of Oil Price Regulation*, p. 19.

28. See Lane, *The Mandatory Petroleum Price and Allocation Regulations*, pp. 57–58.

29. Ibid.

30. Material in this section is adapted from G. Horwich, *Energy: An Economic Analysis* (New York: Joint Council on Economic Education, 1983), pp. 17–25.

31. See figure 7.

32. Calculations were based on data provided by Carmen Difiglio in "Economic Allocation of Gasoline Shortages," in Transportation Research Board, *Considerations in Transportation Energy Contingency Planning: Special Report 191* (Washington, D.C.: National Academy of Sciences, 1980), p. 124.

33. The shift of excess demand can be interpreted as a response to the higher de facto price of gasoline represented by the average shadow price.

34. See chapter 2, table 5.

35. There was, of course, no prohibition against *reductions* in the profit margin, which would be caused by increases in supply or decreases in demand. In the tightly controlled product markets, however, the tendency was not to reduce margins below the allowed maxima. The maximum effectively became the minimum. The usual pressure to reduce margins—the threat of competitive price cutting by existing or newly entered firms—did not operate or operated weakly under the price and allocation controls. The market thus failed to allocate by changes in the profit margin both for market expansion and for contraction.

36. Lane, *The Mandatory Price and Allocation Regulations*, p. 83.

37. Couts and Horwich, "Government Contingency Planning," pp. 150–51.

38. Office of Energy Emergencies, *Preliminary Analysis of Federal Energy Emergency Preparedness Strategies: The EPAA Experience and Current Programs at the Department of Energy* (Washington, D.C.: Department of Energy, 1982), as reprinted in George Horwich, ed., *Energy Use in Transportation Contingency Planning*, special issue of *Energy—The International Journal*, August-September 1983, p. 617.

39. Elasticity estimates, as of August 1983, were provided by the Energy Information Administration, Office of Energy Markets and End Use, forthcoming in the methodology volume of its *Short-Term Energy Outlook*.

40. Consider the following comparative data. Great Britain and West Germany each occupies an area slightly smaller than that of the state of Oregon. There are 53 million Britons, 62 million West Germans, and 2 million Oregonians. The U.S. trend, moreover, is toward decreasing population density. In 1950 the urban areas of the United States contained 70 million people and covered an area approximately the size of the state of Vermont (12,800 square miles). In 1980 the urban area population was 140 million people, but they

occupied an area roughly equal to that of the state of New York (52,000 square miles). Since 1950 the urban population density has thus dropped from 5,469 to 2,692 persons per square mile. These comparisons of urban density were made by Wendell Cox in opening remarks to the Conference on Energy Contingency Planning in Urban Areas, Transportation Research Board, Houston, Texas, April 7, 1983.

41. Lane, *The Mandatory Price and Allocation Regulations*, p. 96.

42. Ibid., pp. 83–84. See also our discussion and analysis of the set-asides in chapter 7.

43. See the accounts in Lane, *The Mandatory Price and Allocation Regulations*, pp. 74–76; John Murray, "Railroads in Emergency Planning," and George G. Cline, "Contingency Planning for Motor Carriers," in G. Horwich, ed., *Energy Use in Transportation Contingency Planning*, special issue of *Energy—the International Journal*, August-September 1983, pp. 669 and 672, respectively.

44. See Office of Energy Emergencies, *Preliminary Analysis of Federal Energy Emergency Preparedness Strategies*, pp. 619–20.

45. Ibid., p. 618.

46. See the rough calculations in G. Horwich, "Planning for the Next Oil Shortage," *Baltimore Sun*, March 7, 1982. Kalt, *The Economics and Price of Oil Price Regulation*, p. 26, estimates that the controls on oil raised U.S. imports 2 million barrels per day. This amount would be added to world excess demand. Natural gas controls may have added another 2 million barrels per day by discouraging natural gas output and stimulating consumption.

47. K. J. Arrow and J. P. Kalt, *Petroleum Price Regulation: Should We Decontrol?* (Washington, D.C., American Enterprise Institute, 1979).

# 4

# The Strategic Petroleum Reserve

The experience with price controls and allocations during the last decade, as detailed in chapter 3, strongly indicates that the United States should not follow similar policies during the next oil supply disruption. Unfortunately, very few, if any, desirable affirmative policies can successfully be initiated and implemented once a disruption has begun. Several desirable policies, however, can and should be implemented in preparation for future disruptions. Of these, the strategic stockpiling of crude oil is by far the most important.

The development of a strategic petroleum reserve became official U.S. policy when President Ford signed the Energy Policy and Conservation Act (EPCA) on December 22, 1975.[1] Congress accepted the Ford administration's proposal that the SPR program should develop government-owned crude oil reserves of 250 million barrels by the end of 1978 and 500 million barrels (then approximately six months of imports) by the end of 1982.[2] Congress later accepted Carter administration amendments to the SPR plan calling for 538 million barrels in storage by the end of 1980 and 1 billion barrels by the end of 1985.[3] At the end of the Carter administration, approximately 100 million barrels were actually in place, and construction of facilities for storage beyond 538 million barrels had not yet begun. The Reagan administration accelerated the rate of fill of existing storage capacity so that more than 380 million barrels were held by January 1984; it has also made a public commitment to developing a reserve of 750 million barrels. Current Reagan administration budget proposals for fiscal years 1984 and 1985, however, would result in about 450 million barrels in storage by the end of 1985 and only about 610 million barrels of available capacity by the end of the decade.

Although it will be useful to consider briefly the reasons why SPR goals have not been met in the past, it is of greater importance to focus on three questions relevant to future policy: (1) How much storage capacity should be developed and at what rate? (2) At what rate should oil be purchased to fill available capacity, and how should the fill be financed? (3) How and when should the SPR be distributed? The history of the SPR program will help us evaluate answers to these questions. First, however, we need a conceptual framework for considering the costs and benefits of strategic stockpiling.

## Why Should the Government Be Involved in Strategic Stockpiling?

Stockpiling can be regarded as a way of transporting goods from one time period to a future period in which they may have a higher economic value. In some ways stockpiling is analogous to the movement of goods among local markets: If the difference in price between two markets is greater than the cost of moving goods from the market with the lower price to the one with the higher price, goods will be transported from the former to the latter. In the case of intertemporal transfers, the "transportation costs" are the costs of storing the goods, including the cost of use forgone while they are in storage. The analogy breaks down, however, in an important way. Whereas firms can readily observe the spatial distribution of prices with considerable accuracy, they can only guess the prices that will prevail in the future. Guessing about future oil prices is particularly difficult because major sources of supply are located in the politically volatile Middle East.

Despite the greater uncertainty in future oil prices, private firms do stockpile to some extent. Petroleum stocks are regularly held by refiners to accommodate the uneven arrival of ship deliveries, to deal with fairly predictable seasonal shifts in the demand for petroleum products, and to take advantage of short-term fluctuations in crude oil prices. In general, we would expect risk-neutral profit-maximizing firms to increase their holdings of speculative stocks of petroleum as long as the present value of the expected price some time in the future is greater than the sum of the current price and the per unit cost of storage from the present to the anticipated time of sale.[4] Previously accumulated speculative stocks that are released during supply disruptions will keep prices from rising as high as they otherwise would, providing economic benefits to all countries that are net importers of petroleum.

We normally assume that private firms move goods among local markets to produce a socially efficient allocation.[5] Is it reasonable to assume that private firms will hold socially optimal levels of speculative petroleum stocks? If the answer were yes, there would be no need for the government to engage in petroleum stockpiling. Unfortunately, several factors lead firms to make stockpiling decisions that are far from the social optimum.

112

First, firms do not bear the full costs and benefits of their stockpiling decisions. When firms purchase oil stocks, they increase the demand for oil in the world market. This increase in turn may raise the world price.[6] Although the stockpilers must pay the higher price for oil, so too must all buyers of oil. The economic costs of the higher prices, however, are external to the profit calculations of the firm. Thus the social costs of stockpile purchases may be larger than the private costs. Similarly, when firms draw down their stocks, a lower world oil price will result, and all users of oil will be economically better off. The social benefits of stockpile drawdowns are therefore larger than the private benefits.

The divergence between the private and social benefits of drawdowns will lead firms to stockpile less than is socially optimal. The divergence between the private and social costs of stock purchases will lead firms to stockpile more than is socially optimal. Which effect dominates? In general, the net effect is probably toward the accumulation of private stocks that are too small from a social standpoint. The reason is that stock accumulations will usually occur gradually, causing small increases in oil prices with negligible economic effects, whereas drawdowns are likely to occur during sharp price rises when even small reductions in price will yield economic benefits. Thus the external costs that cause overstockpiling are likely to be of less significance than the external benefits that lead to understockpiling.

The major exception occurs in situations where firms attempt to build their stocks once supply disruptions have begun. Such buying is rational from the point of view of firms that anticipate the possibility of yet higher prices and fear the loss of market shares if others bid away available supplies. It increases the magnitude of the price shock, however, and exacerbates the economic impact of the disruption. In fact, some observers have argued that the effect of such stockpiling is likely to be greater than the direct effect of the supply disruption triggering it.[7] Thus it appears that the difference between private and social costs and benefits will lead to too little stockpiling during normal periods and to too much at the outset of disruptions.

A second, and perhaps more important, reason why firms normally hold less than socially optimal levels of speculative stocks is that they anticipate the possibility that government will not allow them to sell accumulated stocks at market prices during severe supply disruptions. Even with the elimination of price controls on crude oil and petroleum products in January 1981, firms will include in their calculations the probability that controls will be reinstituted during future oil price shocks. As a result, firms will hold lower levels of speculative stocks than they otherwise would.

A third reason why private speculative stocks are likely to be too small is that the social optimum is determined under the assumption of risk neutrality, whereas firms may actually be risk averse. A decision maker is risk neutral if she or he is willing to accept fair lotteries. That is, a risk-neutral decision maker would be indifferent between receiving a payment of two dollars with certainty and receiving a lottery ticket that would pay either one dollar or three dollars with equal likelihood. If society is assumed to place equal weight on equal changes in net social benefits regardless of the base from which they are measured, and a large number of decisions involving risk must be made (so that extreme outcomes can average out), then social welfare will be maximized if social decisions are made in conformity with risk neutrality.[8] The appropriate cost-benefit criterion under risk neutrality is that choices should be made so as to maximize expected net benefits, where *expected* is used in the mathematical sense.[9]

Now consider a firm that is deciding whether or not to hold speculative stocks. Assume the firm believes that in the coming year there is a 99 percent probability of normal market conditions and a 1 percent probability of a serious disruption that will send prices soaring. Furthermore, assume the firm estimates that it will lose one dollar for the next barrel it stockpiles if normal market conditions prevail but will gain ninety-nine dollars if the market is disrupted. The expected value of adding the marginal barrel is zero $[0.99(-1) + 0.01(99)]$, so a risk-neutral firm would be indifferent between adding and not adding the barrel to its stocks. Yet adding the barrel to its stocks would be 99 percent likely to lose money for the firm. It would not be surprising if the manager of the firm, who must face stockholders and creditors on a regular basis, rejected investments of this sort in favor of ones that involve less risk. The results of this risk aversion would be that, other things being equal, firms would develop speculative stocks smaller than the social optimum.[10]

Because of externalities, fear of government expropriation, and risk aversion, the private sector will accumulate socially inadequate levels of oil stocks during normal market periods for release during supply disruptions. There is, therefore, a rationale for government involvement in oil stockpiling, but for how large an involvement? The first step in answering this question is to enumerate the social benefits and social costs that are likely to result from government stockpiling.

### What Are the Benefits of Strategic Stockpiling?

The primary benefits of a petroleum stockpiling program accrue when previously accumulated stocks are sold during oil supply disruptions. At one extreme, we can imagine a drawdown of stocks sufficiently large to offset the reduction in supply totally, thereby eliminating the price shock that would otherwise result. Even a drawdown that is small relative to the size of the supply reduction, however, will lower the magnitude of the oil price shock. The social benefits associated with attenuation of the price shocks can be described conceptually in the framework we developed in chapter 2.

Changes in social welfare from drawdowns can be approximately measured as changes in real GNP or social surplus in U.S. crude oil markets. We illustrate this point in figure 20, in which a supply loss of size $x$ is followed by a stock drawdown of size $z$ during a specified period of time. The predisruption price $p_0$ is determined in the world market (figure 20b) by the intersection of world supply $S$ and demand $D$. At $p_0$ the world quantity is $Q_0$; the U.S. quantity demanded, given by the demand schedule $D_{US}$ in the figure 20a, is $q_0^D$; the U.S. quantity supplied, determined by $S_{US}$, is $q_0^S$; and U.S. oil imports are $(q_0^D - q_0^S)$.

The disruption of size $x$ shifts the world supply curve leftward to the curve marked $(S - x)$. At the same time, firms may wish to make purchases for their stocks in anticipation of future price increases and supply uncertainties. If they do so, world demand shifts rightward from $D$ to $(D + y)$, where $y$ is the addition to private stocks.[11] The post-disruption price is $p_1$, at the intersection of $(S - x)$ and $(D + y)$. U.S.

FIGURE 20

THE IMPACT OF A STRATEGIC PETROLEUM RESERVE DRAWDOWN ON (a) THE U.S. OIL MARKET AND (b) THE WORLD OIL MARKET

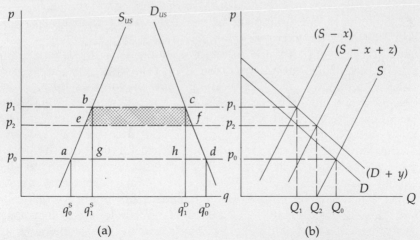

(a)                    (b)

SOURCE: Authors.

115

imports fall to $(q_1^D - q_1^S)$, and the loss of social surplus to the U.S. is measured by the area of the trapezoid *abcd*.[12] The petroleum reserve drawdown of size $z$ shifts the supply curve in the world market to $(S - x + z)$. The postdrawdown price, determined by the intersection of $(S - x + z)$ and $(D + y)$, is $p_2$. The postdrawdown loss of social surplus in the United States is given by trapezoid *aefd*. The gain of social surplus from the drawdown is the difference between the areas of *abcd* and *aefd*, which is *ebcf*. This difference, represented by the shaded area, plus the revenue resulting from the sale of stockpiled oil in the world oil market, $p_2z$, is the direct economic benefit of the stockpile drawdown.

As we noted in chapter 2, the price shock will also impose adjustment costs on the economy that create additional, though temporary, losses in real GNP and social surplus. In the simplest formulation, it is reasonable to assume that the greater the price shock $(p_1 - p_0)$, the greater these adjustment costs. Moreover, the macro simulations cited in chapter 2 (see the references cited in chapter 2, notes 32 to 38) invariably indicate that equal reductions in crude oil supply create successively greater increases in adjustment costs. The basis for this outcome can be described as the fact that short-run supply curves are rising and concave upward. Thus, following a disruption, the attempt to substitute alternative inputs for petroleum and to substitute among final products throughout the economy encounters increasing increments in prices and costs in response to given losses of crude oil and to given increments in oil prices. Our analysis implies that the greater the oil price shock, the greater, to a disproportionate degree, the benefits of an SPR drawdown of any particular size, including, for severe disruptions, very small drawdowns indeed.

Benefits of stockpiling, apart from the direct reduction in the economic costs of a disruption, are even more difficult to measure. A large stockpile expands the range of options the United States can pursue in carrying out foreign policy. Since stockpile drawdown provides a "breathing space" between the time oil supplies from an exporting region are disrupted and the time the full impact of the resulting price increase is felt, diplomatic initiatives can be launched in a less politically volatile domestic environment than otherwise. If the disruption coincides with, or leads to, military intervention, the stockpile will enhance military flexibility by reducing the costs to the United States and its allies of temporary damage that they might inflict collaterally on oil-producing facilities. Although the value of such flexibility is difficult to quantify, it is nevertheless real, especially to a president who must make politically sensitive decisions, such as

116

those concerning the resupply of Israel during a Middle East war or the use of military force to aid the government of Saudi Arabia against foreign-supported insurgents.

A large stockpile may deter embargoes and politically motivated reductions in production. The larger the stockpile, the more severe the reduction in supply must be in order to impose any particular level of economic costs on importers. As long as exporting countries anticipate that they also will suffer economic losses by reducing production, the existence of a large stockpile will deter the use of supply disruptions for political purposes.

Finally, a large petroleum reserve may reduce private stockpiling at the outset of disruptions. If refiners anticipate drawdowns of strategic stocks, they will make smaller additions to their own temporary holdings. The result will be a smaller rightward shift of the world demand curve in figure 20. Furthermore, by reducing the magnitude of price shocks, drawdowns lessen the political panic that can lead to such harmful policies as price controls and mandatory allocations.

### What Are the Costs of Strategic Stockpiling?

Two elements of the social cost of strategic stockpiling are relatively easy to measure because they appear as expenditures in the federal budget. One is the cost of constructing storage facilities, which ranges from approximately four dollars per barrel for water-leached salt-dome caverns to twelve dollars or more per barrel for steel tank or floating tanker storage. The other budgetary cost is the direct outlay on oil. At current prices of twenty-nine dollars per barrel, the budgetary cost of building a strategic reserve of 1 billion barrels exceeds $30 billion.

The largest potential element of cost, however, does not appear in the budget of the stockpiling program. Oil purchases for the reserve may increase the world price that must be paid for all oil. The losses of social surplus associated with such a price rise can be measured in the same way as those caused by a supply disruption. Imagine that the price rise from $p_0$ to $p_1$ in figure 20a was due to purchases for the stockpile, reflected in a rightward shift of $D$ in figure 20b. The area *abcd* would now represent the loss of social surplus due to the acquisition of oil for the stockpile.

The size of the price increase, and hence the magnitude of the loss of surplus, will depend upon the response of producers to the temporary increase in demand. At one extreme we can envision a tight market in which suppliers will not provide more oil at the prevailing price in the short run. Buying oil for the stockpile increases demand, but prices must rise for suppliers to be willing to meet this demand. The size of the resulting price increase will then depend upon the demand price elasticity, which describes the extent to which consumers reduce their purchases as price goes up. In a slack market, on the other hand, producers are willing to supply some additional amounts at the prepurchase price, and as a result, the price does not actually increase. Slack markets may occur in situations where oil exporters have cut back their rates of production in an attempt to maintain higher-than-competitive market prices; they may be willing to meet the increased demand out of unused production capacity at the same price. Obviously, the costs of building a stockpile will be greater the higher the fraction of purchases that must be made in tight markets.

Other costs are related to changes in the behavior of market participants. The existence of a large stockpile controlled by the U.S. government may discourage stockpiling that would otherwise be done by domestic industry. Firms will expect government reserve drawdowns during disruptions to reduce the price at which their own stockpiles could be sold. Although this price-reducing effect will tend to lower the size of private stockpiles, the marginal reduction may be small because firms already anticipate that price controls on and government allocation of private stockpiles will be reimposed during disruptions large enough to trigger use of the government reserve. In fact, if firms believe that larger government stockpiles reduce the likelihood that price controls and allocations will be imposed during disruptions, increasing the size of the government reserve will tend to encourage private stockpiling. Overall, our best guess is that at the present time, displacement of private stockpiling is insignificant and unlikely to be important for currently planned SPR size.

A U.S. strategic petroleum reserve may also discourage foreign governments from stockpiling oil. Because all consumers gain from the lower price resulting from drawdown of the U.S. stockpile, other importing nations may take a "free ride" on large U.S. stockpiles rather than developing their own. This statement implies that each barrel added to U.S. reserves may result in less than a barrel of net additions to world stocks. As of mid-1982, however, free riding did not appear to be a problem. The ratio of all oil stocks, public and private, to total annual oil consumption was 25 percent in the United States, 28 percent in all other Western alliance countries, and 29 percent in Japan. The SPR, still plagued by delays, is thus far more a "beggar-thy-neighbor" than a "help-thy-neighbor" policy.[13]

# How Can the Socially Optimal Stockpile Size Be Determined?

In the next twenty years the Middle East will continue to account for a large fraction of world oil production. During this period the Middle East will continue to be politically volatile. If these commonly advanced assertions are true, we face the possibility that we will experience major disruptions in the world oil market before the end of the century. The variety of circumstances that would lead to sharp reductions in oil exports from the Middle East suggests that the probability of at least one major disruption sometime during this period is quite high. We cannot know with certainty, however, how many disruptions, if any, will actually occur, when they will occur, how severe they will be, or how long they will last. By making assumptions about the probabilities of various types of disruptions, we can convert the problem from one of uncertainty into one of risk. Using the assumed probabilities, we can evaluate stockpiling programs in terms of resulting expected costs and benefits.

The calculation of expected net benefits is conceptually simple if measures of costs and benefits are available. These measures are obtained in the following way. First, an exhaustive set of mutually exclusive future states of the world is specified. Second, the present value of the net benefits (benefits minus costs discounted to the present) associated with each of the possible future states is determined. Third, the total present value of expected net benefits is calculated as the sum of the present value of expected net benefits associated with each state of the world weighted by the probability that the state will occur. The program yielding the greatest present value of expected net benefits would be selected to maximize social welfare.

In practice, the enumeration of the analytically distinct states of the world and their probabilities is tedious, complex, and never fully exhaustive. Nevertheless, by concentrating on representative states of the world (such as slack market, tight market, minor disruption, and major disruption), the best stockpiling program can be found within a decision analysis framework. The life of the program is divided into a number of stages (usually years). At each stage a decision is made concerning changes in the size of the stockpile, given the current state of the market and the probabilities of moving to other states in the future. The decisions translate into costs and benefits, depending on the state of the market that randomly occurs in the next stage. Working through all the possible decisions in this way permits determination of the best decision in the initial period. For problems of even relatively small size (say, two states of the world, forty possible stockpile sizes, and twenty stages), it is impossible to do the decision analysis by hand. Fairly large problems of this type, however, can easily be solved with the use of a computer by a technique known as dynamic programming. In addition to indicating the optimal drawdown or acquisition decision in the current period, dynamic programming permits us to look ahead to determine the largest stockpile that will be optimal at any time in the future.

The dynamic programming approach has been widely used to evaluate alternative U.S. stockpiling programs. Thomas J. Teisberg, who first applied the technique to the oil stockpiling problem, used changes in consumers' and producers' surplus in the crude oil market to measure costs and benefits.[14] Other investigators have used real GNP.[15] These studies, along with others that used different methodologies,[16] employ a wide range of assumptions about future market conditions. Nevertheless, they provide fairly consistent answers to the question of the minimum size of stockpile that is socially desirable: Almost all recommend a reserve of greater than 750 million barrels, and most recommend reserves of greater than 1 billion barrels.

## Are U.S. Stockpiling Goals Appropriate?

To the casual observer of national energy policy, the issue of the ultimate size of the strategic petroleum reserve might appear to have been settled. In April 1977 the Carter administration issued the first National Energy Plan (NEP 1), which called for the establishment of a 1-billion-barrel reserve by the end of 1985.[17] Congress endorsed this goal by allowing amendment 2 to the SPR plan to become effective on June 13, 1978.[18] Establishing a 1-billion-barrel reserve by the end of 1985 still remains the "official" U.S. policy. Thus it might seem that U.S. stockpiling policy is consistent with the weight of analysis on the question of the appropriate size of U.S. reserves.

Yet current budget proposals would result in only about 490 million barrels in storage by the end of 1985 and 700 million barrels of available storage capacity by the end of 1989. Why is there so great a divergence between official goals and actual achievement? One reason is that serious technical and organizational problems were encountered during the first years of the SPR program. Another is that expansion of the SPR beyond 500 million barrels has been an attractive target for budget cutters.

**The 1975 Strategic Petroleum Reserve Plan.** The Energy Policy and Conservation Act created the SPR office in December 1975 and required it to produce a plan for implementation of the SPR program within one year. The plan, which became effective in April 1977, called for storage of approximately 500 million barrels of crude oil by 1982 in salt-dome caverns and salt mines located on the U.S. Gulf Coast. Implementation was expected to proceed in two stages. First, existing salt-dome caverns and mines would be purchased and prepared for oil storage. Second, new salt-dome caverns would be created and existing caverns expanded through a leaching process by which fresh water is injected to dissolve the salt, which is then removed with the water as brine. It was expected that approximately 330 million barrels of existing storage capacity could be purchased through eminent domain. The cost of leaching new caverns was estimated to be about $2 per barrel of storage capacity. This estimate compared favorably to estimates of $12 per barrel for steel tank storage and more than $100 per barrel for *in situ* storage.[19]

Problems were encountered at the very beginning of the effort to implement the SPR plan.[20] Some were of a technical nature, reflecting the inexperience of the SPR office. It was originally assumed that disposal of brine removed from existing cavern storage space would be achieved by pumping it into porous rock below the fresh water table at the storage sites. When the disposal wells failed to take brine at the planned rates, oil deliveries had to be delayed. The problem was compounded by the need to replace about 87 million barrels of existing storage, which could not be used for various reasons, with newly mined caverns. Because the creation of new caverns requires the injection and removal of seven barrels of brine for each barrel of capacity, as compared with the simple removal of one barrel of brine for each barrel of existing capacity, the amount of brine to be disposed of was much greater than anticipated. Construction of a pipeline for disposal of brine in the Gulf of Mexico was delayed for almost two years by the Environmental Protection Agency. Local opposition in Louisiana to the use of eminent domain prompted the governor to prevent the U.S. Army Corps of Engineers from granting permits for pipelines until a general agreement on a large number of issues, including disposal of nuclear wastes, had been reached between the state and the Department of Energy.

**Problems Due to the Department of Energy and the Office of Management and Budget.** Both the resolution of specific technical difficulties and general progress in implementation were hindered by organizational problems created by establishment of the Department of Energy. The SPR office was initially part of the Federal Energy Administration, where it enjoyed the highest priority. The SPR director reported directly to the FEA administrator, enabling the director quickly to obtain resources and to secure decisions critical to implementation. When FEA was subsumed under DOE in October 1977, the SPR program lost its special status. SPR's director had to file requests through a multilevel bureaucracy with competing programmatic interests. The SPR staff was subjected to an agencywide hiring freeze at a time when personnel with technical skills were desperately needed in the field. During a change in emphasis from speedy implementation to cost reduction, contracts for the SPR program were routed through the cumbersome procurement system of the new agency, stretching the approval time from weeks to months. Despite all these problems, the secretary required the SPR office to develop plans for the accelerated implementation of an expanded reserve.

The cumulative effect of these technical and organizational problems has been to delay the anticipated completion date of the first 538 million barrels of storage capacity (phases I and II) to the end of 1985. Although these implementation problems have contributed indirectly to the delayed expansion of the SPR beyond phases I and II by raising doubts about the capabilities of the SPR office, the primary reason for delay lies in the determined efforts of the Office of Management and Budget (OMB) to limit the SPR program to 538 million barrels.[21] The SPR has been an attractive target for budget cutters because it is a costly program with no natural political constituency to oppose the cuts. The SPR does not provide immediate benefits to narrowly defined groups; rather, it provides insurance against widely distributed economic losses that may or may not occur sometime in the future. Defense programs provide benefits of a similar nature, but they enjoy support from the sellers of weapons systems, veterans' organizations, and a large well-established bureaucracy. Firms that sell goods to the SPR program can sell them elsewhere and hence have little to gain from pushing for expansion. The SPR program does not enjoy the interest of organized groups; it is not highly visible to the general public. Delays in funding for facilities that take four or five years to complete may not even come to the attention of many people outside government who support the program. Finally, the SPR program has been part of a multilayered bureaucracy with conflicting interests.

In 1977, the DOE request for funds to begin construction of the second 500 million barrels of storage capacity was cut by OMB from the administration's fiscal year 1979 budget. (Phase III consists of capacity expansion from 538 to 750 million barrels; phase IV is storage capacity for the final 250 million barrels.) In response to an appeal by the DOE secretary, President Carter affirmed the billion-barrel goal but decided to limit the fiscal year 1979 budget request to planning funds for phase III only. OMB initiated a joint study with DOE and the Council of Economic Advisers in 1978 to determine if expansion of the SPR could be justified on economic grounds. Although OMB initially agreed to a set of assumptions to be used in the analysis, the agency repudiated the analysis when it appeared to support an SPR of 1 billion barrels.[22] OMB cut phase III funds from the fiscal year 1980 budget, and DOE did not appeal, perhaps because other programs needing OMB approval had a higher priority. The same pattern characterized the fiscal year 1981 budget cycle. In 1980, OMB again demanded a joint study of the SPR size question. Although agreeing to participate, DOE announced that it would produce its own study (using the more sophisticated dynamic programming approach) and made clear that cuts of funds for phase III from the fiscal year 1982 budget proposal would be appealed to the president. In December 1980, OMB indicated that it would not cut phase III funding. Consequently, as the Reagan administration took office, funding for phase III appeared in the fiscal year 1982 budget.

The Reagan administration initially issued strong public statements in support of the SPR and acted on them by accelerating the SPR fill rate in 1981. Nevertheless, the Reagan OMB attempted to cut funding from the fiscal year 1982 budget for 150 million barrels of phase III to be developed at a new site. Although Congress restored the funds, OMB had moved to defer the funds from the fiscal year 1984 budget and remove them totally from the fiscal year 1985 budget. If OMB had been successful in these efforts, the SPR would have reached a maximum storage capacity of only 610 million barrels in 1989.

## What Should Be the U.S. Storage Development Policy?

The weight of economic analysis supports the official U.S. stockpiling goal of 1 billion barrels. Focusing on the goal of ultimate size diverts attention from the more relevant policy question: What steps should be taken now to influence the storage capacity that will be available in the future? At a minimum, funds should be provided in the current fiscal year to permit work toward completion of all the phase III facilities by 1989. Funding for future years should permit acceleration of the phase III program for completion before 1989. Studies of the timing of SPR expansion suggest that program acceleration is worth substantially higher facility development costs.[23]

Should the development of phase IV facilities also begin immediately? This question is more difficult to answer. Immediate implementation of phase IV appears desirable not only in terms of the cost/benefit perspective but also in terms of regret analysis. If phase IV facilities are built but are never used because of changed circumstances, the United States will have suffered a loss of approximately $1 billion. If, alternatively, phase IV is not implemented and there is a major supply disruption, U.S. economic losses will be tens of billions of dollars above the level that they would reach with the drawdown of a reserve larger by 250 million barrels. As long as the likelihood of deciding in the future that phase IV is unnecessary is not much greater than the likelihood of a major disruption, the United States would minimize the expected future regret by beginning implementation of phase IV.

There are, however, practical difficulties. If phase IV is developed as low-cost salt-dome storage by the SPR office, it probably could not be completed before 1990. During its implementation, it would be a prime target for OMB budget cutters. If we assume that they will be as successful in delaying expenditures as they were with phase III, a realistic completion date would be the mid-1990s. Attempts to speed implementation of phase IV by substituting higher-cost steel tank storage or the purchase of existing facilities from industry would increase budgetary costs and would therefore make the use of delaying tactics even more attractive to OMB.

On balance, it is probably a better investment of political effort to concentrate on ensuring that phase III is fully implemented as quickly as possible than to seek the implementation of both phases simultaneously. Nevertheless, DOE should be alert for opportunities to buy private storage facilities that would permit immediate increases in storage capacity.[24] In summary, the Reagan administration should make a firm commitment to speedy implementation of phase III, also giving direct and explicit White House guidance to OMB. Congress already seems committed to phase III; it should continue its vigilance.

## How Should the Strategic Petroleum Reserve Program Be Funded?

The direct costs of the SPR program are currently being paid out of the general revenues raised by the federal government. Because the benefits that will result from drawdown of the SPR will be widely distributed among participants in the economy, it is reasonable to place the burden of the costs on federal taxpayers. Arguments based on grounds of economic efficiency, distributional fairness, and political behavior, however, can be made in support of an alternative financing method, a petroleum import fee.

Many economists believe that the true social cost to the United States of the marginal barrel of imported oil exceeds its market price. This difference, called the oil import premium, has two major components. The first is based on a recognition that the level of U.S. oil imports influences the world price of oil. An increase in imports that raises price will cost Americans additional dollars that must be paid not only for the increase in imports, but for all oil imports. Let us assume, for example, that the United States imports 5 million barrels per day at the world price of twenty-nine dollars per barrel. If an increase in imports of 1 million barrels per day resulted in a new world price of thirty dollars per barrel, the total oil import bill would rise from $145 million per day to $180 million per day. The additional purchases would cost Americans an average of thirty-five dollars per barrel, five dollars more than the world price. Because individual importers pay only the world price, they will have imported to the point where the social benefits of the last barrel have just fallen to thirty dollars, despite the fact that its social cost has risen to thirty-five dollars. Thus, in effect, society pays a premium of five dollars for the last barrel.

A second component of the import premium arises from the relationship between the costs of supply disruptions and import levels. The larger the postdisruption level of imports, the greater the wealth transfer from U.S. consumers to foreign oil exporters for any given price rise. With reference to figure 20, an increase in the predisruption import level could be represented as a rightward parallel shift of the U.S. demand schedule. The disruption would now inflict larger costs because the increased wealth transfers to foreign producers for postdisruption imports (rectangle *bghc*) are greater. These costs, adjusted to reflect uncertainties in the timing, duration, and severity of future disruptions, constitute the second major component of the import premium.

One way to eliminate the divergence between the private and social costs of imported oil is to impose an import fee equal to the estimated import premium. The result would be more economically efficient levels of oil consumption, domestic oil production, and investment in alternative fuels. Furthermore, the present is an excellent time to impose the import fee. The fee would make it more difficult for OPEC to slow the current market movement toward lower prices, and falling prices would minimize the macroeconomic effects of the fee. Thus imposition of an oil import fee seems to be sound energy policy.[25]

Still, how large should the import fee be? Estimates of the oil import premium fall in the analytically supportable range of $2 to $10 per barrel but have been as ridiculously high as $124 per barrel.[26] It would therefore be conservative to impose an import fee of $2 per barrel on crude oil and petroleum products at current prices and import levels.[27] At 1984 import levels of slightly more than 5 million barrels per day and a world oil price of $29 per barrel, revenues from the fee would be sufficient to cover the costs of facility development and a fill rate of more than 300,000 barrels per day.

An import fee earmarked for the SPR program can be regarded as a user fee. Just as the benefits of public road use are roughly proportional to gasoline consumption, the benefits of SPR drawdowns are roughly proportional to predisruption consumption levels of petroleum products. On equity grounds, therefore, it seems reasonable to make payments for support of the SPR program proportional to petroleum consumption. The import fee would of course have other distributional consequences as well. Perhaps of most significance, the fee would increase the domestic price of oil and profits of U.S. oil producers. Much of these additional profits, however, would be taxed away through existing federal excise and state severance taxes.[28]

The import fee would also make our energy-intensive industries somewhat less competitive in world trade. This effect would tend to offset any gains in the balance of trade that would result from lower oil import bills. One way to reduce the potential competitive disadvantage is to keep the import fee relatively low. Another is to impose the fee in conjunction with other major importers. The coordinated import fee would also result in a greater reduction in total world demand and therefore in a greater reduction in world price.

Earmarking import fee revenues for the SPR program seems desirable in light of political incentives. Although it is generally argued that all federal programs should be funded from general revenues to facilitate their comparison in the political process, it seems reasonable to make an exception in the case of the SPR: Its lack of a vocal constituency makes it an especially attractive target for executive office budget cutters, despite its relatively high expected net benefits. We have already discussed the efforts of OMB to delay implementation of storage capacity expansion. Funding for oil purchases, however, although more politically visible, is also a tempting target. In 1980 the Carter administration was persuaded to resume filling the SPR only after Congress threatened to take away authority for sale of an equivalent amount of oil from the naval petroleum reserve. Although the Reagan administration accelerated the SPR fill rate during its first year in office, its budget proposals called for a rate of 145,000 barrels per day in fiscal year 1984 and 100,000 barrels per day in fiscal year 1985 (though in a compromise with Congress, the rates were raised to 186,000 and 145,000, respectively). This proposed reduction is particularly disturbing because the current slack oil markets provide an opportunity for filling the SPR with minimal impact on world oil prices.

126

Perhaps the best way to neutralize the short-run political incentives that hinder efforts toward the long-run goal of an adequate stockpile would be to arrange SPR funding so that program delays do not translate into immediate budget reductions. This result could be achieved by putting all the revenue from the two-dollar import fee into a fund to be used exclusively for achieving and maintaining a 750-million-barrel SPR.[29] Only when 750 million barrels were actually in storage would revenues be diverted from the fund to the general budget.[30] Under this system, OMB analysts would have incentives for exploring ways of accelerating the SPR program and for monitoring its management.

## When and How Should the Strategic Petroleum Reserve Be Distributed?

The primary benefits of the SPR are realized only during drawdowns. It is therefore important to consider carefully the institutional arrangements for initiating and managing the use of the SPR. There may be substantial opportunity costs in depleting the reserve during an extended minor disruption that could easily turn into a major one. The larger the reserve, however, the greater the relative costs of waiting too long to initiate drawdowns.

**Presidential Authority and Trigger Mechanisms.** EPCA permits the withdrawal and distribution of oil in the SPR upon a finding by the president that a drawdown is required either to counter a "severe energy supply interruption" or to meet U.S. obligations under the International Energy Program.[31] Because the definition is sufficiently vague to allow drawdowns for even relatively minor supply disruptions, and because a very major disruption is needed to obligate drawdowns under the International Energy Program, the president retains virtually complete discretion over use of the SPR. Advocates of more explicit criteria for SPR use have expressed concern that the president and his advisers will be hesitant to initiate drawdowns. Whereas the economic benefits from drawdowns are probably greatest at the onset of disruptions, when consumers and nondisrupted producers have not yet had a chance to adjust to higher prices, fear that the disruptions will be more severe or of longer duration than expected may lead decision makers to delay drawdown until more information is available. Appearing to have used the reserve too quickly is likely to be more politically costly than appearing to have been overly cautious in its use. More information and analysis are necessary to increase the chances of avoiding the former error, but additional study can result in delays that make the latter more likely.

A number of analysts have advocated putting trigger mechanisms in place prior to disruptions as a way of eliminating the political bias toward underutilization. Unfortunately, no simple set of rules can adequately take into account all the factors relevant to drawdown decisions. An unambiguous assessment of current market conditions is often difficult to make from available data. More important, none of the trigger mechanisms that have been proposed adequately takes into account expectations about future market conditions. The myopia is particularly serious for triggers that are based on production or import levels. Estimates of recent changes in these levels provide virtually no information for predicting future changes.

The myopia is less serious for triggers based on observations of market prices. Spot prices and newly negotiated long-term contract prices do incorporate private sector expectations about future market conditions. Spot prices, however, are dominated by current supply and demand conditions, and official long-term contract prices are slow to change and are subject to manipulation. Information about private sector expectations would also be provided by the prices observed in a full-fledged crude oil futures market. Unfortunately, such markets, which are still in their infancy, might not continue to operate efficiently in the face of severe disruptions or manipulations by major producers.

**An Options Plan.** An alternative to having the government make the initial drawdown decision is to allow the private sector the opportunity to purchase SPR oil on a continuing basis.[32] This opportunity could be created through the regular auctioning of options to purchase SPR oil during some future period. Specifically, we propose a plan that would operate in the following way.

Each week the SPR office would announce quantities of the various grades of oil for which options would be sold. The quantities announced would sum to approximately 12 million barrels, the current maximum seven-day drawdown rate for the SPR. For each grade, the SPR office would state a future, or forward, purchase price equal to 110 percent of its estimated current acquisition cost. (The forward price is set above the current price to discourage firms from relying on the SPR for routine inventory management.) Firms would then enter sealed bids for the option to buy some quantity of the oil at the stated forward price any time during an interval between nine and twelve weeks from the date of the auction. Only option bids above a fixed minimum, say 1 cent per barrel, would be accepted. The SPR office would review the bids to find an option price for each grade of oil such that the sum of the quantities requested by all those offering winning bids would be less than or equal to the total quantity offered.[33]

*A numerical example.* Operation of the options system can be illustrated with the simple example presented in table 12.[34] Imagine that the world price of oil is stable at thirty dollars per barrel in weeks 1 to 12. Each week during this period the SPR office offers options for purchase at a forward price of thirty-three dollars per barrel nine to twelve weeks in the future. Because most firms expect prices to remain stable, options for only about 1 million of the 12 million barrels offered each week are sold at the minimum acceptable bid of one cent per barrel. Also, because the world price of oil is lower than the forward price on options sold nine to twelve weeks earlier, no options are being exercised. Now assume that in week 13 a major crisis with potential for disrupting regional oil supplies begins to develop in the Middle East. Spot prices rise to thirty-one dollars as firms seek to expand their stocks. At the same time, firms also seek to purchase options as an alternative to stocks, bidding the price up by ten cents per barrel in week 13 and twenty cents per barrel in week 14. In week 15 a war breaks out, reducing oil supplies from the Middle East. Spot prices rise to thirty-five dollars per barrel, making it profitable for those who purchased options in weeks 3, 4, 5, and 6 to exercise them. The result is a drawdown of 4 million barrels. From week 16 through week 21, options of 1 million barrels per week are exercised. In week 22 the number of options exercised jumps to 12 million barrels as options sold at the first threat of disruption in week 13 mature. Beginning in week 23, oil prices stabilize at forty dollars per barrel, and option prices again fall to the minimum acceptable bid. In week 25 the spot price falls below the forward price for options sold nine weeks before, so those options are not exercised, ending the options system drawdown, which had continued into weeks 23 and 24. For the first ten weeks of the disruption, an average drawdown of 657,000 barrels per day has taken place. The president could order direct auctions of SPR oil to continue the drawdown in week 25 or to supplement the drawdown at any earlier time.

*Advantages and disadvantages.* The options system has several advantages. First, it substitutes the aggregate of private sector expectations for those of the government as to future market conditions. The initiation of drawdowns would thereby become primarily an economic decision rather than a political one. The only decision the president would have to make is whether or not the SPR should continue oil purchases in the world market once firms begin to exercise their options. If he believes the drawdown is not desirable, he can order the SPR to continue its purchases.[35] If he believes an insufficient quantity of options will be available in the near future, he can order SPR to suspend purchases temporarily. Thus the primary drawdown deci-

129

TABLE 12

ILLUSTRATION OF THE OPTIONS SYSTEM DRAWDOWN

| Week | Market Condition | Spot Price ($/bbl) | Options Sold (millions of bbl) | Option Price ($/bbl) | Current Forward Price ($/bbl) | Options Exercised (millions of bbl) | Week of Purchase of Exercised Options |
|------|------------------|--------------------|--------------------------------|----------------------|-------------------------------|-------------------------------------|---------------------------------------|
| 1 | N | 30 | 1 | 0.01 | 33.00 | 0 | — |
| 2 | N | 30 | 1 | 0.01 | 33.00 | 0 | — |
| 3 | N | 30 | 1 | 0.01 | 33.00 | 0 | — |
| 4 | N | 30 | 1 | 0.01 | 33.00 | 0 | — |
| 5 | N | 30 | 1 | 0.01 | 33.00 | 0 | — |
| 6 | N | 30 | 1 | 0.01 | 33.00 | 0 | — |
| 7 | N | 30 | 1 | 0.01 | 33.00 | 0 | — |
| 8 | N | 30 | 1 | 0.01 | 33.00 | 0 | — |
| 9 | N | 30 | 1 | 0.01 | 33.00 | 0 | — |
| 10 | N | 30 | 1 | 0.01 | 33.00 | 0 | — |
| 11 | N | 30 | 1 | 0.01 | 33.00 | 0 | — |
| 12 | N | 30 | 1 | 0.01 | 33.00 | 0 | — |
| 13 | TD | 31 | 12 | 0.10 | 34.10 | 0 | — |
| 14 | TD | 32 | 12 | 0.20 | 35.20 | 0 | — |

| 15 | D | 35 | 12 | 1.00 | 37.50 | 4 | 3,4,5,6 |
| 16 | D | 37 | 12 | 2.00 | 40.70 | 1 | 7 |
| 17 | D | 39 | 12 | 2.50 | 42.90 | 1 | 8 |
| 18 | D | 42 | 12 | 2.00 | 46.20 | 1 | 9 |
| 19 | D | 45 | 12 | 1.50 | 49.50 | 1 | 10 |
| 20 | D | 43 | 12 | 0.90 | 47.30 | 1 | 11 |
| 21 | D | 42 | 12 | 0.50 | 46.20 | 1 | 12 |
| 22 | D | 41 | 12 | 0.10 | 45.10 | 12 | 13 |
| 23 | D | 40 | 6 | 0.01 | 44.00 | 12 | 14 |
| 24 | D | 40 | 2 | 0.01 | 44.00 | 12 | 15 |
| 25 | D | 40 | 1 | 0.01 | 44.00 | 0 | — |
| 26 | D | 40 | 1 | 0.01 | 44.00 | 0 | — |

NOTE: N = normal; TD = threat of disruption; D = disruption. The average drawdown rate during weeks 15–24 is 657,000 bbl/day. At week 25 the president can continue the drawdown by ordering direct auction of SPR oil.

SOURCE: Authors.

sion would be made by the market, with the government making adjustments by changes in the rate of SPR fill. As noted above, if the president at any time believed that the drawdown rate resulting from the exercise of options was too low, he could order supplemental sales through direct auctions of the reserve.

A second advantage of the options system is that it enables the private sector to anticipate SPR drawdowns, thereby lowering not only the expected future price of oil but also the current spot market price by reducing the demand for speculative stocks.[36] In terms of figure 20, the options system reduces the rightward shift in demand caused by desired additions to private stocks at the outset of disruptions; the result is a lower world price during the disruption.

Finally, the use of options removes the temptation of government to allocate SPR oil at less than market prices. Under the options system, SPR oil goes to the highest bidders, who are the firms that place the highest value on its use, and keeps the economic cost of disruptions to a minimum. Government allocation of SPR oil at below market prices not only invites inefficient use but also encourages claims for special treatment from groups throughout the economy. Both tendencies could easily result in government allocation of private oil as well.

The major disadvantage of the options system is that it will not sustain drawdowns once the price stops rising at a rate faster than 3.3 percent per month (10 percent per three-month interval). To maintain the drawdown once the rate of growth in price has slowed, the president would have to order the direct sale of additional oil. Perhaps the best way to do so would be to reduce the stated forward price to 100 percent or less of the current acquisition cost. If firms believe that the world price is going to remain constant for the next three months, and the forward price is set at $(100 - X)$ percent of the current price, we would expect firms to bid up to $X$ percent of the current price for options. In general, other things being equal, the lower the stated forward price, the higher the option bids and the more likely the options will be exercised.

Administrative simplicity is the only reason for limiting the system to the sale of a single type of option. One possibility, which would produce a more graduated drawdown response, would be to sell options with different forward prices. One-third of the weekly offerings, for example, might be for options with a forward price at 100 percent of current price, another third at 105 percent of current price, and the final third at 110 percent of current price. Another possibility is to vary the period during which the options can be exercised. Some options could be exercised between five and eight weeks, for example, as well as between nine and twelve weeks, after purchase. Obviously, a plan that incorporated both these features could be designed. The highest priority, however, should be given to establishing a simple options plan as quickly as possible to increase the likelihood that the SPR will actually be used at the onset of the next disruption.

## Summary

The strategic stockpiling of oil is the most important affirmative step the federal government can take in preparation for oil supply disruptions. Private firms will not stockpile in a socially optimal way because they do not see the full social costs and benefits of their decisions, because they must anticipate the possibility of government expropriation of stockpiled oil, and because they may exhibit risk aversion in their stockpiling decisions. The release of government stocks during disruptions will substantially reduce the losses suffered by the U.S. economy and may reduce political pressure for governmental interference in foreign and domestic petroleum markets. The mere existence of a large government stockpile may deter embargoes and politically motivated reductions in oil output. The costs of government stockpiling include expenditures for storage facilities and oil, higher oil prices during the acquisition of stocks, and the possible displacement of private sector stockpiling. Comparisons of these costs and benefits that take into account the uncertainty surrounding the occurrence of future disruptions strongly suggest the need for a government stockpile of at least 750 million barrels. Although the question of the ultimate size of the reserve is important for long-term planning, the more urgent questions concern concrete actions that should be taken today to realize the stockpiling goals.

The SPR program has failed to reach U.S. stockpiling goals that remain valid. The early stages of the program were plagued with organizational and technical problems that have largely been overcome. Both the Carter and Reagan administrations, however, have delayed investment in storage facilities needed to achieve their putative goals; each has had to be prodded by Congress to fill available storage capacity at a fast rate. To prevent further delay based on short-run budgetary considerations, the SPR should be funded through a petroleum import fee of approximately two dollars per barrel. Revenues from the fee should not revert to general use until 750 million barrels of oil are in storage. An options system, which incorporates private sector expectations in drawdown decisions, should be instituted to increase the likelihood that SPR oil will be used effectively to reduce the costs of oil supply disruptions in the future.

# Notes

1. Title 1, pt. B, of the Energy Policy and Conservation Act (PL94-163) mandated creation of strategic petroleum reserves of between 150 million and 1 billion barrels.

2. Strategic Petroleum Reserve Office, "Strategic Petroleum Reserve Plan," December 15, 1976. The plan was officially received by Congress on February 16, 1977, and became effective, in the absence of a resolution of disapproval from either house, on April 18, 1977.

3. Strategic Petroleum Reserve Office, "Strategic Petroleum Reserve Plan Amendment No. 1: Acceleration of the Development Schedule," Energy Action 12, May 1977; and the "Strategic Petroleum Reserve Plan Amendment No. 2 (Energy Action DOE 1): Expansion of the Strategic Petroleum Reserve," March 1978.

4. Expressed algebraically, a risk-neutral profit maximizing firm would add to speculative stocks as long as

$$(p_0 + s) \leq E(p_1)/(1 + d)$$

where $p_0$ is the per unit price in the present period, $s$ is the per unit cost of storing the oil from the present period to the anticipated time of sale, $E(p_1)$ is the expected or average price the firm anticipates for the future sale period, and $d$ is the discount rate the firm employs when comparing a dollar of revenue or cost today with a dollar of revenue or cost at the anticipated time of sale.

5. A socially optimal allocation is generally defined as one under which no one could be made better off without making at least someone worse off. We will use the related cost-benefit criterion of applied welfare economics to define social optimality: A policy is socially optimal if it provides the greatest net social benefits. If the cost-benefit criterion is satisfied for a policy and net benefits are positive, it would be possible to implement the policy with a set of income transfers so that everyone was made at least as well off as under any other policy.

6. We would expect a higher price if the world market were competitive with an upward-sloping supply curve. If the world market is not competitive, some producers may be restricting their production to maintain higher prices. It may be that some of these producers will be willing to meet the added demand at the existing price by increasing their rates of production. If they were, the purchases for oil stocks would not increase the world price as much as they would under competitive supply.

7. See, for example, M. A. Adelman, "Coping with Supply Insecurity," *Energy Journal*, vol. 3, no. 2 (April 1982), pp. 1–17.

8. Risk-averse decision makers will tend to avoid risky projects that on average are desirable, whereas risk-seeking decision makers will tend to select risky projects that on average are undesirable.

9. Although the measurement of net benefits in terms of expected values is the standard approach, measurement in terms of *option prices* may be concep-

tually more appropriate for situations involving collective risk. See Daniel A. Graham, "Cost-Benefit Analysis under Uncertainty," *American Economic Review*, vol. 71, no. 4 (September 1981), pp. 715–25.

10. One way of modeling risk aversion is to assume that the higher a firm's level of profits, the less value it places on adding another dollar to profits. We might assume, for example, that VPR = lnPR, where VPR is the value to the firm of profit level PR and ln is the natural logarithm function. Consider a firm having a base profit level of 10 that is evaluating a marginal addition to stocks. It believes that there is a 99 percent chance that the addition will decrease PR by 1 and a 1 percent chance that it will increase PR by 99. The expected VPR for not adding to stocks is $[(.99)\ln(10) + (.01)\ln(10) = 2.30]$ and the expected VPR for adding to stocks is $[(.99)\ln(10 - 1) + (.01)\ln(10 + 99) = 2.22]$. Thus, although the expected value of PR from adding to stocks is zero, the expected value of VPR is less for adding than for not adding, so the firm will not add to stocks. What happens if we assume that society is also risk averse? Assume, for example, that SW = lnGNP, where SW is social welfare and GNP is gross national product. Assume that if society does not stockpile, there is a 99 percent probability that GNP will equal 2,000 and a 1 percent probability that GNP will equal 1,000, so that the expected value of GNP is 1,990. Assur·e that if society does stockpile, there is a 99 percent probability that GNP will equal 1,999 and a 1 percent probability that GNP will equal 1,099 so that the expected value of GNP is 1,990. For the case of no stockpiling, the expected value of SW $= (.99)\ln(2,000) + (.01)\ln(1,000) = 7.5940$. For the stockpiling case, the expected value of SW $= (.99)\ln(1,999) + (.01)\ln(1,099) = 7.5944$. Thus society would prefer to stockpile even though the expected value of stockpiling is zero. This example suggests that society will desire to stockpile more if it is risk averse than if it is risk neutral. If we assume that both society and firms are risk averse, the divergence between social and private stockpiling will be greater than if either one is risk neutral and the other risk averse.

11. If $y = 0$, then the demand curve will not shift. If firms draw down their stocks ($y > 0$), then the demand curve shifts leftward. In either case, social surplus changes are measured in the same general way in the U.S. market.

12. See chapter 2, "Direct Costs as Reflected in the Product Markets," including figure 5, for the demonstration that the surplus area in the crude oil market corresponds to equivalent surplus areas in the markets for final products. In figure 20 triangle *hcd* represents losses in welfare to consumers from smaller quantities consumed, a so-called dead-weight loss; rectangle *gbch* represents increased transfers of wealth from U.S. consumers to foreign oil producers; and triangle *abg* represents real resource costs associated with increased domestic oil production. Trapezoid $p_1 bap_0$ represents wealth transfers from U.S. consumers to U.S. producers and is generally not considered a social surplus loss because it simply changes the distribution of wealth within the United States.

13. See William W. Hogan, "Oil Stockpiling: Help Thy Neighbor," *Energy Journal*, vol. 4, no. 3 (July 1983), pp. 49–72, for an analysis of the freeloading character of oil stockpiling. In this connection, it should be noted that oil is not the only commodity whose price rise is restrained by SPR drawdown

during oil supply disruptions. The price of energy, all of whose component prices are highly correlated, is the true SPR target. The U.S. per capita use of all varieties of energy is almost triple that of Japan and is generally more than double that of other industrial countries.

14. Thomas J. Teisberg, "A Dynamic Programming Model of the U.S. Strategic Petroleum Reserve," *Bell Journal of Economics*, vol. 12, no. 2 (Autumn 1981), pp. 526–46. Also see Glen Sweetnam, "Stockpile Policies for Dealing with Oil Supply Disruptions," in George Horwich and Edward J. Mitchell, eds., *Policies for Coping with Oil-Supply Disruptions* (Washington, D.C.: American Enterprise Institute, 1982), pp. 82–96.

15. Hung-po Chao and Alan S. Manne, "Oil Stockpiles and Import Reductions: A Dynamic Programming Approach," Electric Power Research Institute, Palo Alto, California, October 1980; James L. Plummer, "Methods for Measuring the Oil Import Reduction Premium and Oil Stockpile Premium," *Energy Journal*, vol. 2, no. 1 (January 1981), pp. 1–18; and William W. Hogan, "Oil Stockpiling: Help Thy Neighbor."

16. See, for example, Henry Rowen and John Weyant, "The Optimal Strategic Petroleum Reserve Size for the U.S.?" International Energy Program, Discussion Paper, Stanford University, October 1979; Robert E. Kuenne, Gerald F. Higgins, Robert J. Michaels, and Mary Sommerfield, "A Policy to Protect the U.S. against Oil Embargoes," *Policy Analysis*, vol. 1, no. 4 (Fall 1975), pp. 571–97; U.S. Congress, Congressional Budget Office, "An Evaluation of the Strategic Petroleum Reserve" (Washington, D.C., June 1980); Glen Coplon, "DOE Analysis of the Appropriate Size of the Strategic Petroleum Reserve," Working Draft, U.S. Department of Energy, Office of Energy Preparedness, November 30, 1979; and Carlyle Hystad, "Estimating Appropriate Reserve Size: 750 and 1,000 MMB," Federal Energy Administration, Strategic Petroleum Reserve Office, March 24, 1977.

17. Executive Office of the President, "The National Energy Plan," April 29, 1977 (Washington, D.C., 1977), p. 60.

18. Strategic Petroleum Reserve Office, "Strategic Petroleum Reserve Plan Amendment No. 2 (Energy Action No. 1): Expansion of the Strategic Petroleum Reserve," DOE/PA-0032/2, March 1978.

19. Why is *in situ* storage so expensive? The primary reason is that it is practical to produce at most only about one-eighth of an oil reservoir in one year, so that to have a surge capacity of 1 billion barrels in one year, at least 8 billion barrels of reserves would have to be committed, or about 25 percent of proven U.S. reserves. Furthermore, pipelines, including the trans-Alaska pipeline, would have to have sufficient standby capacity to carry the surge production.

20. See David L. Weimer, "Problems of Expedited Implementation: The Strategic Petroleum Reserve," *Journal of Public Policy*, vol. 3, no. 2 (1983), pp. 169–90.

21. For a detailed history of OMB involvement in the SPR size issue, see David L. Weimer, *The Strategic Petroleum Reserve: Planning, Implementation, and Analysis* (Westport, Conn.: Greenwood, 1982).

22. Ibid., pp. 118–24.

23. Dynamic programming analysis of the timing of SPR development, for example, suggests that facility costs of between six and twelve dollars per barrel (as compared with about four dollars under current plans) would be justified to accelerate completion of phases III and IV to 1986. See Glen Sweetnam, "Reducing the Costs of Oil Interruption: The Role of the Strategic Petroleum Reserve," paper presented at the joint national meeting of the Operations Research Society of America/The Institute of Management Sciences at Colorado Springs, Colo., November 10, 1980.

24. In 1978 the SPR office sought bids from the private sector for the development of storage capacity. This effort, called the turnkey program, could have provided phase III (and perhaps phase IV) storage capacity by the end of 1984 at estimated costs only slightly higher than those for government-developed facilities. Although questions of liability and financing remained to be solved, DOE canceled the turnkey solicitation in 1979 for highly questionable reasons. The official explanation given was that the tight crude oil markets after the Iranian revolution constituted a severe constraint on the filling of available capacity in the future (see the statement of DOE undersecretary John Deutch before the House Subcommittee on Energy and Power in U.S. Congress, House, "Strategic Petroleum Reserves: Oil Supply and Construction Problems," in *Hearings before the Subcommittee on Energy and Power of the Committee on Interstate and Foreign Commerce*, 96th Cong., 2d sess., September 10, 1977, p. 26). Probably the prospect of higher short-run budgetary costs, at a time when balancing the budget was taking on greater importance in the Carter administration, was also a factor in cancellation of the turnkey program.

25. For a nontechnical review of the oil import fee issue, see Douglas R. Bohi, Harry G. Broadman, and W. David Montgomery, "Is the Oil Import Fee Sound Energy Policy?" *Challenge*, September-October 1982, pp. 58–62. For an excellent treatment of the technical issues, see Douglas R. Bohi and W. David Montgomery, *Oil Prices, Energy Security, and Import Policy* (Washington, D.C.: Resources for the Future, 1982); and Charles E. Phelps, Frank Camm, and Fred Hoffman, "Issues Surrounding an Oil Import Premium," Rand Paper Series, P-6903 (Santa Monica: Rand, September 1983).

26. See the survey by Harry G. Broadman, "Review and Analysis of Oil Import Premium Estimates," Discussion Paper D-82C, Resources for the Future, Washington, D.C., 1981. Also see William W. Hogan, "Import Management and Oil Emergencies," in David A. Deese and Joseph S. Nye, eds., *Energy and Security* (Cambridge, Mass.: Ballinger, 1981), pp. 261–301.

27. To avoid a socially inefficient shift from crude oil to petroleum product imports, the fee must be applied to both.

28. The federal windfall profits tax, for example, really an ad valorem excise tax coupled with a per unit excise subsidy, would take about 60 percent of the total increase in revenues going to domestic producers. This percentage would gradually decline as older fields, taxed at a 70 percent marginal rate, were exhausted and as newer fields, taxed at a 15 percent marginal rate, made up a larger fraction of total domestic production. The increase in domestic oil prices caused by an import fee can in fact be justified as a means of offsetting

some of the deterrent effect of the windfall tax on domestic production. For a discussion of that deterrent, see Joseph P. Kalt, *The Economics and Politics of Oil Price Regulation* (Cambridge, Mass.: MIT Press, 1981), pp. 93–96, 201–05, 287–88.

29. This approach might even make practical the official U.S. goal of 1 billion barrels. If Congress were to decide to implement the billion-barrel goal, it would be wise to keep the revenues in the SPR fund until 1 billion barrels were actually in storage.

30. In some ways this approach resembles that taken by the Federal Republic of Germany. German refiners and importers are required to hold strategic stocks separate from working inventories. A public corporation, the Erdölbevorratungsverband (EBV), holds required stocks for firms for a fee proportional to the amount of each type of petroleum product refined or imported. These fees can be regarded as excise taxes. Because Germany produces almost no crude oil, the fees are conceptually equivalent to a petroleum import fee. In summary, the Federal Republic of Germany set a stockpiling goal and gave the EBV the fiscal authority to carry it out.

31. EPCA defines *severe energy supply interruption* as: "A national energy supply shortage which the President determines—A. is, or is likely to be, of significant nature; B. may cause a major adverse impact on national safety or the national economy; and C. results, or is likely to result, from an interruption in the supply of imported petroleum products, or from sabotage or an act of God" (Energy Policy and Conservation Act, Public Law 94-163, Title I, sec. 3 [8]).

32. Adelman recommends allowing purchase of SPR oil at any time at a price equal to the highest price being charged anywhere in the world on the day of purchase or on the day of delivery, whichever is greater, plus the cost of a year's storage. See M. A. Adelman, "Coping with Supply Insecurity." The options plan we propose is similar to that suggested by the Industrial Oil Consumers Group in its November 5, 1982, comments on the strategic petroleum reserve drawdown plan proposed by the Department of Energy. See "Energy Emergency Preparedness: Pre-Crisis Forward Sales of Strategic Petroleum Reserve Oil," *Federal Register*, vol. 48, no. 69 (April 8, 1983), pp. 15320–23. The major difference is that our plan would permit the initiation of a drawdown without a presidential declaration of emergency.

33. An alternative bidding scheme is to fill the bids in descending order at the price bid. This approach, which economists call price discrimination, attempts to capture the consumer surplus of the bidders. Experimental studies by Vernon Smith suggest, however, that participants will offer bids closer to their true marginal valuation if the auction is competitive (that is, if all winners pay the market-clearing price). Furthermore, if the proportion of rejected bids is low or moderate, the competitive auction is more likely to yield higher total receipts. See Vernon L. Smith, "Experimental Studies of Discrimination versus Competition in Sealed-Bid Auction Markets," *Journal of Business of the University of Chicago*, vol. 40, no. 1 (January 1967), pp. 56–84; and "Relevance of Laboratory Experiments to Testing Resource Allocation

Theory," paper presented at the Conference on Criteria for Evaluation of Econometric Models, Ann Arbor, Mich., June 9–10, 1977.

34. It is worthwhile to distinguish the options plan from the operation of a futures market. A futures market allows both buyers and sellers to hedge against price changes by guaranteeing buyers an opportunity to purchase, and sellers an opportunity to sell, oil at a fixed price at a future date. Typically, futures contracts involve the actual buying and selling of oil at the expiration of the contract. The options plan we suggest involves sales of oil only if the option holder chooses to exercise his or her claim.

35. For a discussion of this point, see Hank Jenkins-Smith, "Futures Markets," Office of Oil and Gas Policy Working Paper, Department of Energy, October 14, 1982.

36. For a discussion of this benefit, see Shantayanan Devarajan and R. Glenn Hubbard, "Drawing Down the Strategic Petroleum Reserve: The Case for Selling Futures Contracts," Energy and Environmental Policy Center, John F. Kennedy School of Government, Harvard University, June 1982; and R. Glenn Hubbard and Robert Weiner, "When the Oil Spigot Is Suddenly Turned Off: Some Further Thoughts," *Journal of Policy Analysis and Management*, 2 (Winter 1983), pp. 299–302.

# 5
# Emergency Fiscal Transfers

We have argued that reliance on market prices to allocate petroleum products during oil supply disruptions is the most economically efficient policy. The alternative, price controls with administrative allocation, would involve greater loss to the U.S. economy. Nevertheless, at the onset of the next oil supply disruption, price controls and allocations will be advocated by those who believe government intervention in petroleum markets will result in a more equitable distribution of the disruption costs. Although there is merit in their argument if equity is viewed solely in terms of changes in the distribution of expenditures and revenues in petroleum markets, a broader definition of the costs of oil supply disruptions makes their case less convincing. Under price controls and allocations, consumers pay lower dollar prices but must also pay nonpecuniary prices in terms of queuing time, search costs, and uncertainty of supply. In addition, because price controls and allocations result in inefficient use of available supplies, and therefore greater economic loss, unemployment will be greater than under market pricing. Thus price controls and allocations will create a larger number of big losers—people who lose their jobs. Although it is clear that those who have invested in alternative energy sources, petroleum inventories, and crude oil reserves are better off under market pricing than under price controls, it is not clear that consumers are worse off.

If the results of market pricing were judged to be inequitable by policy makers, it would be possible to use taxes and subsidies to redistribute wealth so that the combined effects of market pricing and redistribution of money would be viewed as more equitable. Economists usually find it useful to separate the concepts of efficiency and equity in evaluating alternative allocations of society's resources. By focusing first on the questions of efficiency, they hope to find the policies that will provide the greatest aggregate net benefits to society.

After we have found the policy that gives society the biggest pie, secondary policies can be put in place to make the distribution of slices more equitable.[1] The distributional consequences of economically efficient policies are likely to be diverse and hence possibly offsetting. Economists therefore generally advocate that redistribution be handled through a single set of tax and income transfer programs rather than with specific redistributions for each of the many policies that are adopted.

### Why Should Emergency Fiscal Transfers Be a Component of Federal Energy Policy?

We believe that policies intended to achieve general redistributions of income after market-accommodated oil price shocks are undesirable. Any broad-based redistribution, such as income tax credits for energy expenditures by all economic units, would result in transfers to the majority of consumers who can cope with substantially higher petroleum product prices without severe hardship. Still, there are several reasons why special fiscal transfers from the federal government to particular groups of petroleum consumers are a desirable complement to market pricing during oil supply disruptions.

1. A relatively small number of consumers have both very low income and great difficulty in reducing their short-run consumption of petroleum products, causing them real hardship during oil price shocks unless they are provided with financial assistance. Heating oil rather than gasoline is likely to be the critical product.[2] Even a sudden doubling of gasoline prices is unlikely to cause severe hardship for significant numbers of consumers—gasoline accounts for a relatively small fraction of consumer expenditures, and behavioral changes, such as switching to public transportation, carpooling, and reduction of nonessential automobile use, permit major reductions in consumption levels (see the account of the New York State response in 1979, which appears in chapter 2). Obviously, consumption of fuel oil may be reduced by turning down the thermostat. Substantial reductions in temperature, however, may involve health risks for small children, for the elderly, and for people already ill. Low-income families in cold climates who heat with fuel oil are therefore most likely to suffer real hardship during price shocks, particularly if the shocks occur during the heating season. Households with negligible savings who rely upon Aid to Families with Dependent Children (AFDC), Supplemental Security Income (SSI), or old age and survivors insurance (OASI) as their primary source of income and who heat with fuel oil are likely candidates for emergency cash grants intended to reduce hardship.

141

2. State and local governments face short-run budget constraints that make it difficult for them to maintain essential public services during severe oil price increases. In 1980, state and local governments purchased over $4.6 billion worth of gasoline and fuel oil for use in the provision of police, fire, and other services.[3] Because local governments are usually legally required to operate on a balanced budget and because immediate increases in tax revenues are not readily obtainable, substantial increases in gasoline and oil prices would have to be offset by major reductions in service delivery. Although states have greater taxing powers and financial resources than local governments, they also face short-run fiscal problems during oil price shocks. With the exception of royalty payments for oil produced from state lands, endogenous state revenues are likely to decline: gasoline taxes because of lower unit sales and sales taxes, and state income taxes because of reduced levels of economic activity. At the same time, state expenditures for unemployment benefits and welfare payments are likely to increase. Without federal assistance, state and local governments will be forced to curtail public services. These curtailments, if large, may threaten public safety and may interfere with commerce.[4] Therefore, increased federal assistance to state and local governments during oil supply disruptions may be desirable.

3. Sharp increases in petroleum product prices might cause serious temporary problems for particular sections of the economy that cannot immediately pass along higher energy costs to their customers. Farmers may have difficulty securing loans to cover higher energy costs, especially if they are already heavily in debt and crop prices are not expected to rise immediately. Truckers and taxicab operators who are subject to price regulations may also have difficulty borrowing to cover higher fuel costs. Without the availability of government-subsidized emergency loans, it is possible that a large number of firms will go out of business because of short-run cash flow problems rather than because of the competitive environment that results after the stabilization of petroleum prices. Therefore, it might be argued that federal funds should be made available for emergency loans to firms in agricultural and price-regulated sectors.

4. We might reject the preceding three arguments on their merits yet favor emergency federal assistance because it would help defuse political pressures for direct government involvement in the allocation of petroleum products. It is quite possible that local public and private resources will be mobilized to relieve the vast majority of severe hardships suffered by low-income consumers. Nevertheless, those few cases that fall through the cracks and end in tragedy are likely to receive extensive media coverage and to serve as rallying points for

groups advocating direct federal intervention in petroleum markets. Will a congressman continue to support market pricing when his or her constituents are furiously protesting that an elderly couple died of hypothermia because they could not pay higher heating bills? Similarly, although state and local governments may be able to cope with price shocks without weakening essential services, and although the private capital market may be adequate to help all efficient firms to stay in business, major affected interests will undoubtedly seek relief through the political process. In the past, the relief gained has been in the form of special treatment under a general system of petroleum product allocations; we should fear the possibility of a similar outcome in the future (see the discussion of this point in chapter 3). If the political process is going to result in some administrative allocation of resources, it is better that these resources be federal money rather than private petroleum.

5. Federal transfers to petroleum consumers may be desirable to help counter the oil price drag that accompanies oil supply disruptions. Higher oil prices result in major flows of money away from consumers to foreign and domestic crude oil producers and to the federal government. The revenue going to oil producers increases because the short-run demand for oil is price inelastic. The windfall profits tax and the corporate income tax will enable the federal government to capture a substantial fraction of these increased revenues. The federal government will also realize revenues from sale of SPR oil. If oil producers and the federal government delay in spending these funds, however, and government reduces its borrowing, aggregate demand will be depressed and the recessionary effects of the disruption will be exacerbated.[5] Federal transfers to petroleum consumers would, as a side benefit, help offset any price drag that does occur. We will argue in the next chapter that the drag problem is less serious than is generally supposed. We will also argue that oil price drag is best countered by monetary policy. Nevertheless, the likely existence of some degree of drag suggests that federal emergency transfers initiated for other reasons will be helpful, or at least not very harmful, from the macroeconomic perspective.

### What Are the Major Considerations in Designing an Emergency Transfer Program?

In 1981 Senators Bill Bradley (D-N.J.) and Charles Percy (R-Ill.) introduced a bill (S. 1354) requiring the president to establish a plan for the distribution of increased federal revenues to the states and consumers following a severe oil supply disruption.[6] Although S. 1354 did not become law, researchers have developed a number of proposals that would satisfy its provisions.[7] Most involve widespread distribution of revenues through adjustments to existing tax and benefits programs coupled with block grants to the states. Before discussing our specific proposal, which relies solely on block grants to the states, it will be useful to consider briefly the attributes of a desirable emergency fiscal transfer program.

Because the program is a temporary measure intended to reduce the hardship associated with adjustments to sudden price shocks, we must consider how the transfers will be initiated and terminated. The ideal program would distribute revenue from the very onset of the price shock, not only to maximize the relief of hardship but also to defuse political pressure for market interventions. This statement implies that the transfer system must be designed prior to the disruption so that it can quickly be implemented. The design should include explicit mechanisms for initiation and termination of the transfers. Government programs tend, of course, to assume a life of their own, particularly if they develop a constituency of beneficiaries.

The question of how much money should be transferred is more difficult. Transfers on the order of tens of millions of dollars would probably be adequate, if efficiently used, to prevent life-threatening hardship among low-income individuals. Transfers of billions of dollars, however, would be necessary for a substantial impact on the budgets of state and local governments and on their emergency relief services.[8] The choice of particular transfer levels will depend upon how much weight is placed on the various programs involved. It also seems reasonable to assert that more money should be transferred the more severe the disruption.

There are numerous ways of distributing the transfers. Although it is desirable to direct a high proportion of the funds to the people who are suffering the most, it is also important, if for no other reason than political feasibility, for the distribution to be viewed as fair. Because the manifestations of hardship will vary greatly among locales, it is desirable for the program to provide at least some flexibility below the federal level over the ultimate distribution of the transfers. Other things being equal, the lower the administrative costs, the better. The program should involve a minimum of planning, monitoring, and decision making at the federal level, and it should rely as much as possible on existing agencies at the state and local level.

### A Proposal for an Emergency Transfer Program

The emergency transfer program we propose is the immediate distribution to the states of the revenue realized by the federal government

144

from the sale of SPR oil. A major advantage of this proposal is that it clearly specifies when transfers will begin, how large they will be, and at what rate they will be made. The proposed distribution also contributes to a political environment that encourages sound SPR policies: It creates a politically active constituency of state and local public officials whose jurisdictions will benefit if the federal government builds a large SPR, actually uses it during disruptions, and sells it at market prices. Because the transfer would be in the form of automatic, direct grants to the states, the program would involve minimal administrative costs at the federal level and maximum flexibility in use at the state level.

The program would operate in the following way: Revenue collected by the federal government from the sale of SPR oil or from the sale of options to purchase SPR oil, would be deposited in a special account. At the end of each week the total amount would be divided according to a predetermined formula into shares for each of the states and for the District of Columbia. Each state would then be sent a check in the amount of its share. The checks would be sent to the public official designated by the governor (or by the mayor in the case of the District of Columbia). A state that intended to use the transfers to assist low-income consumers, for example, might designate the official in charge of the state's AFDC program as the recipient. At the direction of the governor, the recipient would make arrangements to disburse the funds as grants or loans to persons and firms. Aside from a general statement of purpose to the effect that the funds must be used to reduce the adverse impact of sudden increases in petroleum prices, the federal government would impose no restrictions or requirements except that public records be kept, showing the way in which the funds are used.

As an illustration, consider a severe oil supply disruption that results in a doubling of crude oil prices from twenty-nine dollars per barrel to fifty-eight dollars per barrel. Assume that during a six-month period, 250 million barrels of SPR oil are sold at an average price of forty dollars per barrel, yielding total receipts of $10 billion. If we use 1980 figures for consumption of motor gasoline and fuel oil, state and local government expenditures would increase by $4.6 billion, agricultural expenditures by $8.1 billion, and total consumer expenditures by $116.6 billion for these products (we are assuming perfectly inelastic demand).[9] These amounts would therefore represent upper bounds on the increase in expenditures. The $10 billion transferred to the states during this period could be used to offset increased expenditures by state and local governments, by the agricultural sector, or by a portion of both. Overall it could be used to offset about 6 percent of the total increase of expenditures on fuel oil and motor gasoline. If the distribution of the $10 billion were based solely on population, New York State would receive $775 million, which it might use to aid low-income consumers, while Iowa would receive $128 million, which it could earmark for low-income consumers and for emergency loans to farmers. These amounts are substantial; they would, of course, be greater the higher the average sale price of SPR oil and the larger the drawdown.

These latter observations suggest that the transfer program would indeed create a political constituency for a more effective SPR program. State officials would have an incentive, the prospect of greater future revenues, for advocating achievement of the SPR goals: drawdown at the onset of disruptions, increasing the likelihood that the SPR will actually be used, and the sale of SPR oil at market prices to maximize the transfers. The support of the states would help Congress resist the pleas for special access to the SPR that will undoubtedly be made during the next disruption.

### How Should the Transfers Be Distributed among the States?

The transfer program requires the specification of a formula for dividing SPR revenues among the states and the District of Columbia. Because the objectives of the program are multiple, there is no single distribution formula that is obviously best from the social perspective. At the same time, we can expect congressmen to favor formulas that will maximize the transfers to their states. Nevertheless, we will consider a few of the possible distribution formulas that seem most reasonable.

The simplest formula would distribute funds on a per capita basis. The formula is also somewhat simplistic in that it implicitly assumes that hardship is distributed uniformly across the population. Recognizing that hardship is most likely to be prevalent among low-income consumers, we might distribute the transfers in proportion to the population of each state below the poverty line. Hardship will, however, also be related in some degree to base levels of petroleum product use. We might therefore adopt a formula that allocates transfers in proportion to consumption of fuel oil and gasoline. Alternatively, allocations could be made on the basis of narrower categories of fuel oil and motor gasoline expenditures. Concern about the continuity of essential public services, for example, might lead to a distribution proportional to state and local government expenditures on these products; concern about maintaining agricultural production might lead to a distribution proportional to farm expenditures on petroleum.

Table 13 shows the amount each state would receive from the

# TABLE 13

## ALTERNATIVE DISTRIBUTIONS OF $10 BILLION OF STRATEGIC PETROLEUM RESERVE REVENUES
### (millions of dollars)

| State | Per Capita | Proportional to Persons below Poverty Line[a] | Proportional to Total Expenditures on Fuel Oil and Motor Gasoline[b] | Proportional to State and Local Government Expenditures on Oil and Gasoline[c] | Proportional to Agricultural Expenditures on Oil and Gasoline[d] | Proportional to Oil and Natural Gas Expenditures Weighted by Percentage of Population below Poverty Line |
|---|---|---|---|---|---|---|
| Alabama | 172 | 265 | 173 | 106 | 132 | 248 |
| Alaska | 2 | 15 | 27 | 35 | 1 | 22 |
| Arizona | 120 | 129 | 122 | 57 | 123 | 121 |
| Arkansas | 101 | 156 | 108 | 68 | 245 | 162 |
| California | 1045 | 968 | 931 | 540 | 733 | 842 |
| Colorado | 128 | 105 | 133 | 86 | 190 | 109 |
| Connecticut | 137 | 90 | 148 | 185 | 21 | 103 |
| Delaware | 26 | 25 | 29 | 39 | 17 | 28 |
| District of Columbia | 28 | 42 | 20 | 111 | — | 30 |
| Florida | 430 | 474 | 407 | 352 | 183 | 423 |
| Georgia | 241 | 325 | 250 | 213 | 213 | 328 |
| Hawaii | 43 | 34 | 37 | 21 | 33 | 30 |
| Idaho | 42 | 43 | 48 | 44 | 169 | 49 |
| Illinois | 504 | 454 | 426 | 613 | 559 | 392 |
| Indiana | 242 | 190 | 261 | 283 | 322 | 205 |
| Iowa | 129 | 105 | 148 | 194 | 598 | 111 |

(*Table continues*)

147

## TABLE 13 (continued)

| State | Per Capita | Proportional to Persons below Poverty Line[a] | Proportional to Total Expenditures on Fuel Oil and Motor Gasoline[b] | Proportional to State and Local Government Expenditures on Oil and Gasoline[c] | Proportional to Agricultural Expenditures on Oil and Gasoline[d] | Proportional to Oil and Natural Gas Expenditures Weighted by Percentage of Population below Poverty Line |
|---|---|---|---|---|---|---|
| Kansas | 104 | 86 | 126 | 109 | 404 | 103 |
| Kentucky | 162 | 231 | 179 | 98 | 171 | 264 |
| Louisiana | 186 | 282 | 203 | 61 | 145 | 307 |
| Maine | 50 | 52 | 62 | 112 | 32 | 64 |
| Maryland | 186 | 149 | 191 | 261 | 63 | 151 |
| Massachusetts | 253 | 196 | 250 | 655 | 26 | 196 |
| Michigan | 409 | 349 | 367 | 476 | 212 | 326 |
| Minnesota | 180 | 138 | 196 | 263 | 449 | 146 |
| Mississippi | 111 | 216 | 107 | 49 | 177 | 210 |
| Missouri | 217 | 215 | 226 | 164 | 321 | 224 |
| Montana | 34 | 35 | 51 | 38 | 147 | 51 |
| Nebraska | 69 | 60 | 81 | 91 | 469 | 67 |
| Nevada | 35 | 25 | 44 | 23 | 24 | 30 |
| New Hampshire | 41 | 28 | 43 | 69 | 9 | 30 |
| New Jersey | 325 | 254 | 353 | 376 | 41 | 274 |
| New Mexico | 57 | 83 | 72 | 40 | 82 | 100 |
| New York | 775 | 848 | 570 | 1171 | 198 | 625 |
| North Carolina | 259 | 309 | 263 | 395 | 322 | 307 |
| North Dakota | 29 | 29 | 48 | 51 | 258 | 49 |
| Ohio | 477 | 402 | 469 | 287 | 291 | 394 |

148

| | | | | | | |
|---|---|---|---|---|---|---|
| Oklahoma | 134 | 145 | 152 | 116 | 223 | 162 |
| Oregon | 116 | 101 | 136 | 187 | 120 | 123 |
| Pennsylvania | 524 | 446 | 501 | 414 | 212 | 421 |
| Rhode Island | 42 | 35 | 38 | 75 | 3 | 31 |
| South Carolina | 138 | 184 | 136 | 121 | 99 | 173 |
| South Dakota | 30 | 42 | 42 | 47 | 227 | 54 |
| Tennessee | 203 | 271 | 216 | 175 | 135 | 294 |
| Texas | 628 | 751 | 737 | 297 | 830 | 873 |
| Utah | 65 | 55 | 68 | 45 | 53 | 58 |
| Vermont | 23 | 22 | 27 | 25 | 25 | 25 |
| Virginia | 236 | 225 | 242 | 280 | 130 | 223 |
| Washington | 182 | 146 | 177 | 217 | 161 | 144 |
| West Virginia | 86 | 106 | 86 | 63 | 23 | 101 |
| Wisconsin | 208 | 147 | 208 | 172 | 340 | 141 |
| Wyoming | 21 | 13 | 58 | 29 | 51 | 37 |

a. Number of persons below the poverty line in 1979: Bureau of the Census, *Statistical Abstract of the United States, 1982–1983* (Washington, D.C., 1983), pp. 443–444.

b. Assumes a 1980 average heating oil price of $0.978/gal. and a 1980 average retail motor gasoline price of $1.221/gal. Energy Information Administration, *Monthly Energy Review: March 1983* (Washington, D.C.: U.S. Department of Energy, March 1983), pp. 92–94. Quantities of distillate and motor gasoline consumed in 1980 were collected from Energy Information Administration, *State Energy Data Report, 1960 through 1980* (Washington, D.C.: U.S. Department of Energy, July 1982), pp. 13, 23–429.

c. Based on estimates of 1980 state and local government expenditures for gasoline and fuel oil. Jack Faucett Associates, *Preliminary Analysis of Economic Impacts of Petroleum Shortages with Tax Rebates*, DE-AC01-79PE70050, April 1981.

d. Based on estimates of 1980 fuel and oil expenses for farm vehicles provided by Sandy Suddendorf, Economic Research Service, U.S. Department of Agriculture.

SOURCE: Authors except as indicated in the notes.

distribution of $10 billion of SPR revenues under each of these formulas. With the exception of less populous states, such as Alaska and Wyoming, distributions based on population, persons below the poverty line, and total consumption yield fairly similar allocations. The only clear regional pattern is that southern states do much better under the formula based on persons below the poverty line than under either of the other two criteria. The formula based on total consumption yields the narrowest range of transfers of the three: $20 million to $931 million versus, for the per capita formula, $2 million to $1,045 billion and, for the number of persons below the poverty line, $13 million to $968 million. The distributions based on state and local government expenditures and agricultural expenditures differ considerably from those resulting from the other formulas. The former distribution tends to be relatively favorable to northeastern states and the latter to midwestern states.

Reasonable arguments can be made in support of any one of these five formulas. We believe the one based on total expenditures on fuel oil and motor gasoline is the most appropriate because it relates transfers to the aggregate economic harm likely to be suffered by the states. There is of course no reason to limit attention to these particular formulas. Weighted averages or more complicated combinations might be viewed as more equitable. The last column in table 13, for example, is based on total expenditures on fuel oil and motor gasoline in each state weighted by the fraction of the state population below the poverty line. It represents an attempt to allocate funds proportionately to the likely hardship of low-income consumers.

## Summary

It is much more efficient to allocate dollars rather than petroleum products during oil supply disruptions. If the fiscal transfer program is to be an effective mechanism for reducing hardship and for shielding the market system from political attack, however, it should be designed so as to distribute funds automatically at the very onset of a severe price shock. We believe that the distribution of SPR drawdown revenues according to a predetermined formula offers the best prospect for an effective transfer program. It has the merit of creating incentives for state and local officials and their constituencies to support early SPR drawdown at market prices—goals consistent with optimal use of the reserve.

# Notes

1. Unfortunately, the pie has a tendency to shrink the more nearly equal we try to cut the pieces. If we guaranteed everyone the same after-tax income, for example, we would destroy the incentive for work effort and would shrink the pie greatly. There is always some trade-off between equity and efficiency. For an excellent discussion of this issue, see Arthur M. Okun, *Equality and Efficiency* (Washington, D.C.: Brookings Institution, 1975).

2. If the oil supply disruption leads to long-term increases in oil prices, the prices of natural gas, electricity, and other fuel oil substitutes would also be expected to rise. Long-term contracts and public utility regulations, however, would most likely result in gradual increases in fuel oil substitutes. Existing income transfer programs, particularly those like social security retirement benefits, which have built-in cost-of-living adjustments, would help low-income consumers accommodate these gradual price increases. Also, consumers anticipating the price increases would be able to make long-term adjustments in life style, for example by living in smaller and more energy-efficient dwellings. The sudden increase in heating oil prices requires special attention.

3. Jack Faucett Associates, "Preliminary Analysis of Economic Impacts of Petroleum Shortages with Tax Rebates," DOE Contract DE-AC01-79E70050, April 1981.

4. States might reduce their highway patrols, for example, and might thus contribute to higher accident rates; local governments might reduce the frequency of refuse collection and might thus create a potential threat to public health; and school districts might eliminate bus service, thus contributing to a net increase in gasoline consumption and perhaps to losses of employee time as parents provide transportation by private automobile instead.

5. See the discussion on "Oil Price Drag" in chapter 2.

6. For discussion of S. 1354, see U.S. Congress, Senate, "Government Responses to Oil Supply Disruptions," in *Hearings before the Committee on Natural Resources*, 97th Cong., 1st sess., July 28 and 30, 1981; and U.S. Congress, Senate, "Standby Revenue Recycling Authority to Deal with Petroleum Supply Disruptions," in *Hearing before the Subcommittee on Energy and Agricultural Taxation of the Committee on Finance*, 97th Cong., 1st sess., December 8, 1981.

7. See, for example, Michael Barth and Edwin Berk, "Administering Revenue Recycling: Options and Analytical Framework," ICF, Inc., Washington, D.C., 1982; and Steven Kelman and Eugene Peters, "A Single-Agency Emergency Recycling Plan Using Checkwriting," Harvard University, Kennedy School of Government, Energy and Environmental Policy Center, 1982.

8. To put matters in perspective, we should recall that the total expenditures by state and local governments amounted to $355 billion in 1980 (Bureau of the Census, *Statistical Abstract of the United States* [Washington, D.C., 1981], p. 248).

9. For state and local government fuel expenditures, see the reference cited below in table 13, n.c; for agricultural expenditures, see table 13, n.d; and for total expenditures, table 13, n.b.

# 6
# Macro Fiscal-Monetary Policies

Macro stabilization measures are a relevant part of the policy response to an oil supply disruption. Expansive monetary or fiscal policy can, to some degree, ameliorate the fall in real GNP caused by the adjustment to higher energy prices and has the potential to offset fully any decline in aggregate demand and any further fall in real GNP due to oil price drag. We shall deal with the drag phenomenon first. Oil price drag, the possible mass transfer of purchasing power from the nonpetroleum goods markets to the oil industry, was viewed by the Council of Economic Advisers in 1979–1980 as the central economic problem occasioned by an oil supply disruption. The following section presents the methodology and empirical results of our estimates of drag during 1969–1980. Subsequent sections will address monetary policy and a fiscal measure, the reduction of payroll taxes, as possible stabilizers. We argue that expansive monetary policy will facilitate the intermarket movement of resources following the oil price shock and can efficiently counter any oil price drag. Our preliminary findings do not indicate that reductions in payroll taxes are an effective offset to the employment and income-reducing effects of increased energy costs.

## The Measurement of Oil Price Drag

Our basic source of data on oil price drag is the aggregate balance sheet and income and expense statements for the twenty-five largest American-based oil companies. These statements have been collected and published annually since 1968 by the American Petroleum Institute (API). Supplementing the API data in several important respects, particularly since 1977, are data published as part of the Financial Reporting System (FRS) of the Energy Information Administration (EIA). The FRS provides information similar to, though somewhat

## FIGURE 21

SCHEMATIC REPRESENTATION OF OIL AND OTHER COMPANY-PRODUCT
TRANSACTIONS

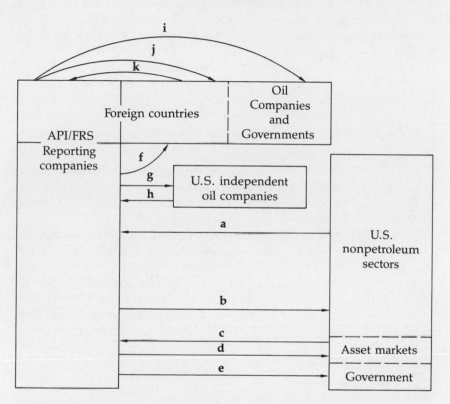

SOURCE: Authors.

more detailed than, that of the API sample for twenty-six major en-
ergy-producing companies. There is an approximate 83 percent
overlap in the companies in the FRS and the API samples.

**Conceptual Framework.** Figure 21 presents a schematic drawing of
the relevant expenditures between the API/FRS reporting companies
and other domestic and foreign sectors. The sectors involved in the oil
trade are represented by labeled boxes. Vectors linking the boxes show
the directional movement of money against oil; other goods and services, including interest and dividends; and payment of taxes to domestic and foreign governments. Our task is to organize and adjust

these flows so as to leave a net measure of expenditures on oil not recycled to domestic goods and services markets in the current period.

The box on the left represents the reporting companies; the one above, all foreign countries. The intersection of the two boxes at the upper left denotes the companies' foreign operations. At the far right of the foreign sector box is a subsector corresponding to foreign oil companies and governments. The box at the far right represents the United States exclusive of petroleum-producing companies. Two subsectors are designated, the financial and other asset markets and government at all levels. The small box in the center represents U.S. oil-producing companies other than those in the API and FRS sample. They are designated as *independents*.

The labeled vectors represent the following flows:

$a$ = API/FRS company receipts from the U.S. nonpetroleum sector.

$b$ = API/FRS company expenditures to the U.S. nonpetroleum sector for goods (capital goods and other supplies of equipment and raw materials) and services (payroll and benefits, including consultants' services) and interest and dividend payments.

$c$ = funds raised by API/FRS companies by short- and long-term borrowing and by the sale of shares and fixed assets in domestic asset markets.

$d$ = funds invested by API/FRS companies in domestic asset markets; this item includes the companies' additions to cash balances.

$e$ = taxes paid by API/FRS companies to domestic government at all levels.

$f$ = net imports of petroleum (crude and product) by API/FRS companies into the United States.

$g$ = API/FRS company purchases of petroleum from the independent oil companies in the United States.

$h$ = API/FRS company receipts from petroleum sales to the independents.

$i$ = API/FRS company purchases of petroleum from foreign oil companies and governments for resale in foreign countries.

$j$ = API/FRS company purchases of goods (capital and raw materials) and services (payroll and benefits) and taxes paid in foreign countries.

$k$ = API/FRS company receipts from petroleum sales in foreign countries.

*A sources and uses statement.* Sources of funds of the API/FRS companies are on the left side of the following summary equation; uses

154

are on the right side:

$$a + c + k + h = b + d + e + f + g + i + j \qquad (1)$$

Oil price drag occurs when the oil companies delay in spending their additional receipts on domestic goods (other than petroleum) and services. We identify oil price drag by taking first differences of equation 1 and subtracting from $\Delta a$ on the left side those incremental company outlays that are added to the domestic nonpetroleum goods and services markets in the current period. All other components of equation 1 are transferred to the right side of the equation and are grouped.

$$\Delta a - \Delta b = (\Delta j + \Delta i - \Delta k) + (\Delta g - \Delta h) + \Delta f + (\Delta d - \Delta c) + \Delta e \qquad (2)$$

On a first approximation, oil price drag is thus the sum of the terms on either side of equation 2. On the left side, drag is expressed as the oil companies' net withdrawal of funds in any period from the domestic markets for nonpetroleum goods and services; on the right side, drag appears as the sum of additional expenditures by the companies in markets other than domestic nonpetroleum goods and services. Since there are no direct data on $a$, receipts from the domestic nonpetroleum sectors, our measurement of drag is cast in terms of the right side, where

$(\Delta j + \Delta i - \Delta k) = D_1 = $ the increment in payments less receipts by the reporting companies from foreign operations

$(\Delta g - \Delta h) = D_2 = $ the increment in payments less receipts by the reporting companies for oil from the U.S. independent oil industry

$\Delta f = $ reporting companies' incremental net imports of petroleum (crude and product) into the United States

$(\Delta d - \Delta c) = D_3 = $ reporting companies' incremental net (mainly financial) investment in domestic asset markets

$\Delta e = $ the companies' additional tax payments to domestic governments

We expect equation 2 generally to be positive, although the parenthetical terms, $D_1$, $D_2$, and $D_3$ will tend to be positive or negative. If $D_1$, $D_2$, or $D_3$ is positive, its sign indicates that part of the incremental net receipts from domestic nonpetroleum goods markets is diverted to foreign countries, to the domestic oil independents, or to the domestic financial markets, respectively. If $D_1$, $D_2$, or $D_3$ is negative, then oil price drag, as measured by the remaining terms in equation 2, is overstated, since a portion of the remaining outlays is funded not by receipts from domestic nonpetroleum goods markets but by a surplus of incremental company sales in foreign countries or to domestic independent oil companies or by a reduction in additions to company-owned financial assets.

*Sources of data.* The available API company data used in estimating the right side of equation 2 are presented in appendix B. These data include aggregate payments for goods and services [the sum $(b + j)$, excluding taxes paid to foreign governments], the net increase in financial and other assets $(d - c)$, and total taxes paid by the companies to all governments (the sum of $e$ plus that part of $j$ representing tax payments to foreign governments). Major components of $(b + j)$ are also available, although, like taxes, they are not divided between domestic and foreign disposition.

Important additional data are provided by the FRS for 1977–1980. Included, for the reporting companies, are net petroleum imports into the United States $(f)$, payments and receipts from foreign oil operations $(i$ and $k)$, tax payments to foreign governments (a component of $j$), and the balance of trade with the domestic independent oil companies $(g - h)$. These data, for the years in which they are available, are used as if the FRS and API samples had been composed of the same companies. For earlier years in which these data are unavailable, we make extrapolations using the API company series. These and several other adjustments and interpretations that complete the estimates of oil price drag are the following.

1. The trade balance $(g - h)$, between the majors and the independent oil sector, as reported for the FRS companies in 1977–1980, is negative, indicating a net inflow of funds to the majors. The increment $D_2 = (\Delta g - \Delta h)$, a component of drag, is also negative, averaging $-\$6.40$ billion for the 1978–1980 interval. $D_2$ is thus an offset to the oil price drag attributable to the reporting companies. For the pre-1978 period, we make the simplifying assumption that $D_2 = 0$. This conservative assumption tends to raise our drag estimates for the reporting companies and for the industry as a whole.

2. The variables $i$ and $k$, whose increments are components of $D_1 = (\Delta j + \Delta i - \Delta k)$, are reported for the FRS companies for 1977–1980. The variable $j$ is estimated from API company total outlays on goods, services, and taxes by a procedure described in point 3 below. The sum $(j + i - k)$, so derived, averages $\$0.91$ billion for the period 1977–1980, and its increment, $D_1$, averages $-\$1.38$ billion for 1978–1980. Receipts and payments from foreign operations of the majors

156

thus tend to be roughly in balance, and the increment of net payments, small but negative, indicates a net domestic inflow of funds and an offset to oil price drag. For the pre–1978 years, however, we assume that $D_1 = 0$, again, from the available evidence, tending to bias upward our estimates of drag.

3. Data on the API and FRS company foreign expenditures are incomplete, but a rough general estimate usable for the 1968–1980 period can be pieced together. The components of total expenditures on goods and services plus taxes paid are given in equation 5 and in table 21 in appendix B. The major items are listed in table 14 and are assigned percentages indicating the portion spent abroad. The companies' payroll expenditures in foreign countries are believed to be a relatively small part (10 percent) of their total payroll. On the assumption that most interest and dividends go to domestic claimants, the foreign component is set at 5 percent. For the late 1970s and 1980, about 30 percent of capital expenditures were made in foreign countries, as reported in API and FRS publications.[1] This percentage is assumed to prevail for the entire period 1968–1980 and is entered in the table for both capital expenditures and additions to inventory. Since an average of 40 percent of the companies' income is earned abroad,[2] 40 percent of nonoil expenses, the single largest cost item other than the purchase of oil, is also assumed to be incurred in foreign countries. Finally, FRS company current taxes paid to foreign governments during 1977–1980 average 62 percent of their total current taxes, and this percentage is entered in table 14 for all of 1968–1980.

TABLE 14

MAJOR COMPONENTS OF REPORTING COMPANIES' FOREIGN-BASED
OUTLAYS ON GOODS, SERVICES, AND TAXES, 1968–1980

|  | % Foreign Expenditures | Weight |
|---|---|---|
| Payroll and benefits | 10 | 0.14 |
| Interest and dividends | 5 | 0.07 |
| Taxes paid | 62 | 0.25 |
| Capital expenditures | 30 | 0.19 |
| Other costs and expenses, nonoil | 40 | 0.32 |
| Additions to inventories | 30 | 0.03 |
| Total |  | 1.00 |

SOURCES: American Petroleum Institute, Energy Information Administration, and assumptions described in text.

Weights for each of the categories in table 14 are taken as the percentage that each bore to total outlays on goods, services, and taxes in 1979. A more precise year-by-year weighting was deemed unnecessary in view of the general imprecision involved in assigning the foreign-based percentages. Moreover, our estimates of oil price drag will not be very sensitive to alternative weighting procedures.

The weighted average percentage in table 14 is 36.65, or simply 37. That is, on average, 37 percent of the companies' outlays on goods, services, and taxes is taken as occurring in foreign countries.

4. Information on net petroleum imports into the United States is available only for the FRS reporting companies during 1977–1980. In that period the companies' net imports (crude and product) average 0.88 of total U.S. net petroleum imports. This same proportion, 0.88, is assumed to hold for the API companies from 1968–1976.

We shall follow the Council of Economic Advisers in assuming that any increase in oil imports is offset in the current year by an increase in U.S. exports in general equal to 20 percent of the additional imports.[3] An increase in oil imports will, of course, tend to raise the exchange rate and will induce a balancing increase in exports of goods and services and an inflow of capital. In the short period, the dominant response will be the capital inflow. As time passes, exports of goods and services will rise, and the capital inflow will stimulate domestic goods expenditures (although, as indicated in point 5 below, the induced expenditure response to the capital inflow is likely to be quite delayed).

5. The accumulation of assets, of which $(d - c)$ is the net flow, includes financial instruments of all kinds, including cash held by the companies plus investments and advances. The latter are mainly loans to oil industry subsidiaries (90 percent of the total) but include direct acquisition of subsidiaries, including extraordinary purchases of banks, manufacturing facilities, and so forth. All of these assets, financial and real, share the characteristic that funds expended on them are at least temporarily diverted from the expenditures stream of currently produced goods and services. Additions to cash balances would, of course, represent a more or less permanent diversion from the goods markets, but available evidence from the API sample companies, presented in table 15, indicates that during the critical period, 1977–1980, increases in cash holdings were insignificant.

The generally accepted view is that, under normal circumstances, there is a six- to nine-month lag between the injection of additional funds into financial markets and the induced response of investment and consumer durables spending. For a six-month lag, one-half of all funds that entered (and left) financial markets uniformly over the

TABLE 15
CASH BALANCES OF AMERICAN PETROLEUM INSTITUTE
REPORTING COMPANIES, 1977–1980
(billions of dollars)

|  | Cash Balances | Annual Change |
|---|---|---|
| 1977 | 2.18 | — |
| 1978 | 2.89 | 0.71 |
| 1979 | 3.73 | 0.84 |
| 1980 | 3.52 | −0.21 |

SOURCE: American Petroleum Institute, work sheets from C. A. Pendzich.

course of a year would be converted into additional investment and consumer expenditures by the end of the year. For a nine-month lag, one-fourth of such funds would reach the goods markets. The circumstances of an oil supply disruption are not, of course, normal. Late 1973, 1974, 1979, and 1980 were all periods of sluggish economic activity, either prerecession or actual recession. We therefore assume that additional financial accumulations by the oil companies do not succeed in stimulating any net additional spending on goods and services during those periods or in any other part of the decade. This assumption is relatively conservative, particularly in view of the evidence on the small increments in the companies' cash balances in the later 1970s. All of financial assets (FA) are thus included in our measure of oil price drag, where FA, the change in the balance sheet category "Financial Assets," is our approximation to $(d - c)$.

6. We make an assumption analogous to that in point 5 on the disposition of taxes paid to domestic governments. Any increase in government receipts is assumed to reduce government borrowing in the current period by an equal amount. The reduction in borrowing releases an equivalent amount of private saving, which becomes available for nongovernmental borrowing and fund raising. Like oil company financial asset acquisition, however, such released saving entails the transfer into financial markets of funds, none of which is assumed to reach currently produced goods and services markets in the current period. We also abstract from any increase in government expenditures automatically triggered by the disruption-induced decline in economic activity.

7. After we have secured measures of the drag terms on the right side of equation 2, the sum of these terms is deflated by the ratio of the current year's GNP deflator to the deflator of the preceding year. Drag

occurs only when funds leave the domestic goods markets at a rate greater than the current inflation rate.

8. The drag attributable to the reporting companies must be enlarged to include drag that occurs vis-à-vis the domestic independents. Enlargement is achieved simply by multiplying the total drag of reporting companies by 1.33, since the latter are approximately 75 percent of the oil industry, or by subtracting $D_2$ from the estimate, whichever results in a larger number. $D_2$, the net flow of funds from the majors to the independents, is, if negative, a drag component attributable to the independents.

**Empirical Results.** Estimates of oil price drag for 1969–1980, based on the above sources and procedures, are reported in table 16. Since drag is generated by *increments* in the flow variables ($a, b \ldots, k$), the first drag estimate is for 1969, even though data on the flows begin in 1968.

A drag total, for the reporting companies only and unadjusted for inflation, appears on line 11. This is an approximation to the right side of equation 2: the sum of $D_1$ (line 4), $D_2$ (line 6), $\Delta f$ (line 7) less $0.2\Delta f$ (line 8), $D_3$ (line 9), and $\Delta e$ (line 10). Line 12 is the value of the GNP deflator for each year divided by that of the preceding year. The drag estimates on line 11 are adjusted for the current year's inflation relative to that of the preceding year by dividing them by the ratios on line 12 and entering the result on line 13 (see adjustment 7). Line 14 raises the estimates thus obtained for the reporting companies to encompass the entire domestic oil industry by multiplying them by 1.33, except in 1980, when the alternative procedure noted in adjustment 8 is followed. In that year, $D_2$, a drag component attributable to the independent oil companies, is subtracted from line 13, after adjustment for inflation. The drag total obtained by this method exceeds that resulting from multiplication of line 13 by 1.33.

As promised in point 2 above, $D_1$ is assumed to be zero (line 4) until its components, $\Delta i$ and $\Delta k$, become known in 1978. As noted in point 1, $D_2$ is simply set at zero (line 6) until estimates of its component ($\Delta g - \Delta h$), are available in 1978.

*Comparative analysis.* These procedures yield estimates of oil price drag for the entire industry (line 14) that fall at or below $3.19 billion for 1969–1972. In 1973, the first year of disruption, drag reaches $11.05 billion, and in 1974, $26.74 billion. Both totals reflect increases in all the measured components, though they are dominated in 1974 by an astonishing increase in the incremental cost of imports (line 7). In 1975, drag is −$16.20 billion, indicative of a net injection of funds by the companies into domestic nonpetroleum goods markets. The negative drag is essentially explained by a sharply reduced rate of increase

160

in financial assets (line 9) while the other drag components are quiescent. Drag increases significantly to $13.40 billion in 1976 and more moderately to $3.97 billion in 1977. Both increments are strongly influenced by the rise in oil imports stimulated both by the recovering economy and by the imposition of the entitlements program. In 1976 an increase of $7.22 billion in the rate of growth of financial assets supplements the rise in imports, but in 1977 a decrease of −$3.96 billion in the rise of the financial flow partially offsets the imports. In 1978, drag at −$4.22 billion is again negative, explained by inflows from foreign operations ($D_1 = $ −$4.57 billion) and domestic independents ($D_2 = $ −$4.41 billion) and a reduction of imports due to the introduction of Alaskan oil, all countered somewhat by an acceleration of financial asset accumulation ($5.71 billion).

The second and third disruptions generate drag of $33.50 billion in 1979 and $11.94 billion in 1980. As in 1974, the oil import bill accounts for a major portion of the 1979 drag, though the largest rate of increase of the decade in financial assets (reflecting major acquisitions of subsidiaries) also contributes. In 1980, the import bill again rises, though at only half the 1979 rate. Meanwhile, financial asset accumulation falls off sharply from its 1979 pace, the new windfall profits tax pushes net incremental tax payments to their highest level (line 10), and the majors enjoy a dramatic incremental surplus with the independents ($D_2 = $ −$11.50). The net effect of these factors is a virtual zero drag, though, by adjustment 8, the subtraction of $D_2 = $ −$11.50 creates a net positive sum.

The 1979 drag of $33.50 billion is the highest of the period, but not in relation to the scale of the economy. On line 15 all of the drag estimates are expressed as percentages of the current year's nominal GNP. The percentage is 1.86 in 1974, the highest of the decade. In 1979 it is 1.39. The 1973 and 1976 percentages are comparable at 0.83 and 0.80, respectively, whereas in 1980 the percentage is only 0.45.

*General assessment.* It does not follow, however, that GNP is an appropriate base against which to assess the economic or deflationary impact of the drag. We saw in chapter 2 that less than one-third of total expenditures on petroleum is made by purchasers for whom the petroleum is final product.[4] Such purchasers would be limited, by national accounting convention, to households and government. More than two-thirds of the outlays are for oil as an intermediate product, an input in the process of production. Thus, for the overwhelming portion of oil expenditures, total transactions, which are at least twice the magnitude of GNP, are the appropriate reference for assessing the size of the oil price drag.

A limitation of our measurement of drag as the first difference of

## TABLE 16
### DERIVATION OF ESTIMATES OF OIL PRICE DRAG BASED ON API/FRS REPORTING COMPANIES, 1969–1980

| | 1969 | 1970 | 1971 | 1972 | 1973 | 1974 | 1975 | 1976 | 1977 | 1978 | 1979 | 1980 |
|---|---|---|---|---|---|---|---|---|---|---|---|---|
| 1. Foreign expenditures on goods, services, and taxes (change): $\Delta j$ | 1.55 | 1.41 | 1.77 | 1.34 | 3.36 | 11.14 | 0.75 | 1.42 | 4.49 | 2.52 | 13.70 | 14.85 |
| 2. Oil purchases in foreign operations (change): $\Delta i$ | — | — | — | — | — | — | — | — | — | 2.83 | 46.36 | 47.86 |
| 3. Receipts from foreign operations (change): $\Delta k$ | — | — | — | — | — | — | — | — | — | 9.92 | 62.48 | 59.85 |
| 4. $D_1$: 1969–1977, 0; 1978–1980, lines 1 + 2 − 3 | 0 | 0 | 0 | 0 | 0 | 0 | 0 | 0 | 0 | −4.57 | −2.42 | 2.86 |
| 5. Net oil purchases from independents: $(g - h)$ | — | — | — | — | — | — | — | — | −18.43 | −22.84 | −26.14 | −37.64 |
| 6. $D_2$: 1969–1977, 0; 1978–1980, change in line 5 | 0 | 0 | 0 | 0 | 0 | 0 | 0 | 0 | 0 | −4.41 | −3.30 | −11.50 |
| 7. Net petroleum imports (change): $\Delta f$ | 0.24 | 0.15 | 0.50 | 0.93 | 2.84 | 16.05 | −1.18 | 6.11 | 7.37 | −1.33 | 17.99 | 9.38 |

| | | | | | | | | | | | | |
|---|---|---|---|---|---|---|---|---|---|---|---|---|
| 8. 0.2 × line 7 | 0.05 | 0.03 | 0.10 | 0.19 | 0.57 | 3.21 | −0.24 | 1.22 | 1.47 | −0.27 | 3.60 | 1.88 |
| 9. Increase in financial assets (change): $D_3$ = ΔFA | 0.74 | −0.32 | −0.40 | 1.35 | 4.73 | 5.02 | −13.60 | 7.22 | −3.96 | 5.71 | 15.98 | −4.16 |
| 10. Domestic tax payments (change): Δe | 0.24 | 0.55 | 0.78 | 0.40 | 1.76 | 3.94 | 1.26 | −1.54 | 1.21 | 0.93 | 2.61 | 5.78 |
| 11. Oil price drag (unadj.): lines 4 + 6 + 7 − 8 + 9 + 10 | 1.17 | 0.35 | 0.78 | 2.49 | 8.76 | 21.80 | −13.28 | 10.57 | 3.15 | −3.40 | 27.26 | 0.48 |
| 12. Adjustment for inflation: $P_0/P_{-1}$ | 1.051 | 1.054 | 1.050 | 1.042 | 1.057 | 1.087 | 1.093 | 1.052 | 1.058 | 1.073 | 1.085 | 1.090 |
| 13. Line 11/line 12 | 1.11 | 0.33 | 0.74 | 2.39 | 8.29 | 20.06 | −12.15 | 10.05 | 2.98 | −3.17 | 25.12 | 0.44 |
| 14. Oil price drag, total: line 13 × 1.33 | 1.48 | 0.44 | 0.99 | 3.19 | 11.05 | 26.74 | −16.20 | 13.40 | 3.97 | −4.22 | 33.50 | 11.94[a] |
| 15. Line 14/GNP (%) | 0.16 | 0.04 | 0.09 | 0.24 | 0.83 | 1.86 | −1.05 | 0.80 | 0.21 | −0.20 | 1.39 | 0.45 |

a. Line 13 − Line 12 (see adjustment 8 in text).

NOTE: All figures except those in lines 12 and 15 are in billions of dollars. Line 1: table 22, line 3; see explanation in text, adjustment 3. Line 2: 1968–1977: unreported; 1978–1980: from worksheets on FRS companies provided by the Energy Information Administration. Line 3: see line 2. Line 4: 1969–1977: assumed to be zero (see text, adjustment 2); 1978–1980: lines 1 + 2 − 3. Line 5: 1968–1976: unreported; 1977–1980: from worksheets on FRS companies provided by the Energy Information Administration. Line 6: 1969–1977: assumed to be zero (see text, adjustment 1); 1978–1980: change in line 5. Line 7: table 22, line 11; see explanation in text, adjustment 4. Line 8: table 22, line 12; see explanation in text, adjustment 4. Line 9: table 22, line 8; see discussion in text, item 5. Line 10: table 22, line 5; see discussion in text, item 6. Line 12: see explanation in text, adjustment 7. For GNP deflators, see Council of Economic Advisers, *Economic Report of the President* (Washington, D.C., February 1983), p. 168. Line 13: see explanation in text, adjustment 7. Line 14: see explanation in text, adjustment 8. Line 15: see line 12 for GNP source.

SOURCE: Authors except as indicated in the notes.

flow variables is that it ignores any possible carry-over of drag from one period to the next. If oil imports are normally $40 billion a year, for example, and suddenly increase by $15 billion, measured drag would go up by that increment for one year only. An ongoing $55-billion-a-year import level, however, could entail drag in subsequent months or years until a new steady-state equilibrium, with imports and exports both at $55 billion, had been reached. Our measurement of drag as the first difference of imports would not capture this continuing drag tendency. The same possibility exists with respect to the lag between the first difference of company financial asset acquisitions and induced investment spending or between additional company tax payments, reduced government borrowing, and added private expenditures.

This lag does not, however, limit the accuracy of our estimates in the periods when oil price drag is at its maximum—during the actual disruption episodes. The disruptions struck spontaneously, with very little, if any, buildup. Thus carry-over of drag would be reflected in post–1974 or post–1979 years, during which measured drag was significantly negative (1975) or, under the circumstances, relatively low (1980).

Overall, oil price drag does not appear to have been as serious a deflationary force as feared by the CEA in the 1970s and in 1980. Our estimate for 1979 is 62 percent, and for 1980, half or less of the CEA's, depending on which CEA projection is used.[5] As a percentage of GNP, our 1980 estimate is less than one-half of one percent, as compared with the CEA's anticipated 3 percent. The CEA's estimate appeared in its January 1980 report, which expressed no expectation that crude oil prices would rise more in 1980 than they had in 1979 (the de facto price increase in 1980, reflected in our drag estimate, was 58 percent, as compared with 42 percent in 1979). Had the CEA been aware of the oil price developments, it would surely have projected an even greater drag than it did.

It is true that our estimates of drag, like those of the CEA, are predicated on the actual regulatory environment of the period, which included the whole network of crude oil and product price controls and allocations. U.S. crude oil prices were on average three to seven dollars below the world price—approximately 10 percent to 30 percent in relative terms—and product prices 10 percent to 15 percent below world levels. If freeing the market raised prices by roughly these percentages, it seems unlikely that our drag estimates, already small or moderate, would rise more than proportionately. Drag would still be much less than the CEA believed it to be. We have, moreover, argued that there is evidence that U.S. controls, by limiting domestic petroleum output and stimulating consumption, may have raised world crude oil prices, an effect that decontrol would reverse. Oil price drag could thereby remain roughly the same whether it occurred in a controlled or an uncontrolled environment. Our estimates would then fall in the upper range of those that would have prevailed in the 1970s under any market conditions, free or otherwise.

## A Role for Monetary Policy

Whether or not oil price drag is viewed as a serious deflationary force in the nonpetroleum sectors of the economy, the proper response, in our opinion, is a loosening of the money supply. As we mentioned in chapter 2, drag is a siphoning of cash balances away from current goods markets into financial markets where they are held to support a temporarily increased demand for money or are used to pay off bank loans, which reduces the stock of money. In either case an increase in the money stock, or, more accurately, in its growth rate, is the natural countermeasure.

Monetary policy is, of course, an extremely flexible macro instrument and would not appear to operate with any greater lag than characterizes the buildup of oil price drag. The oil companies are very efficient managers of their cash balances, and there is no evidence that their dispositions of revenues that appear in our annual data did not proceed more or less uniformly over the course of each year. The quarterly API release, *Petroleum Industry Profits*, gives every indication that industry outlays on capital equipment and raw materials were synchronized with the inflow of revenues. The ability of the companies to respond so immediately to additional revenues with new projects was, in fact, rather remarkable.

The proper amount and timing of monetary ease will obviously vary with the size of the disruption and the increase of oil prices. The increased growth rate of money will be appropriate and should be continued as long as oil prices or expenditures are rising and, perhaps, for several quarters following. The optimal amount of money is, of course, a function of the increase in the oil magnitudes and the extent to which funds are thereby diverted from nonpetroleum goods and services markets. The danger of adding to the energy-induced inflation is balanced by the fact that the proposed policy is an offset to oil price drag, a concomitant deflationary force. If significant drag actually materializes and the monetary injection is too large, only the excess of new money over drag—not the whole injection—will tend to be inflationary.

Even if the monetary increase exceeds the amount needed to

offset any drag, the outcome could easily have net positive effects. Although monetary expansion is not an appropriate antidote to the direct energy-induced loss of output, additional money can limit further contraction of output by facilitating the numerous interproduct market shifts of the adjustment process in the year or so following an oil disruption. With a sufficient increase in money, the loss of demand in declining product markets would be moderated. Since prices tend to be inflexible downward, the short-run loss of output and employment resulting from leftward shifts of demand would be reduced. In expanding markets, where output tends to be inflexible upward, increased demand and prices would be financed both by new money and by transfers of demand from declining markets, rather than by transfers of demand only. On net, the economy would experience a gain of output and employment in exchange for some increase in inflation.[6]

On the negative side, any additional inflation will, through economywide indexation of wages and other resource prices, raise production costs and reduce aggregate output. Nevertheless, if the interproduct market shifts are numerous enough, the gain of output and employment from monetary expansion and moderate inflation could easily outweigh any negative GNP effects. In fact, given the monetary authority's policy of restraint in the previous disruptions, a case can probably be made for urging the authority to err, if at all, on the side of overease. In the context of an oil disruption, there would appear to be a broad range of inflation rates for which the resulting welfare losses are not as severe as those resulting from monetary increases that are noninflationary but insufficient, that is, that do not fully offset drag or raise demand adequately in individual product markets. The losers from inflation caused by a limited monetary overdose are those whose incomes are not indexed—a minority in the present economy. To a large extent, these individuals are reachable through the financial assistance programs commonly proposed as part of the disruption response (see chapter 5). Moreover, their losses will be picked up by others, who gain disproportionately, if, in the aggregate, the monetary increase is income sustaining. In the case of noninflationary but insufficient money relative to the stabilization task, there is a clear reduction of real GNP, income, and employment that can only be a net loss of social welfare.[7]

## Should Payroll Taxes Be Reduced?

A policy measure that in principle could be a useful offset to a loss of oil supply is a reduction in payroll taxes. Whereas the oil shock shifts the aggregate supply schedule to the left, a reduction in production taxes will tend to shift it to the right. The parallel, symmetrical character of such targeted tax reductions, vis-à-vis the energy shock, makes them an appealing and potentially efficient policy response. Several writers, notably including Mork, alone and with Hall and Gilbert,[8] place great weight on this approach.

On the micro level, payroll tax reductions obviously cannot be as efficient in maintaining firm output as can drawdown of SPR or other stockpiled oil. In a free market, additional oil from any source will tend to replace reduced supplies in their most-valued uses. The reduction of payroll taxes, however, encourages firms to maintain output by substituting labor for energy or, where firms have low energy inputs, by simply hiring additional labor. Firms in the former category are likely to respond to the temporary tax cut by accelerating what they view as an increase in the long-run optimal labor/energy ratio. Firms in the latter category, with low energy costs, would appear less likely to respond to a temporary reduction in labor costs under disruption conditions. For these firms, the tax cut would instead generate a rent that plays no useful role in the adjustment process.

What evidence do we have regarding the likely targeting of reduced payroll taxes and labor costs to firms classified by the size of their energy costs? A preliminary evaluation can be made with industrial data generated by the Data Resources, Inc. model. The percentage of total cost due to labor and energy inputs is provided for each of the seventy-seven domestic private-sector U.S. industries. Table 17 presents a 3 × 3 contingency table summary of the DRI data. Each variable, the percentage of total cost represented by refined petroleum products and labor, respectively, is divided into three groupings of roughly equal numbers of industries: low, medium, and high. Low cost for petroleum is defined as 0 percent to 0.88 percent, medium cost as 0.89 percent to 1.74 percent, and high cost as 1.75 percent to 9.91 percent. For labor, low, medium, and high costs are, respectively, 4.5 percent to 26.0 percent, 26.1 percent to 33.0 percent, and 33.1 percent to 71.6 percent. The entry in each cell is the number of industries having the indicated attributes. There are, for example, six industries whose percentage costs for both petroleum and labor are low (we designate the cell LL) and ten industries whose petroleum cost is in the highest category but whose labor cost is in the lowest category (cell HL).

At this level of analysis, and by the criteria suggested above, the clearest support for the use of the payroll tax as an offset of petroleum costs would be a concentration of frequencies in cells on or below the downward diagonal. Cells above the diagonal are those for which the

## TABLE 17
### FREQUENCY DISTRIBUTION OF PRIVATE DOMESTIC INDUSTRIES, CLASSIFIED BY RELATIVE PETROLEUM COSTS AND RELATIVE LABOR COSTS, 1981–1982

| Petroleum Cost | Labor Cost | | | Total No. of Industries |
| | Low (4.5–26.0%) | Medium (26.1–33.0%) | High (33.1–71.6%) | |
|---|---|---|---|---|
| Low (0–0.88%) | 6 | 10 | 11 | 27 |
| Medium (0.89–1.74%) | 9 | 8 | 8 | 25 |
| High (1.75–9.91%) | 10 | 7 | 8 | 25 |
| Total no. of industries | 25 | 25 | 27 | 77 |

SOURCE: Data Resources, Inc. printout furnished by Energy Information Administration.

percentage petroleum cost is relatively low and labor cost is relatively high. In these cells a temporary payroll tax reduction confers a significant windfall on firms whose petroleum costs may not be high enough to justify more than a token temporary expansion of the work force. On a first approximation, we assume that all the frequencies in the cell LH and one-half of the frequencies in cells LM and MH receive rents from a tax reduction that exert little or no positive employment effect. The calculation yields a total of 11(LH) + 5(LM) + 4(MH) = 20, or 20/77 = .26, of the total number of industries for whom reduced payroll taxes do not appear to be a socially efficient offset to increased oil costs.[9]

On the basis of these data, we must express serious reservations regarding the usefulness of payroll tax cuts as a counterdisruption policy tool. Fully one-fourth, and perhaps more, of all industry would be receiving benefits that are poorly targeted. This is a high percentage as compared with the universal effectiveness and efficient individual response to petroleum reserve drawdown under free market prices or the imposition of a petroleum import tariff. If we take into account also the severe political resistance that any tampering with social security taxes is likely to encounter, very definitive evidence regarding the benefits of variable tax rates would seem to be required before they could be recommended.[10]

**Summary**

This chapter has investigated the magnitude of so-called oil price drag, the loss of purchasing power in nonpetroleum goods markets as a result of oil supply disruption, during the period 1969–1980. Our empirical estimates, based on assumptions that seem to bias the results upward, point to significantly lower levels of drag, in absolute and relative terms, than those found by the CEA. Since more than two-thirds of petroleum products purchased are for use as intermediate goods, we do not regard GNP as an appropriate reference base for evaluating the size of drag. Relative to total transactions in the economy, our drag estimates would be only half as large as in relation to GNP.

Expansion of money is seen as a useful policy measure during and following a disruption. In contrast to the tight monetary policies actually pursued during the oil disruptions of the 1970s, monetary ease would offer some trade-off between possibly increased inflation and unemployment caused by the induced intermarket demand shifts. Monetary ease is a natural offset to oil price drag, whether the magnitude of the drag is large or small.

We have also examined the case for using payroll tax reductions as a symmetrical supply-side offset to increased petroleum costs. Preliminary evidence from the domestic private-sector industries indicates a lack of correlation between labor costs and petroleum costs for a significant part of the economy. Payroll tax cuts are unlikely to be efficiently targeted as a compensator for increased oil costs.

# Notes

1. See appendix B.
2. Ibid.
3. Council of Economic Advisers, *Economic Report of the President* (Washington, D.C., January 1980), p. 65.
4. See chapter 2, n. 17.
5. Ibid., n. 12 and related text.
6. In terms of aggregate supply and demand schedules, an increase in the rate of monetary growth shifts $AD$ to the right along $AS$. We are arguing that as an offset to interproduct market shifts, the movement along $AS$ is quite flat, with output ($Q$) increasing relatively more than the price level ($P$). By comparison, an increase in $AD$ not specifically designed to facilitate the intermarket shifts (or to offset a leftward shift of $AD$ itself owing to oil price drag) would encounter a much steeper $AS$ schedule and a much less favorable trade-off between $Q$ and $P$. The flatter $AS$ slope in the case underlying the use

169

of monetary policy to facilitate intermarket shifts may be interpreted as resulting from a rightward shift of the entire $AS$ schedule. The reader will recall in chapter 2 (see figure 10, shift "2") that the intermarket shifts, though involving a shift among demands, is manifested in the aggregative framework as a leftward shift of aggregate supply. The monetary increase will thus shift both $AD$ and $AS$ simultaneously, to the right, though $AS$ by a smaller amount.

7. The lag in the effect of monetary policy may in fact justify some overcompensation in the amount of money introduced early in the disruption period. There is, of course, some increase in the size of the monetary injection that will compensate for any tendency of money to lag the effects of the disruption—the rise in oil prices, possible oil price drag, and the intermarket shifts of demand. Such additional amounts of money could be removed later, although there would probably be less damage if the resulting higher price level were simply allowed to remain.

8. See chapter 2, n. 40 and related text.

9. We may argue that a more meaningful comparison is between labor and all energy costs rather than petroleum only. All energy includes electricity, in addition to the direct use of oil, gas, and coal. If we substitute all energy for petroleum in table 17, the resulting matrix of frequencies is changed only slightly:

|    |    |    |
|----|----|----|
| 6  | 10 | 11 |
| 7  | 9  | 9  |
| 12 | 6  | 7  |

The low, medium, and high intervals for the percentage energy cost are 0 percent to 2.3 percent, 2.4 percent to 4.2 percent, and 4.3 percent to 77.4 percent, respectively. Then 11(LH) + 5(LM) + 4.5(MH) = 20.5, or 20.5/77 = .27, of all industries still remain above the diagonal and, by hypothesis, gain rent from a temporary payroll tax reduction that is at least questionable in terms of stimulating employment. Total energy costs in the LH cell are more than triple the cost of petroleum but are still a small 3.9 percent of labor cost, compared with 1.2 percent for petroleum only. Although all energy costs rise more or less in tandem, the nonpetroleum costs, particularly those for electricity and coal, will rise much less than petroleum and with some delay.

10. None of the foregoing analysis is intended to challenge the very real evidence that the containment of wage costs and the avoidance of profit squeeze have been key factors in the speed and depth of the recovery following the oil supply disruptions. In the United States, where wage moderation characterized the 1975–1979 recovery from the (at least partially) energy-induced recession of 1973–1975, the recovery exceeded that of all other major industrial countries. See the comparative analysis of Jeffrey Sachs, "Stabilization Policies in the World Economy: Scope and Skepticism," *American Economic Review*, vol. 72, no. 2 (May 1982), pp. 56–61. To judge from the strength of the recovery in 1983 in the United States and somewhat earlier in Japan, in both of which countries wage moderation has prevailed, a similar interpretation can be made of the role of reduced real wages in stimulating growth after

the 1979–1980 energy shock. None of our discussion implies, however, that payroll tax reductions are an effective substitute for the selective industry-by-industry bargaining process or, preferably, for the firm-by-firm bargaining process that determines real wages and, under appropriate macro incentives, keeps real wages at the full-employment level.

# 7
# Other Crisis Measures

We shall now analyze several other policies proposed to alleviate the costs of an oil supply disruption. We shall consider an oil import tariff that is levied during disruption periods; demand restraint measures, including coupon rationing of gasoline; the use of so-called set-asides of petroleum products for allocation by state governments; and participation in the programs of the International Energy Agency (IEA), particularly its sharing agreements.

## Disruption Tariffs

We have argued that the imposition of a moderate tariff on petroleum imports is a desirable way to finance the strategic petroleum reserve. A tariff of about two dollars per barrel corresponds to a very conservative estimate of the oil import premium, which measures the divergence between the world price and the marginal social cost of imported oil during normal market periods. It is economically efficient to impose a tariff that raises the acquisition cost of oil (the world price plus the tariff) to the social cost. Because many analysts believe that the premium increases during oil supply disruptions, they advocate the imposition of a still higher petroleum import tariff, called a disruption tariff, during periods of increased oil prices. Although disruption tariffs appear desirable when viewed solely from the perspective of oil markets, their macroeconomic effects and the political difficulties associated with their implementation suggest that they should not be used.[1]

The rationale for disruption tariffs is illustrated in figure 22.[2] Figure 22b shows the world market with demand curve $D_W$ and normal period supply curve $S_W$, determining a price of $p_0$. In figure 22a, $D_{US}$ represents the U.S. demand for petroleum imports (U.S. total petroleum demand minus domestic supply); at price $p_0$, a quantity $q_0$

172

FIGURE 22

THE IMPACT OF A DISRUPTION TARIFF ON (a) THE U.S. OIL MARKET AND
(b) THE WORLD OIL MARKET

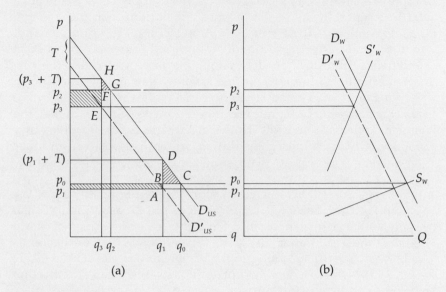

(a)

(b)

SOURCE: Authors.

is demanded. Imposition of a per unit tariff, $T$, shifts the U.S. demand, as seen by suppliers of oil, to $D'_{US}$. (To consumers, the effective price is now the stated price plus the tariff; at any price on the vertical axis, the relevant demand quantities are thus lower, or at any quantity, the demand, or offered, price to sellers is lower by the amount of the tariff.) Because the United States is a major importer of petroleum, the shift to $D'_{US}$ causes a sympathetic shift in the world total demand to $D'_W$, resulting in a new world price of $p_1$, below $p_0$. U.S. consumers, however, see a price of $(p_1 + T)$, which is higher than $p_0$. When $(p_1 + T)$ is projected to the demand curve $D_{US}$, which, for prices inclusive of the tariff, is still the relevant curve, the quantity demanded falls from $q_0$ to $q_1$. The social loss due to this reduced consumption is the change in consumers' surplus, represented by the area of trapezoid $(p_1 + T)DCp_0$. Society gains the revenue from the tariff, however, which is represented by the area of rectangle $(p_1 + T)DAp_1$. These two areas overlap in rectangle $(p_1 + T)DBp_0$. The net gain (or loss) from the tariff is thus given by the difference between the area of rectangle $p_0BAp_1$

(gain) and the area of triangle *BCD* (loss). As drawn, the revenue from the tariff, which is assumed to be redistributed among consumers, is only slightly larger than the loss in consumers' surplus. The optimal tariff would be the one that maximizes the net gain.

Now consider a disruption in the world market that shifts the supply curve from $S_w$ to $S'_w$. Because the new supply curve is less price elastic (steeper) in the region of price equilibrium than the original, the imposition of a U.S. tariff, *T*, will, in shifting the world demand, produce a greater price decline than occurred under normal market conditions. Following the disruption, the tariff will cause the disrupted price to fall from $p_2$ to $p_3$ and quantity demanded from $q_2$ to $q_3$. The net gain to the United States from the tariff is represented by the area of rectangle $p_2FEp_3$ minus the area of triangle *FGH*. As drawn, the net gain appears to be large. Thus a given tariff of size *T*, which may produce virtually no net gains during normal periods, can produce substantial gains during disruptions, suggesting that a relatively larger tariff will be optimal in the latter conditions.

In our illustration, this conclusion resulted primarily from the assumption that disrupted supply is less price elastic than normal supply. Other assumptions, involving the price elasticities of world demand and U.S. import demand, can influence the conclusion as well. It is also worth noting that the benefits of the tariff will be greater, in either normal or disrupted markets, the greater the fraction of world petroleum consumption affected by the tariff. In terms of figure 22, the shift from $D_w$ to $D'_w$ will be greater if the United States and other major importers impose the tariff simultaneously than if the United States does so alone. The greater the shift of $D_w$, the greater the price reduction and hence the smaller the loss in consumers' surplus. Clearly there are potential benefits to be gained from international coordination of tariff policy.

Uncertainty about the magnitudes of the various supply and demand parameters assumed in the analysis makes it difficult to calculate optimal tariffs with any degree of confidence. Even if available data permitted accurate calculation within the narrow perspective of the oil market, the resulting estimates of the optimal size of tariff would be overstated because of failure to take into account the widespread adjustment costs experienced following oil price shocks. As we observed in chapter 2, disruption of supply arrangements and changes in the composition of aggregate demand, combined with downward rigidity in nominal wages and prices, prevent the economy from moving instantaneously to a new efficient equilibrium. Because disruption tariffs increase the magnitude of the price rise seen by consumers, the tariffs increase the adjustment costs. Hence the actual

174

net social benefits of disruption tariffs will be smaller than estimates based on a partial analysis and perhaps even negative.

If it were possible to take into account all economic effects, optimal disruption tariffs could be calculated with accuracy. Their imposition would require the understanding and the will of political decision makers to take actions that were counterintuitive and were likely to elicit hostile public response. Even if both politicians and voters fully understood that disruption tariffs can produce net social benefits, the question of how the costs and benefits are to be distributed would still remain to block political action.

Perhaps the only politically feasible way to implement disruption tariffs is to establish a permanent ad valorem oil import tax.[3] The ad valorem tariff would raise the price of imports by a fixed percentage, so that if the world price doubled, so would the per barrel fee paid by importers. Unfortunately, it would be only by coincidence that any ad valorem tariff was optimal. In fact, the ad valorem rate that is optimal in normal market conditions might result in a tariff that is much too high during disruptions. Although the likelihood of this possibility could be reduced by establishing the rate so that it is consistent with conservative estimates of the normal-period premium, the uncertainty involved in all the premium estimates means that the ad valorem approach is of doubtful merit.

## Demand Restraint Measures

The equilibrium price in a product market depends on both supply and demand. Although a leftward shift in the supply schedule will cause an increase in the market-clearing price, a simultaneous downward shift of sufficient magnitude in the demand schedule can leave the price unchanged. A strategy for reducing price shocks is to force downward shifts in effective demand through the imposition of demand restraint measures, which coercively restrict consumer access to the market. Demand restraints invariably result in substantial losses in consumer welfare, and they are difficult and costly to implement. These costs will almost always outweigh any distributional benefits they produce. Hence demand restraints should generally be rejected as policies for dealing with petroleum price shocks.

**Coupon Rationing.** The most commonly discussed demand restraint is coupon rationing of gasoline.[4] Under coupon rationing, consumers would be allowed to purchase a quantity of gasoline only less than or equal to the allotment provided by the number of coupons they hold. The total number of coupons issued would determine the effective market demand. That demand is equal to the quantity supplied at the market price. The price, by law, is below market clearing. The role of coupons is thus to do what price is not permitted to do—to constrain demand to the supply level.

Rationing plans that do not allow consumers to sell unused coupons result in gross allocational inefficiency, because there is no practical way to distribute coupons to consumers who place the highest value on them. Distribution according to historical consumption patterns may be the best that central administrators can do, but it fails on efficiency grounds because different consumers have different demands. Limitations in data-handling capabilities may make even historically based allocations impractical. Although the standby gasoline rationing plan developed by the Carter administration called for allocations of coupons to firms according to historical use, for example, it would have allocated coupons to consumers on a per vehicle basis.[5]

The initial distribution of coupons, however it is determined, is inevitably allocationally inefficient. Some consumers will receive more coupons than they want at the ceiling price and will place a below-market value on their excess supply. Others will want to purchase more gasoline than is possible with their coupon allocation. They would value an additional coupon at the price they would have been willing to pay for another gallon of gasoline in the unconstrained market (the shadow price) minus the market price of gasoline. Clearly, both groups of consumers would be better off if coupons could be bought and sold, which the Carter administration plan permitted.

If the coupon resale market is efficient, the price of coupons will equal the vertical distance between the market supply and the unrestrained market demand curve at the quantity corresponding to the number of coupons issued. With reference to figure 17, the coupon price will equal $(p_3 - p_2)$, the difference between the shadow price and the ceiling price. Still, although the coupon market, in the absence of constraints, may be expected to function smoothly, the fact that gasoline remains under price controls makes it difficult for the coupons and gasoline supplies to come together. We have seen that under the gasoline price controls used in the 1970s, price could not function effectively as an allocator. Price increases had to be preceded by eligible cost increases; profit margins were frozen and inflexible except under occasional permitted adjustments. Supply and demand shifts were thus ineffective in altering the price and allocation of gasoline. Under these circumstances, gasoline lacks the price signals that would direct it to where the coupons are, and it would not move appropriately except in response to time-consuming, ad hoc monitoring of the coupon distribution.[6]

**Gasoline Tax/Rebate Option.** The same distribution of gasoline and money created under ideal circumstances by coupons could be obtained by imposing an excise tax on gasoline equal to the market price of coupons. The resulting revenues would be sent to everyone by a check equal to the market value of the coupons they would have received. The excise tax and rebate system would entail much lower administrative costs than coupon rationing, which involves the printing, distribution, use, and monitoring of an entirely new currency. The logistics involved in putting the coupons into circulation are staggering. It has been estimated that 5 billion coupons would have to be introduced every three months (the Treasury Department prints about 4 billion currency bills each year).[7] In contrast, there is already an administrative mechanism in place to collect gasoline excise taxes, and the government could as easily distribute rebate checks as coupon packets to motorists and firms.

A fundamental contradiction with both coupon rationing and gasoline tax/rebate systems is the fact that in time, all markets, controlled or otherwise, tend to clear. As we noted in chapter 3, the short-run search and queuing in a controlled market are gradually replaced by deterioration of product quality and transfer of unsatisfied demand to alternative markets. Both processes reduce the effective market-clearing price to the level of the ceiling price, which itself tends to rise as crude oil and other costs are passed through. The artificially created shortage gradually disappears. By the time coupon rationing or tax/rebate systems come on stream—for coupons, at least, the lags are believed to be anywhere from three to nine months—they will very possibly be superfluous in that ad hoc market clearing will already obtain. By then the price of coupons in the resale market and the appropriate excise tax on gasoline will both approach zero.

As long as coupons and the excise tax do have positive values, one of the ongoing administrative tasks will be to estimate their appropriate levels. Since the number of coupons that equal the available quantity of gasoline and the size of the tax that clears the gasoline market will both vary from month to month, estimating the relevant amounts of each would be a formidable econometric undertaking.

**Additional Demand Restraints.** Other demand restraint measures are less effective than coupon rationing and are equally undesirable. They fall into two categories: access restrictions and transaction restrictions.

Access restrictions attempt to depress demand by limiting the time or frequency with which a product may be purchased. A ban on the weekend sale of gasoline, for example, discourages recreational intercity travel, which some observers view as having low social value. Even if we were to accept this doubtful value judgment, the weekend ban has the unfortunate effect of also hindering business and high-priority personal travel that is most efficiently done on weekends. As long as consumers see the market price of gasoline, it is best to let them decide whether weekend travel is desirable.

The other access restriction that has been used, alternate-day gasoline purchases, is a response to the queuing caused by gasoline price controls. Consumers are allowed to purchase gasoline only on either even or odd days of the month, depending on their license plate number or on some other numerical identification. Therefore, roughly only half of potential consumers are permitted to wait in queues each day. If queues are actually shortened, less time and energy (literally) will be wasted. Because most consumers would in any event not elect to wait in queues every day, it is unlikely that alternate-day purchases will do anything more than slightly inconvenience some buyers. If gasoline prices are left uncontrolled, of course, there is no need to worry about queuing in the first place.

The major transaction restrictions that have been used in the past are maximum and minimum purchases of gasoline. The rationale for maximum purchases is to spread the limited supply under price controls over a larger number of consumers. An undesirable side effect, however, is to aggravate queuing; people who have a strong desire for a full gasoline tank can simply get back in line. Minimum-purchase restrictions make somewhat more sense. During times of supply uncertainty, it is not unreasonable for people to want to keep their tanks as full as possible. Continually topping off tanks, however, increases queue lengths. If purchases are restricted to some minimum quantity, people simply waiting to top off can be eliminated from the queue. Maximum purchases would be harmful, and minimum purchases largely irrelevant, in the absence of queuing induced by price controls.

### Petroleum Product Set-Asides

Refiners secure crude oil from a variety of sources: through standing agreements with foreign producers, through spot market purchases, and through ownership of domestically produced oil. A sudden reduction in oil exports from a disrupted foreign producer will affect some refiners more than others. In the very short run, refiners who rely most heavily on the disrupted producer will be forced to reduce their sales of petroleum products unless they have significant stocks of crude oil to replace lost inputs or significant stocks of petroleum products to offset reduced outputs. Market forces, however, will lead to a rearrangement of crude oil supplies throughout the refining sector, so that available supplies can be refined in the most efficient

178

manner. Nevertheless, under either the initial postdisruption crude oil distribution or the more efficient one that follows, some petroleum product consumers will be unable to satisfy their demands solely through transactions with their regular suppliers.

Are there any factors that interfere with the smooth transition from the predisruption to the postdisruption pattern of relationships among buyers and sellers? One possibility is that the provisions of established contracts might prevent refiners from legally shifting significant fractions of their sales from regular customers to those who must seek new sources of supply. A recent study conducted for the Department of Energy by the Rand Corporation concluded, "Formal contract provisions would not be major impediments to market adjustment, even in quite severe crises."[8]

There is also the possibility that refiners will voluntarily continue to supply regular customers rather than divert products to new customers willing to pay slightly higher prices. By forgoing the maximization of short-run profits, the refiners may expect to gain a reputation for reliability that will strengthen their long-term market position. The refiners may also fear that undesirable political consequences might result if they are perceived as "profiteering" during troubled times.

Even if refiners favor regular customers, the overall impact on retail consumers will be largely mitigated by the organization of the petroleum product distribution system. Refiners sell large fractions of their outputs to "jobbers" who act as wholesalers. Jobbers usually buy from more than one refinery, and most locales are served by more than one jobber. These diversifications tend to spread production cutbacks by individual refiners over a wide area. Furthermore, because jobbers rely primarily on road transport, they can easily change the geographic range of their operations. Price differences only slightly greater than transportation costs will make it profitable for them to extend their operations to locales that have been particularly hard hit.

Price controls of course remove the incentive for jobbers to seek out locales where their products are most valued. An approach used to reduce the local shortages caused by federal price controls and allocations in the 1970s was to allow states to allocate a fraction of refinery output directly to priority users. In effect, petroleum products were set aside from the federal allocation system to create a separate state allocation network. Because of better information at the state level about local circumstances, the state network offered at least the possibility of reducing the worst inefficiencies and hardship caused by the cumbersome federal regulations.

In the absence of federal price controls and allocations, the case for state set-asides is not strong. Set-asides should be viewed as desirable only if we believe that refiners and jobbers will consistently forgo increased profits and that some consumers will therefore not be able to find sellers at prevailing prices. It might then be desirable for states to be able to require refiners to sell a fraction of their output to new customers at market prices.

Several states have contingency plans to implement set-aside programs during oil supply disruptions even in the absence of federal price and allocation regulations. A particularly thorough plan has been prepared by the California Energy Commission.[9] It recommends that as much as 5 percent of the total monthly supply of petroleum products expected to be available to the state be set aside during supply emergencies for priority bulk consumers who have difficulty securing supplies at market prices. During severe fuel emergencies, emergency services such as police and fire would have the highest priority, following in descending order by health and safety services, agricultural services, trucking, and other bulk purchasers. Priority users would make monthly requests to the proposed fuel allocation office, which would determine how much each user would be allowed to purchase at market prices from the state set-aside. The plan establishes monthly deadlines for administrative action so that the set-aside is never physically removed from the distribution system. Although the plan allows considerable discretion regarding the initiation of the set-aside program, it does have clear criteria for termination.

On its surface, the California plan appears quite reasonable; modest administrative costs provide insurance against the costs of a possible, if unlikely, gross failure of the petroleum distribution system to adjust to new supply conditions. A hidden cost of the program is that the anticipation of its implementation may discourage priority users from diversifying their sources of supply, from holding emergency stocks, and from taking other actions that would reduce their vulnerability to supply shocks. Of much greater significance, however, is the danger that the fuel allocation office will succumb to pressure to force sales of set-aside product at below market prices. The pressure will arise from priority users who face economic hardship during the crisis. If they are politically powerful, they may be successful in securing changes in regulations that give them access to set-asides at prices below market. Once this occurs, the fuel allocation office would likely be faced with a dramatic increase in requests for allocations as other users seek similar bargains. The task of selecting among priority users would then become much more difficult; it might entail an expansion of the set-aside program and other interventions in the market system.

180

Perhaps a safer approach is to establish state set-aside programs that do not involve administrative allocation. The state could simply require refiners to sell the set-aside amounts of products by auctions open to all bidders. Such a requirement would guarantee all consumers access to new sources of supply without requiring the states to set priorities. States might play a role in helping refiners coordinate and publicize auctions.

## Participation in the International Energy Agency

The International Energy Agency was established in November 1974 through the International Energy Program Agreement, which was signed by sixteen of the twenty-four members of the Organization for Economic Cooperation and Development.[10] The current IEA membership includes the United States, Japan, and all the major industrial countries of Western Europe except France. One goal of the IEA is to facilitate cooperation among its members that will reduce their dependence on imported oil and their vulnerability to oil supply disruptions. Although we might question the ability of the IEA to promote such cooperation, the goal itself is desirable. The other major IEA goal, however, the administration of a plan for mandatory sharing of petroleum during oil supply disruptions, is neither practical nor desirable, as we shall shortly argue. The United States should work to eliminate mandatory oil sharing from the IEA charter.

There are several areas of cooperation in which the IEA might play a useful role. One is in the coordination of petroleum import tariffs. All countries that are net petroleum importers gain when a major importer such as the United States imposes a tariff that reduces the world price. If other countries join the United States in a common tariff policy, the reduction in price will be greater. Because all countries receive the benefits of a lower world price whether or not they share in the costs of imposing tariffs, negotiation through an agency such as the IEA may be desirable to prevent "free riding." Similarly, the IEA might provide a framework for coordinating petroleum stockpiling policies. In fact, an IEA goal is that all members develop stockpiles equivalent to ninety days of petroleum imports. Although the actual impact of the establishment of this goal has probably been very modest, it nevertheless points in the right direction. The same can be said about other IEA activities, such as information gathering and the support of basic energy research.

**The Sharing Agreement.** The International Energy Program Agreement sets out a mandatory sharing system to be implemented by the IEA during oil supply emergencies. The IEA secretariat has discretion

181

to initiate emergency sharing whenever the IEA or any of its members sustains, or is expected to sustain, a reduction of 7 percent or more in the average daily rate of petroleum consumption relative to that of the previous year. A decision by the secretariat to initiate the sharing system can be overruled only by special majorities (more than simple majorities of voting "weights") of the membership. Under emergency sharing, each country has a supply right that depends on its base-year consumption, demand restraint level, and petroleum reserve commitments that correspond to ninety days of base-year imports. Basically, each member is supposed to prepare demand restraint measures that will reduce petroleum consumption by 7 percent to 10 percent of base-year consumption, depending on the size of the shortfall. During a shortfall of as much as 12 percent, members have a supply right equal to 93 percent of their base-year consumption minus an amount proportional to their base-period imports.[11]

The actual sharing would be based on the difference between de facto supply (domestic production and imports) and the supply right of each member. Members for whom actual supply exceeds their supply rights would be required to sell petroleum to members for whom supply rights exceed de facto supply.[12] Although the agreement states that pricing should be based upon "price conditions prevailing for comparable commercial transactions," the actual determination of prices could be made by the secretariat subject to special majority overrule. In other words, it is possible for sharing to be mandated at prices lower than the world market price.

In fact, it is unlikely that any country would choose to exercise its buying right unless the price was below the world level. Imagine a 7 percent reduction in world supply. The world price would rise to distribute the reduced supply among the various countries. Each country would face the same higher price, apart from differences in the cost of transporting oil from its particular supply sources. At that price, demand quantities in individual countries would be reduced in accordance with demand price elasticities. Those countries with greater-than-average absolute elasticities (flatter demand schedules) would reduce consumption and imports more than 7 percent, whereas those with smaller-than-average elasticities (steeper demand schedules) would reduce consumption and imports less than 7 percent. Granted that the price paid is the world market price, however, markets will clear in individual countries that will then have no incentive to exercise their buying rights. Simply put, there will be no unsatisfied demand.[13]

**The Impact of Sharing in the World Market.** The price and welfare

# FIGURE 23

## The Effect of International Energy Agency Sharing on Two Trading Countries, A and B

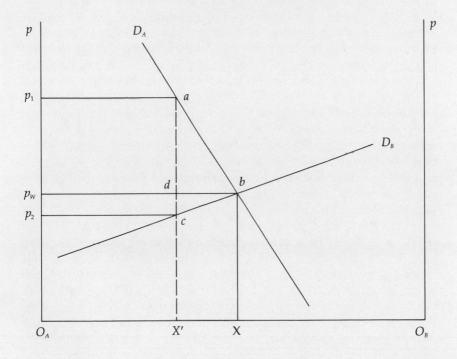

SOURCE: Authors.

effects of sharing on IEA membership as a whole are shown in figure 23. The diagram, which plots the demand schedules of two prototypical IEA countries, A and B, assumes the existence of a fixed total amount of oil equal to the length of the horizontal axis. The amount consumed by country A is measured from the origin on the left, $O_A$, with increasing amounts scaled, as usual, from left to right. The amount of oil consumed by country B is the distance between A's quantity, wherever it happens to be, and the origin on the right, $O_B$. B's consumption is thus scaled so as to increase from right to left, starting at $O_B$.

A's demand schedule, drawn with reference to origin $O_A$, is $D_A$, and B's demand is $D_B$, drawn with respect to origin $O_B$. $D_B$ slopes down and to the left since, relative to $O_B$, quantities increase to the

183

left. The two schedules intersect to determine a world price, $p_W$, at which the quantity of oil going to country A is $O_A X$ and the quantity going to country B is $XO_B$. The market clears at $p_W$, since at that price the sum of the demand quantities ($O_A X + XO_B$), is exactly equal to the total supply quantity, which is the length of the horizontal axis.

The picture of the market equilibrium given in figure 23 may be interpreted as the free-trade outcome resulting from an earlier reduction in world supply. Suppose that under the sharing agreement, country A, whose schedule is less elastic than B's and has therefore sustained a smaller loss from the disruption, is now required to sell oil in the amount of $X'X$ to B. Country A can secure the oil from its consumers only by raising the domestic price, either directly through taxes or import restrictions or indirectly through demand restraint measures. The oil can also be obtained from firms by moral suasion or other varieties of mandatory allocation. In the diagram we see that the requisite quantity $X'X$ would be surrendered by country A's consumers at price $p_1$, which is above the world market-clearing price, $p_W$. When it is transferred to country B, however, the quantity $X'X$ will lower the price in country B below $p_W$ to $p_2$, which is the highest price at which $X'X$ will be accepted by B's consumers. The fact that the price is now different in each country implies that the transfer has created a net loss of welfare. The oil given up by country A has a domestic value equal to the area of the inscribed trapezoidal bar, $abXX'$. In country B, the value of the additional oil received is given by the area of $cbXX'$. The result is a net loss of $abc$ in total consumer welfare as a result of the transfer of oil between the two countries.

If market forces again prevail, the excess of A's valuation of its oil at $p_1$ over that of country B at $p_2$ will quickly lead to sales from country B to country A. This process will continue until the quantity consumed rises in country A by $X'X$ and falls by $X'X$ in B and the price is again the same at $p_W$ in both countries. As long as the trade is carried out at prices below $p_1$ and above $p_2$, countries A and B will both benefit. If the sale price is $p_W$, for example, country A would gain consumer surplus of $abd$ and B would enjoy a seller's surplus of $dbc$, exactly reversing the losses imposed by the sharing agreement. In fact, it is questionable whether the IEA or any other agency without supranational price-setting authority or global control over all exports can prevent such a free-trade offset from occurring immediately following any mandatory sharing. In a world of many trading partners, the offset would materialize not through formal and highly visible transfers but by silent market-induced readjustments in the rate of flow of each country's net imports. The oil flow would increase to countries such as A, where the price is higher than elsewhere, and would decrease to countries such as B, where the price is lower than elsewhere, until all prices (net of transportation costs) are again equal everywhere and the presharing distribution of oil has been restored.[14]

Another possible impact of the sharing agreement is that donor countries will employ mandatory allocations to secure oil to meet their international obligations. There are only two market-oriented methods that avoid the expropriation of domestic supplies. One is for government to offer a sufficiently high price (above the world level) at which domestic companies will supply the oil voluntarily (as in figure 23 at price $p_1$). A higher price is necessary since, at the world market price, there is no excess supply. Even though the purchase price would remain above the world price only temporarily, however, this is a most improbable procedure—imagine the public reaction to purchases from oil companies at above market prices! A second alternative, which is more viable, is to transfer publicly owned reserves, such as SPR oil, to companies that fulfill the country's international obligation by diverting oil from overseas sources to recipient countries. This will entail a de facto temporary price increase, since SPR drawdown would normally lower the price, which under the circumstances would simply remain constant (supply from the SPR and the demand for oil to transfer abroad would have risen equally).[15]

Apart from these two market-oriented methods, governments will, through moral suasion, "fair sharing," or other de facto coercive tactics, require domestic companies to provide supplies for international transfer at prices that do not really justify the transfer.[16] Thus, even though a country, such as the United States, may be committed to the avoidance of price controls and of mandatory allocations, international sharing could readily impose such a regime on broad segments of its domestic oil industry.

**Is Sharing Necessary?** In view of the net welfare and efficiency losses created by IEA sharing, we may wonder why there is any world sentiment for the agreement. The fact is, however, that even though the group as a whole loses, and future market trading does not perpetuate the diminished levels of social surplus, the initial transfer of oil under sharing is both wealth enhancing and welcome to recipient countries. Even nonrecipient countries may view the efficiency losses as an acceptable cost for achieving desirable wealth transfers. Still, is there a particular reason for making the transfers according to relative price elasticities of petroleum demand rather than by some other more broadly based criteria involving national wealth? Furthermore, why not, under any criteria, carry out wealth redistribution by transferring money, rather than oil or other tangible property, among IEA members? The economic cost of moving oil or other real assets is surely greater than that of moving money.

A final question is relevant. Is not an emergency sharing system needed to ensure that IEA members do not suffer unduly from being the targets of selective embargoes by oil producers? A basic factor motivating the creation of the IEA was the 1973 embargo against the United States and the Netherlands by the Organization of Arab Petroleum Exporting Countries. Flexibility of the world petroleum market, however, made that effort ineffective; neither the United States nor the Netherlands suffered a disproportionate share of the economic losses caused by the supply reduction that accompanied the embargo. The market process described above as acting to offset IEA transfers under sharing will tend to neutralize, more or less, any contramarket alteration of supply. Price is inevitably higher in embargo-targeted countries than elsewhere and acts as a powerful magnet attracting oil from every corner of the globe.

The greater diversity of supply sources today makes the likelihood that a selective embargo will be effective even smaller than it was in the past. At worst, the country targeted by the embargo would have to pay a slightly higher delivered price to move petroleum over different transportation routes. Any such embargo-induced price differences could be largely eliminated through informal agreements among IEA members to circumvent the embargo. Among these agreements should be a willingness to allow anyone in any IEA country to export oil to any place in the world.

It should be noted, finally, that the emergency sharing system could probably not be effectively implemented for any purpose. Buying rights would have to be based on information about consumption levels that invariably would be out of date. More important, the IEA has no sanctions to force compliance. Some of the mandated sellers would quite possibly refuse to make sales to designated buyers at subsidized prices. These factors make implementation difficult and uncertain. The harmful effects of sharing are not contingent, however, upon its actual implementation. Anticipation by the private sector that sharing could be triggered in the future provides the same disincentives to precrisis planning and self-insurance as does the expectation of any system of price controls and mandatory allocations. Once implemented, moreover, sharing of U.S. supplies is likely to provoke broader interventions as domestic interest groups petition for treatment at least as favorable as that of the foreign beneficiaries.

# Notes

1. Readers should note that a tariff is the preferred mechanism for reducing imports below market-determined levels. The usual alternative, a quota, is equivalent in its effects to a tariff if the world oil market is competitive. If the market is not competitive, however, firms exercising market power will respond to the demand "kink," which a quota introduces, by raising the world price. A tariff, by contrast, is perceived by suppliers as a downward shift of the entire demand schedule, which tends, in some degree, to lower the world price whether the market is competitive or not. On the subject of tariffs versus quotas as instruments of import restraint, see Edward J. Mitchell, "Oil Import Quotas Won't Work," *Wall Street Journal*, August 17, 1979.

2. For a fuller discussion, see Douglas R. Bohi and W. David Montgomery, *Oil Prices, Energy Security, and Import Policy* (Washington, D.C.: Resources for the Future, 1982).

3. Because it is more difficult to observe the price than the quantity of imported oil, an ad valorem tax would be easier to administer if it were based on average market prices rather than on the prices actually paid by importers, which might be manipulated. Another approach, making the ad valorem tariff payable in kind, is suggested by David L. Weimer in "Routine SPR Acquisitions: The In-Kind Import Fee and Spot Market Purchase Authority," in George Horwich and Edward J. Mitchell, eds., *Policies for Coping with Oil-Supply Disruptions* (Washington, D.C.: American Enterprise Institute, 1982), pp. 124–28.

4. For a comparison of coupon rationing with other allocation policies, see Nancy S. Dorfman, "Gasoline Distribution Policies in a Shortage: Welfare Impacts on Rich and Poor," *Public Policy*, vol. 29, no. 3 (Fall 1981), pp. 473–505. Also see Martin L. Weitzman, "Is the Price System or Rationing More Effective in Getting a Commodity to Those Who Need It?" *Bell Journal of Economics*, vol. 8, no. 2 (Autumn 1977), pp. 517–24.

5. U.S. Department of Energy, "Standby Gasoline Rationing Plan," Economic Regulation Administration, Office of Regulations and Emergency Planning, DOE/RG-0029, June 1980, pp. 15–22.

6. See Joe Cobb, "The Gasoline Rationing Myth," Reprint Paper 14 of the International Institute for Economic Research, Los Angeles, Calif., June 1980.

7. Richard Corrigan, "The Next Energy Crisis—A Job for the Government or the Free Market?" *National Journal*, vol. 13, no. 25 (June 20, 1981), pp. 1106–09.

8. Fred Hoffman, David Seidman, and John Haaga, Rand Corporation, *Legal Constraints on Market Response to Supply Disruptions*, DOE Contract DE-AC01-79PE70078 (Santa Monica: Rand, June 1982), p. 54.

9. Staff Draft, "California Energy Shortage Contingency Plan," pt. 3: "Executive Summary of the Operational Elements of California's Energy Shortage Contingency Plan" and "Appendix D: California Fuel Set-Aside Programs," California Energy Commission, Sacramento, January 1983.

10. For a detailed history of the IEA, see Elena M. Folkerts-Landau, Stephen W. Salant, Warren F. Schwartz, and Rodney T. Smith, "Cooperative Efforts in International Security," Draft, September 1982.

11. Algebraically, the supply right is

$$r = 0.93 \, c_{-1} - \frac{m_{-1}}{M_{-1}} (0.93 C_{-1} - S)$$

where $c_{-1}$ is the individual country's base-year petroleum consumption, $m_{-1}$ its base-year net imports of petroleum (crude and products), $M_{-1}$ is base-year total net imports for all IEA countries, $C_{-1}$ is total IEA petroleum consumption in the base year, and $S$ is the total available supply of petroleum from current production and imports in all IEA countries. As noted above, in place of the ratio of imports, we can write the ratio of individual country petroleum reserve requirements to total IEA petroleum reserve requirements, which are specified at ninety days' supply of imports. For shortfalls greater than 12 percent, 0.90 replaces 0.93 in the above formula. The information given here and in n. 12 below is drawn from an undated OECD publication, *The International Energy Agency of OECD*.

12. The allocation to or from each country is its supply right less its available supply of oil from current production and imports:

$$a = r - s$$

where $a$ is the allocation obligation (positive for recipients of oil and negative for those who must give), $r$ is the supply right as defined in n. 11, and $s$ is the individual country's current available supply. The IEA has ruled that the allocation obligation under sharing can be met by drawdown of the petroleum reserve.

13. In two historical instances in which IEA members suffered reductions in consumption greater than 7 percent and requested initiation of the sharing system, they were in effect seeking petroleum at less than the world price. In 1979 Sweden requested relief when its imports fell because of the system of price controls it maintained. During the Iran-Iraq war, Turkey sought assistance when its supplies from Iraq were reduced. The Turks, however, declined to purchase oil offered at the market price. See Robert O. Keohane, "International Agencies and the Art of the Possible: The Case of the IEA," *Journal of Policy Analysis and Management*, vol. 1, no. 4 (Summer 1982), pp. 469–81.

14. Complete freedom granted to individuals in IEA countries to export oil to each other at the world price would facilitate the price-equalizing adjustment process.

15. The more direct route of simply exporting SPR oil is, of course, impossible under the present U.S. crude oil export ban.

16. Government's failure to pay a price above the prevailing market level simply forces companies who have sold their supplies at market price themselves to bid—at a higher price—for replacement supplies. In all cases, there-

fore, the implementation of the sharing program in countries having a supply obligation raises the domestic price temporarily above the world level: directly, by government bidding; indirectly, by the failure of SPR drawdown to lower the price; in a delayed response, when companies who are forced to sell at the market price attempt to replenish their supplies. The only case in which the domestic price would remain constant would be if it were subject to a legal ceiling. In that event, domestic companies from whom supplies were expropriated at below-market price to meet the international obligation would face a higher shadow price or be forced to buy imports and add upward pressure to the already higher world price. Notice in all cases, whatever the initial impact on price, that if domestic supplies are used to meet the supply obligation, the donor country's imports will rise to replace those supplies and create a greater future obligation under the agreement.

# 8

# Conclusions

The world energy picture appears bright from the U.S. perspective: petroleum prices have declined in nominal as well as real terms during the last two years; U.S. petroleum imports are at a ten-year low; and unused crude oil production capacity, estimated to be about 10 million barrels per day worldwide, suggests continuing downward pressure on prices. Nevertheless, the United States remains vulnerable to the adverse economic consequences of petroleum price shocks caused by oil supply disruptions. For the next few years, at least, most minor oil supply interruptions would probably be accommodated in the world market with only moderate price rises. A major interruption, or immediate threat of a major interruption, of supplies from the Persian Gulf, however, where about 70 percent of the world's excess crude oil production capacity is currently located, could cause absolute price rises greater than those experienced during the Arab oil embargo or the Iranian revolution. The preparations that the United States makes *now* will largely determine how costly future price shocks will be to the U.S. economy.

Once a disruption has begun, there are very few actions the government can initiate to reduce its costs. If the government turns again to petroleum price controls and allocations, as it has in the past, the costs to the U.S. economy will actually be increased. There are, however, policies that should be implemented prior to the next disruption, such as accelerated oil stockpiling and the preparation of emergency fiscal transfers. These policies are desirable not only because they will lower the costs of future disruptions but also because they will reduce the political pressure for unproductive government interventions in disrupted petroleum markets.

Rather than repeating the detailed arguments we have made for our position, we shall conclude by highlighting what we believe to be the seven most important points of relevance to the development of effective public policies for reducing the costs of oil supply disruptions.

1. *Petroleum price shocks are costly, but reliance on market allocation will keep costs to a minimum*. As long as the United States is a net importer of petroleum, steep price increases will be costly to individual consumers and to the economy as a whole. By allowing petroleum to reach its most-valued uses, however, market allocation by price ensures that the aggregate microeconomic costs of reduced petroleum supply are minimized. Because the microeconomic costs translate into unemployment and inflation in the macroeconomy, allowing the market to provide the efficient, cost-minimizing allocation of petroleum has important implications for equity as well. Although the higher prices will involve some hardship for all consumers and considerable hardship for many in low-income brackets, it reduces to a minimum the number of people who suffer the severe hardship of loss of employment.

2. *Petroleum price controls and allocations increase the costs of disruptions; they should be rejected*. Price ceilings on domestically produced crude oil are counterproductive, particularly since they cannot be applied to imports. They discourage domestic oil production and, if coupled with an entitlements system to distribute access more fairly, they lower the effective price of crude oil seen by domestic refiners. This lower price acts as a subsidy for oil imports, which, combined with reduced domestic production, increases U.S. net demand for imports and thus contributes to higher world oil prices.

Government programs that mandate the sale of crude oil at prices below those of the world market are also counterproductive. They tend to shift oil from most-valued to less-valued uses, increasing the costs of disruptions. Administrative allocation tends to freeze historical relationships between suppliers and refiners directly (the supplier/purchaser freeze) and indirectly by slowing market entry and raising the costs of exit. The result is reduced competition and shelter for the inefficient. Because the beneficiaries of the allocations receive economic rents, individual firms and groups of firms have an incentive to invest in political activity to increase their allocations. Consequently, allocation programs of initially limited scope, such as the allocation of oil from the strategic petroleum reserve at below market price, face intense political pressure for expansion. Finally, the anticipation of allocations discourages private stockpiling and other forms of self-insurance against disruption costs.

Attempts to keep petroleum product prices below market-clearing levels lead to consumer costs in the form of queuing, search, uncertainty of supply, and product deterioration. Consumers end up paying effective prices that are at or above free market levels. These nonmarket mechanisms clearly divert products from their most-valued use and thus contribute to greater economic costs; their impact on income redistribution is less clear and cannot be fully evaluated without taking into consideration their effects on employment.

The inefficiency of price ceilings is magnified by the need for government allocation of petroleum products in the absence of market signaling. The information demands for efficient administrative allocation are simply too great. Reliance on historical patterns that are inevitably out of date causes severe regional misallocations that raise the aggregate costs of disruptions.

3. *Revenue from a two-dollar-per-barrel import fee should be earmarked for meeting the stockpiling goals of the strategic petroleum reserve program.* The drawdown of oil stocks is one of the few actions that can be taken to reduce the costs of an oil supply disruption directly. Obviously, stocks must be accumulated before they can be drawn down. Because of fears of price controls and allocations, and because of external costs and benefits associated with stockpiling, the private sector will accumulate less than the socially optimal level of stocks during normal market periods. It is therefore desirable for the government to stockpile oil through the strategic petroleum reserve program. A large number of studies employing a variety of methodologies suggest that the SPR should be built to at least 750 million barrels and preferably to 1 billion barrels.

Both the Carter and Reagan administrations took actions to accelerate the SPR immediately upon taking office. Because the SPR lacks a vocal political constituency, and because it involves immediate costs in return for potential future benefits, the SPR has been a prime target for budget cutters who have been successful in slowing development in the later years of each administration. It is therefore desirable to remove the SPR from the yearly budget cycle of the federal government.

The SPR should be funded through a two-dollar-per-barrel fee on imported crude oil and petroleum products. The revenue from the fee should be earmarked for the SPR, reverting to general revenues only when legally mandated stockpiling goals have been met. This measure would encourage administration budget analysts to look for ways of improving the management of the SPR rather than delaying its implementation. The import fee is attractive for other reasons as well. It brings the private cost of imports closer to economists' estimates of the true social cost. Because the benefits of the SPR will be distributed roughly in proportion to petroleum use, it seems reasonable to pay for the SPR with a fee that distributes costs in the same way. The fee would also put additional downward pressure on world petroleum prices, would increase federal revenues through the windfall profits tax on domestic oil, and would stimulate domestic oil production through increased domestic oil prices.

4. *Regular sales of options for the purchase of SPR oil should be initiated to increase the likelihood of expeditious drawdowns.* The value of SPR drawdowns is greatest during the early months of a disruption while private firms are attempting to increase their stockpiles and before demand and alternative energy supplies can respond fully to higher prices. Fear that disruptions will be more severe or of longer duration than expected may lead decision makers to delay drawdown until more information is available. Such fears ignore the tendency of supply and demand elasticities to increase over time. During the six months for which the currently available reserve would last (at the maximum drawdown rate of about 2 million barrels per day), higher prices would stimulate increased oil production in nondisrupted regions of the world and would reduce consumer demand through purchase of more energy-efficient capital goods. After six months, increased U.S. oil and alternative energy production and conservation measures in response to even moderately higher prices could easily be more than 2 million barrels per day. The longer the disruption continued, the greater the market response would be and therefore the smaller the relative value of SPR drawdowns. As long as there is a funding mechanism to facilitate refilling, such as the import fee, the errors of drawing down too soon or too fast should be given little weight relative to the errors of drawing down too late or too slowly.

An alternative to government's making the initial drawdown decision is for the private sector to have the continuing opportunity to bid on the right to purchase SPR oil at a specific price during some future period. Firms would, for example, be able to bid for the right to purchase SPR oil between nine and twelve weeks in the future at a forward price equal to 110 percent of the current market price. The more likely it is that firms believe the future market price will exceed the forward price, the more they will be willing to bid for the purchase options. At the onset of the disruption, a drawdown will result as firms find it worthwhile to exercise previously purchased options. Once price stabilizes or begins to decline so that firms no longer find it profitable to exercise options, the government could continue the drawdown through normal auction sales for current delivery. The options system would increase the likelihood that at least some drawdown would take place at the onset of disruptions when political decision makers are least likely to act. It would also give firms an alternative to adding to stocks from private sources at the beginning of disruptions.

5. *An emergency fiscal transfer system should be put in place to enable states to provide relief for cases of extreme hardship immediately after the onset of a severe price shock.* The relatively small number of consumers who have both very low income and great difficulty in reducing their short-run consumption of petroleum products are likely to suffer real hardship during oil price shocks unless they receive financial assistance. In addition, local governments may have temporary difficulty providing public services, and particular sections of the economy, such as regulated trucking, which cannot immediately pass along higher costs to consumers, may face serious short-run liquidity problems. Federal funds, distributed to the states during price shocks, could be used to reduce the seriousness of these problems and to defuse the political pressure for price controls and allocations that would otherwise emerge.

If the transfer program is to succeed, it must be set in place prior to the disruption. It must have clear mechanisms for the initiation, termination, and distribution of the transfers. An excellent way to meet these requirements is to implement a formula for the immediate distribution of all revenues realized from the sale of SPR oil and options. Although a variety of formulas would be reasonable, one based on historical patterns of petroleum consumption seems most appropriate. This program would involve minimal administrative costs at the federal level and a maximum of flexibility at the state level. It would also create an active political constituency of state and local officials who would be better able to serve their jurisdictions if the federal government built a large reserve, actually used it during disruptions, and sold it at market prices—all of which are desirable SPR policies.

6. *Some degree of expansionary monetary policy should be implemented during a disruptive episode and for a period following, depending on the severity of the disruption.* Monetary ease, a demand-side measure, is not and should not be viewed as an antidote to an energy shock, which is fundamentally a supply-side disturbance. Additional money can, however, reduce the costs of an oil supply disruption insofar as demand-side adjustments are required. In particular, the numerous induced shifts of demand between individual markets can be facilitated by some monetary increase. The trade-off is between some additional inflation and smaller losses of real gross national product and employment.

194

Monetary ease is ideally suited as an antidote to oil price drag, the tendency for oil price shocks to drain funds from nonpetroleum markets to the oil sector. The task of monetary policy in this case is to counter the resulting deflationary force in the markets for nonpetroleum goods and services. Our empirical analysis does not support the claim that oil price drag was a serious problem during the disruptions of the 1970s. Nevertheless, insofar as any drag at all materializes, a loosening of the money supply can offset the drag without, in principle, increasing the inflation rate at all.

7. *The United States should withdraw from participation in the mandatory sharing rules of the International Energy Agency.* The IEA sharing rules are intended to ensure that no member country bears a disproportionate share of the costs of oil supply disruptions. The rules appear to call for government-directed transfers of oil at market prices. If the transfers are in fact made at market prices, they will be largely irrelevant: Countries with a right to receive oil will be indifferent between buying in the spot market and accepting transfers. More likely, members will be pressured to transfer oil at prices below market. There is the danger that government interventions to secure oil for the transfers could turn into full-scale programs of price controls and mandatory allocations. If the United States continues to participate in the IEA sharing agreement, it should meet any responsibilities for sharing with SPR drawdowns. A still better approach would be to replace the sharing rules with an agreement among members not to restrict their oil companies from exporting or reexporting oil during disruptions. The United States should, however, continue to participate in the information-sharing, basic research, and stockpiling-coordination activities of the IEA.

# Appendix A
## A Note on Crude Oil Prices

Throughout our analysis we will refer to *the* free market price of crude oil. In reality, however, there is no single price at which crude oil is sold at any particular time. Price will vary, depending upon the intrinsic qualities of the oil, including sulfur content and distillation fractions, as well as upon the costs of transporting it from its source to the market in question. These price differences are irrelevant to our conceptual analysis—we can measure quantities of oil in quality-adjusted units, and we can limit our attention to specific geographic markets. Still, prices also reflect the nature of the contractual arrangements under which transactions are made. The distinction between long-term contract prices and spot prices is potentially relevant to our analysis and therefore deserves discussion.

Most crude oil is sold initially in the world market under the provisions of long-term contracts between private firms that are buyers and government-controlled firms that are sellers. Although the contracts are typically multiyear, they have very flexible pricing provisions.[1] Some contracts, such as those with Petromin, the Saudi Arabian selling agent, tie prices directly to OPEC official prices. More commonly, prices are set for three-month periods subject to renegotiation for successive periods. It would be a mistake, however, to view prices as firmly fixed for even these three-month intervals. Sellers may offer discounts and, because contract provisions binding governments are largely unenforceable, governments may unilaterally impose premiums and altered credit terms. Furthermore, contracts often give the sellers some discretion over the quantities actually delivered, allowing them to shift supplies to spot sales.

The spot market encompasses sales where the contractual arrangements cover single transactions. Spot prices reflect the day-to-day balancing of supply and demand. Only about 10 percent of total crude oil supply is traded through the spot market. Reported crude oil spot prices are based on a sampling of transactions in key locations, including export centers, by publications such as *Petroleum Intelligence Weekly* and *Platt's Oilgram*. Spot prices are also reported for petroleum products at Rotterdam and other major refining centers. The spot prices of products can be used to estimate the end-use value of particular crude oils and thus can provide an indirect crude oil spot price.[2] Although both the direct and indirect crude oil spot prices fluctuate considerably on a day-to-day basis, their weekly averages are probably the best indication of market-clearing prices for various grades of crude oil.

During normal market periods spot prices tend to fluctuate around contract prices, although they generally fall below; during supply disruptions, increases in spot prices tend to lead increases in stated contract prices. If the spot market is the marginal source of supply, then petroleum product prices will reflect spot prices and will yield a profit to those who can buy oil at lower contract prices.[3] To the extent that they do, our analysis interpreting spot prices as market prices will somewhat overstate the social costs of disruptions by overstating the wealth transfers to foreign producers and understating the gains of the domestic oil industry.[4]

Philip Verleger, Jr., argues that the lower contract prices will keep petroleum product prices from rising as rapidly as they otherwise would and that this restraint will increase demand, which can only be met by increased spot market purchases.[5] Such an increase in turn will cause spot prices to rise further, eventually raising crude oil contract prices more than they would have risen if the gap between contract and spot prices had closed more quickly. The alleged link between higher spot market prices and an eventually higher level of contract prices is the increased panic and hoarding to which the increased spot price gives rise. Verleger accordingly recommends an import tariff to speed the rise of the contract price during a disruption.

It is not clear to us that the lower contract prices of crude oil will in fact restrain the rise of petroleum product prices, since the spot market is likely to be the marginal source of supply. Even if lower contract prices restrain product prices, however, and the process envisioned by Verleger unfolds, we argue (see chapter 4) that the costs of the adjustment can most effectively be reduced by drawdown of the strategic petroleum reserve. We see the merits of disruption tariffs (chapter 7), although more with a view to reducing the wealth transfer abroad and to reducing the world price of oil than to raising the contract price to the level of the spot price. Indeed, a tariff would tend to raise all oil prices—contract and spot—without necessarily closing any gap between them. During a disruption, there are also macroeconomic costs, along with any possible benefits, involved in raising the domestic price of oil that we prefer to avoid.

Finally, it should be noted that a higher spot price due to a once-and-for-all increase in inventory demand will not last. In the subsequent weeks and months the price will fall as the flow components of oil supply and demand again assert control over the equilibrium price. Only if crude oil supply is permanently reduced as a result of the temporarily higher spot price—an unlikely occurrence—will the increased inventory demand exert a permanent influence on price. As the spot price gradually drops and the contract price rises, the profits that initially gave rise to the higher spot prices will thus disappear.

# Notes

1. See Fred Hoffman, David Seidman, and John Haaga, *Legal Constraints on Market Response to Supply Disruptions* (Santa Monica: Rand, June 1982), pp. 10–12.

2. The procedure involves multiplying the percentage yield of each type of product from the barrel of crude by the spot prices of these products and summing over all products. This weighted average is then adjusted by marginal refining costs and transportation costs to give an implied spot price for the crude oil at its loading port. See Marshall Thomas, "The ABCs of Measuring Oil Market Price Trends," *Petroleum Intelligence Weekly*, February 2, 1981, supp., pp. 2–5. For a general discussion of the Rotterdam market, see Joe Roeber, *The Rotterdam Oil Market* (London: Petroleum Economist, April 1979).

3. The profit is not a windfall but rather a return that has to be balanced against the premium paid in buying oil on contract rather than on the spot market, where prices often dip below contract prices.

4. Independent refiners who rely primarily on spot market purchases for supplies would be the hardest hit during disruptions when spot prices lead contract prices. They would lose the advantage they enjoyed during normal periods of being able to buy on the spot market when spot prices were lower than long-term contract prices. They could protect themselves by diversifying their supply to include some oil purchased under long-term contracts. In fact, some collectives have been formed to gain favorable term contracts through bulk purchases. See Burt Soloman, "Strength in Numbers: Independent Refiners Seek Own Access to Crude," *Energy Daily*, March 4, 1981, p. 3.

5. See Philip K. Verleger, Jr., *Oil Markets in Turmoil* (Cambridge, Mass.: Ballinger, 1982); and "When the Oil Spigot Is Turned Off," *Journal of Policy Analysis and Management*, vol. 1, no. 4 (1982), pp. 541–45.

# Appendix B
## Data from the American Petroleum Institute

This appendix reprints the annual data collected by the American Petroleum Institute from the twenty-five largest American-based oil companies during the period 1968–1980.[1] Income and expense and balance sheet data are incorporated by the API into a sources and uses statement, which we modify for purposes of measuring oil price drag in chapter 6.

### The American Petroleum Institute Sample

The companies in the API sample are:

Amerada Hess Coporation
American Petrofina, Inc.
Ashland Oil, Inc.
Atlantic Richfield Company
Cities Service Company
Conoco, Inc.
Diamond Shamrock Corporation
Exxon Corporation
Getty Oil Company
Gulf Oil Company
Kerr-McGee Corporation
Marathon Oil Company
Mobil Corporation
Murphy Oil Corporation
Occidental Petroleum
    Corporation

Pennzoil Company
Phillips Petroleum Company
Shell Oil Company
Standard Oil Company of
    California
Standard Oil Company
    (Indiana)
Standard Oil Company (Ohio)
Sun Company, Inc.
Superior Oil Company
Texaco, Inc.
Union Oil Company of
    California

As a rough measure, these companies constitute about 75 percent of total assets or sales of the U.S. oil industry. Although they are all based in the United States, the companies have substantial foreign operations. In 1978, 60 percent of their net income was earned in the United States; in 1979, 51 percent; and in 1980, 56 percent.[2]

Tables 18 and 19, reprinted from the API publication,[3] present basic revenue and expenditure data of the twenty-five companies. Table 16 draws on these tables, which we shall describe in some detail before reorganizing them for our own measurement purposes. Table 18 derives net income for the API sample; table 19 is a sources and uses statement in which the sources build upon the net income statistic of table 18.

**The Income Statement.** Table 18 begins with total revenue of the twenty-five companies, from which it subtracts payroll and benefits; depreciation, depletion, and amortization; interest; other costs and expenses; and total taxes to arrive at net income. The largest charge against total revenue is other costs and expenses, which is described as largely "purchased crude oil and refined products, exploration expense, income applicable to minority interests, and general administrative and operating costs."[4] The crude oil and refined products purchases were 83 percent of other costs and expenses in 1980 and averaged more than 80 percent in the postembargo period; they were only 60 percent during 1968–1972. The oil purchases are interfirm intermediate transactions and purchases from domestic independent and foreign producers. The "exploration expense . . . and general administrative and operating costs" include tangible drilling or development costs, such as outlays for power, equipment rental, repair and maintenance of the general infrastructure, and consulting fees. Income payments to other companies who have an interest in an operating subsidiary are also included in this category.

The remaining deductions from total revenue, payroll and benefits, depreciation, interest, and total taxes are typical charges made in arriving at net income. They include several imputed costs, however, that are not actual cash flows. These imputations are restored to net income in table 19, a sources and uses statement involving only cash transactions.

**Sources and Uses of Funds.** Net income from table 18 is entered on the top line of table 19, the sources and uses statement for the API sample firms. On the second line, depreciation and other noncash charges, the sum of depreciation, depletion, and amortization and the deferred portion of total taxes in table 18, is added to yield the third line, funds from operations. This is the oil companies' cash flow from operations.

The next component of table 19 is funds raised from security

## TABLE 18

### SUMMARY OF INCOME STATEMENTS OF TWENTY-FIVE LEADING U.S. OIL COMPANIES, 1968–1980

(millions of dollars)

| | 1968 | 1969 | 1970 | 1971 | 1972 | 1973 | 1974 | 1975 | 1976 | 1977 | 1978 | 1979 | 1980 |
|---|---|---|---|---|---|---|---|---|---|---|---|---|---|
| Total revenue | 61,178.3 | 67,478.8 | 73,499.2 | 81,297.0 | 88,581.5 | 110,348.2 | 194,355.9 | 202,114.8 | 225,540.2 | 250,402.4 | 273,805.8 | 364,830.0 | 486,608.5 |
| Deductions | | | | | | | | | | | | | |
| Payroll and benefits | 6,587.5 | 7,198.5 | 7,746.9 | 8,765.4 | 9,407.2 | 10,042.6 | 11,532.3 | 13,630.6 | 14,666.3 | 16,210.4 | 18,344.8 | 22,043.8 | 26,404.4 |
| Depreciation, depletion, and amortization | 4,130.6 | 4,426.4 | 4,871.4 | 5,221.5 | 5,509.5 | 6,140.0 | 7,102.7 | 8,030.6 | 8,008.9 | 9,134.2 | 10,889.6 | 12,741.2 | 15,226.2 |
| Interest | 763.3 | 1,007.0 | 1,183.5 | 1,304.6 | 1,381.7 | 1,509.3 | 1,719.6 | 1,773.2 | 2,048.0 | 2,942.4 | 3,602.8 | 3,883.1 | 4,194.6 |
| Other costs and expenses | 35,125.2 | 39,451.2 | 42,946.1 | 46,768.1 | 51,460.1 | 63,919.6 | 129,988.4 | 136,988.6 | 159,347.8 | 175,856.6 | 190,082.2 | 255,896.3 | 345,583.8 |
| Total taxes | 8,772.0 | 9,590.5 | 10,956.6 | 13,147.7 | 14,781.5 | 19,325.5 | 30,829.1 | 31,788.1 | 29,846.3 | 34,150.6 | 37,539.1 | 47,310.6 | 65,586.5 |
| Total deductions | 55,378.6 | 61,673.6 | 67,704.5 | 75,207.3 | 82,540.0 | 100,937.0 | 181,172.1 | 192,211.1 | 213,917.3 | 238,294.2 | 260,458.5 | 341,875.0 | 456,995.5 |
| Net income | 5,805.1 | 5,635.7 | 5,796.7 | 5,846.8 | 5,783.6 | 9,467.5 | 13,149.0 | 9,901.2 | 11,640.9 | 12,089.7 | 13,385.2 | 22,983.0 | 29,612.7 |

SOURCE: *Key Financial Data of Leading U.S. Oil Companies, 1968–1980*, p. 23 (table 1).

# TABLE 19

## SUMMARY OF SOURCES AND USES OF FUNDS FOR TWENTY-FIVE LEADING U.S. OIL COMPANIES, 1968–1980

### (millions of dollars)

| | 1968 | 1969 | 1970 | 1971 | 1972 | 1973 | 1974 | 1975 | 1976 | 1977 | 1978 | 1979 | 1980 |
|---|---|---|---|---|---|---|---|---|---|---|---|---|---|
| *Sources of funds* | | | | | | | | | | | | | |
| Net income | 5,805.1 | 5,635.7 | 5,796.7 | 5,846.8 | 5,783.6 | 9,467.5 | 13,149.0 | 9,901.2 | 11,640.9 | 12,089.7 | 13,385.2 | 22,983.0 | 29,612.7 |
| Depreciation and other noncash charges | 4,755.1 | 5,232.6 | 5,596.7 | 6,077.4 | 6,940.6 | 7,485.6 | 9,588.4 | 8,157.5 | 10,246.2 | 12,486.3 | 15,181.2 | 19,952.7 | 25,504.8 |
| Funds from operations | 10,560.2 | 10,868.3 | 11,393.4 | 11,924.2 | 12,724.2 | 16,953.1 | 22,737.4 | 18,058.7 | 21,887.1 | 24,576.0 | 28,566.4 | 42,935.7 | 55,117.5 |
| Net long-term debt issued | 2,780.8 | 1,000.0 | 1,996.6 | 1,712.4 | 51.3 | 493.5 | 2,346.2 | 3,568.0 | 4,114.9 | 2,674.2 | (792.4) | 1,156.1 | 3,796.6 |
| Net stock issued | 145.4 | 709.1 | 423.2 | 147.8 | 221.9 | 199.2 | 364.9 | 413.5 | 452.4 | 1,202.3 | 292.8 | 56.1 | (277.9) |
| Fixed assets sold/retired | 471.5 | 957.9 | 437.3 | 657.5 | 923.3 | 1,150.2 | 1,480.0 | 1,497.8 | 1,881.1 | 1,418.2 | 1,528.0 | 2,423.5 | 3,286.7 |
| Other | 635.9 | 187.7 | 380.5 | 613.1 | 752.4 | 990.8 | 1,507.6 | 1,741.1 | 1,130.0 | 794.2 | 1,445.5 | 1,996.6 | 1,401.6 |
| Total sources | 14,593.8 | 13,723.0 | 14,631.0 | 15,055.0 | 14,673.1 | 19,786.8 | 28,436.1 | 25,279.1 | 29,465.5 | 30,664.9 | 31,040.3 | 48,568.0 | 63,324.5 |
| *Uses of funds* | | | | | | | | | | | | | |
| Capital expenditures | 9,578.3 | 9,671.7 | 9,636.5 | 9,733.7 | 10,078.7 | 12,032.1 | 18,890.6 | 20,138.1 | 21,298.3 | 22,517.2 | 23,998.4 | 30,620.2 | 41,044.7 |
| Investments and advances | 853.0 | 1,382.6 | 634.0 | 936.4 | 714.0 | 458.9 | 1,092.6 | 1,433.8 | 1,865.7 | 1,314.5 | 847.3 | 7,105.9 | 9,854.9 |
| Dividends | 2,953.4 | 3,197.7 | 3,279.8 | 3,311.9 | 3,301.8 | 3,469.5 | 4,017.5 | 4,325.9 | 4,542.2 | 5,174.4 | 5,775.7 | 6,621.7 | 8,791.7 |
| Other | 284.7 | 444.5 | 300.5 | 436.1 | 332.6 | 330.9 | 609.9 | 401.3 | 607.0 | 950.1 | 827.7 | 124.5 | 1,444.2 |
| Total uses | 13,669.4 | 14,696.5 | 13,850.5 | 14,418.1 | 14,427.1 | 16,291.4 | 24,610.6 | 26,299.1 | 28,313.2 | 29,956.2 | 31,449.1 | 44,472.3 | 61,135.7 |
| Change in working capital | 924.4 | (973.5) | 780.5 | 636.9 | 246.0 | 3,495.4 | 3,825.5 | (1,020.0) | 1,152.3 | 708.7 | (408.8) | 4,095.7 | 2,188.8 |

SOURCE: *Key Financial Data of Leading U.S. Oil Companies, 1968–1980*, p. 29 (table 3).

issues: net long-term debt issued and net stock issued. These entries are followed by fixed assets sold/retired, which are funds raised by the sale of properties, such as old oil rigs and other wholly owned items. The final source, "other," is simply a catchall taken from company annual reports.

Among the uses of funds, the major entry is capital expenditures, which are outlays for plant and equipment. Lease acquisition costs, which are bonus payments for exploration and drilling rights, are also included here and compose about one-fifth of total capital expenditures.[5] The plant and equipment includes refineries, pipelines, tankers, storage facilities, and nonexpensed drilling and exploration outlays.

Investments and advances, shown on the second line under uses of funds in table 19, are largely loans to oil industry subsidiaries. Net acquisition of subsidiaries, including the purchase of Bellridge by Shell, International Paper by Mobil, and Transamerica by Sun, are also included. Apart from these extraordinary purchases, the loans to subsidiaries are generally 90 percent of investments and advances. The final two uses are dividends and "other," which is a miscellaneous balancing item that cannot easily be characterized.

The difference between total sources and uses is the bottom line of table 19, the change in working capital, which is the difference between current assets and current liabilities. These are shown in detail in the balance sheet of the API's twenty-five companies in table 20. Current assets are cash and marketable securities, receivables, inventories, and a small "other" category. Current liabilities are notes, loans, and accounts payable; taxes payable; and an "other" component.

## A Modified Sources and Uses Statement

For measuring oil price drag, we reorganize the data in tables 18 and 19, replacing net income with its components and classifying flows into more convenient groupings. We begin by expressing the derivations in tables 18 and 19 algebraically. We use the following symbols:

$$CE = \text{capital expenditures}$$
$$DDA = \text{depreciation, depletion, and amortization}$$
$$Div = \text{dividends}$$
$$FAST = \text{financial assets, short term (change)}$$
$$FL = \text{financial liabilities, short term (change)}$$
$$Fx = \text{fixed assets sold/retired}$$
$$Int = \text{interest}$$

Inv = inventories (change)
IA = investments and advances
NI = net income
Sec = securities issued = net long-term debt issued + net stock issued
OCE = other costs and expenses (equal to the sum of nonoil and oil costs and expenses)
OCEN= other costs and expenses, nonoil
OCEO= other costs and expenses, oil
OS = other sources of funds
OU = other uses of funds
PB = payroll and benefits
SD = statistical discrepancy
TR = total revenue
TxD = taxes deferred
TxP = taxes paid
TxT = total taxes = taxes deferred + taxes paid

The change in working capital, the bottom line of table 19, is broken down into its components, the change in short-term financial assets (FAST) plus the change in inventories (Inv) less the change in short-term financial liabilities (FL). Notice that these symbols denote the *change* in the variable in question. The variables themselves are stocks whose levels are altered each period by expenditure flows. The item statistical discrepancy (SD) is added to the deductions in table 18 to bring their sum to the level consistent with the indicated entries for net income.

Equation 3 expresses the derivation of net income in table 18, and equation 4, the equality between sources and uses of funds plus the change in working capital, as expressed by its separate components, in table 19:

$$NI = TR - (PB + DDA + Int + OCE + TxT + SD) \tag{3}$$

$$NI + TxD + DDA + Sec + Fx + OS = CE + IA \\ + Div + OU + FAST + Inv - FL \tag{4}$$

We solve for net income (NI) in equation 4:

$$NI = CE + IA + Div + OU + FAST + Inv \\ - FL - TxD - DDA - Sec - Fx - OS \tag{4'}$$

In equation 3 we substitute (TxD + TxP) for TxT and (OCEN + OCEO)

# TABLE 20

## SUMMARY OF END-OF-YEAR FINANCIAL POSITIONS OF TWENTY-FIVE LEADING U.S. OIL COMPANIES, 1968-1980

(millions of dollars)

| | 1968 | 1969 | 1970 | 1971 | 1972 | 1973 | 1974 | 1975 | 1976 | 1977 | 1978 | 1979 | 1980 |
|---|---|---|---|---|---|---|---|---|---|---|---|---|---|
| *Assets* | | | | | | | | | | | | | |
| Cash and marketable securities | 5,915.9 | 5,626.2 | 6,009.3 | 6,033.4 | 6,850.0 | 10,282.8 | 13,804.7 | 14,344.2 | 16,717.7 | 14,209.7 | 17,053.6 | 22,409.5 | 23,817.0 |
| Receivables | 11,545.9 | 12,761.2 | 13,842.7 | 14,322.6 | 16,066.0 | 19,809.9 | 27,513.4 | 27,063.0 | 28,990.6 | 31,408.4 | 35,463.7 | 45,537.7 | 51,822.1 |
| Inventories | 6,308.1 | 6,738.5 | 7,530.8 | 8,026.8 | 8,125.3 | 9,975.6 | 17,097.0 | 17,849.4 | 19,353.2 | 22,158.6 | 21,669.9 | 26,746.7 | 31,877.8 |
| Other current assets | 498.2 | 539.5 | 616.7 | 800.3 | 619.4 | 804.5 | 1,051.6 | 736.3 | 742.0 | 1,399.3 | 1,360.8 | 2,219.5 | 4,594.8 |
| Total current assets | 24,268.6 | 25,665.5 | 28,000.2 | 29,183.1 | 31,660.9 | 40,872.8 | 59,466.7 | 59,992.7 | 65,803.6 | 69,176.5 | 75,547.8 | 97,913.4 | 112,111.7 |
| Investments and long-term receivables | 5,050.6 | 5,678.8 | 6,243.4 | 7,120.7 | 7,529.2 | 7,860.5 | 7,671.1 | 10,474.6 | 11,506.9 | 12,406.8 | 12,151.0 | 12,605.9 | 16,190.9 |
| Property, plant, and equipment | 48,788.2 | 54,436.4 | 58,169.8 | 61,723.0 | 64,653.8 | 68,759.8 | 78,422.5 | 86,422.0 | 97,885.8 | 113,668.4 | 125,816.5 | 146,127.8 | 173,344.3 |
| Other | 1,045.7 | 1,421.9 | 1,518.2 | 1,738.4 | 1,978.0 | 1,723.1 | 2,090.8 | 2,606.6 | 3,077.3 | 3,399.9 | 3,061.4 | 3,692.4 | 4,693.6 |
| Total | 54,884.5 | 61,537.0 | 65,931.3 | 70,582.2 | 74,160.9 | 78,343.5 | 88,184.5 | 99,503.2 | 112,470.0 | 129,475.1 | 141,028.9 | 162,426.1 | 192,228.8 |
| Total assets | 79,153.3 | 87,202.6 | 93,931.4 | 99,765.7 | 105,822.1 | 119,216.0 | 147,651.2 | 159,496.3 | 178,273.7 | 198,651.5 | 216,576.9 | 260,339.5 | 306,340.5 |
| *Liabilities* | | | | | | | | | | | | | |
| Notes, loans and accounts payable | 10,692.2 | 12,335.9 | 13,247.5 | 13,034.4 | 15,174.5 | 18,852.4 | 30,491.3 | 33,065.4 | 36,456.0 | 39,530.3 | 43,769.7 | 50,619.0 | 55,062.5 |
| Taxes payable | 2,728.6 | 3,044.8 | 3,685.8 | 3,974.1 | 4,042.8 | 5,540.9 | 8,204.0 | 6,968.5 | 8,072.4 | 7,279.3 | 9,364.8 | 15,937.4 | 20,496.5 |
| Other current liabilities | 138.1 | 218.1 | 218.4 | 789.7 | 811.6 | 1,323.0 | 1,789.0 | 2,109.2 | 2,273.4 | 2,616.8 | 3,035.9 | 7,515.5 | 10,522.2 |
| Total current liabilities | 13,559.0 | 15,598.6 | 17,151.7 | 17,798.2 | 20,028.9 | 25,716.0 | 40,484.0 | 42,142.8 | 46,801.9 | 49,426.6 | 56,170.4 | 74,071.9 | 86,081.2 |

| | | | | | | | | | | | | | |
|---|---|---|---|---|---|---|---|---|---|---|---|---|---|
| Long-term debt | 12,810.4 | 14,101.2 | 16,096.1 | 17,861.5 | 18,044.4 | 18,551.7 | 20,970.1 | 24,603.8 | 28,704.4 | 38,201.9 | 37,731.7 | 39,231.0 | 43,117.5 |
| Other | 5,060.8 | 5,597.7 | 5,890.4 | 6,615.8 | 7,537.5 | 8,874.9 | 10,758.4 | 13,495.3 | 16,009.5 | 17,215.6 | 21,156.8 | 29,018.5 | 38,330.4 |
| Total | 17,871.1 | 19,699.1 | 21,986.5 | 24,477.2 | 25,581.9 | 27,426.5 | 31,728.6 | 38,098.9 | 44,713.9 | 55,417.5 | 58,888.5 | 68,249.5 | 81,447.9 |
| Total liabilities | 31,430.5 | 35,297.7 | 39,138.3 | 42,275.5 | 45,610.8 | 53,142.3 | 72,212.4 | 80,241.8 | 91,516.0 | 104,843.9 | 115,059.0 | 142,321.4 | 167,529.1 |
| Total stockholders' equity | 47,723.0 | 51,905.3 | 54,793.3 | 57,490.2 | 60,211.4 | 66,073.6 | 75,438.5 | 79,254.5 | 86,757.8 | 93,807.7 | 101,517.8 | 118,018.1 | 138,811.4 |
| Total liabilities and stockholders' equity | 79,153.3 | 87,202.6 | 93,931.4 | 99,765.7 | 105,822.1 | 119,216.0 | 147,651.2 | 159,496.3 | 178,273.7 | 198,651.5 | 216,576.9 | 260,339.5 | 306,340.5 |

SOURCE: *Key Financial Data of Leading U.S. Oil Companies, 1968–1980*, p. 31 (table 5).

for OCE. After equating the right sides of equations 3 and 4' and regrouping, we obtain the following sources and uses statement:

$$
\begin{aligned}
\textit{Sources} \quad & (TR - OCEO) + FL + Sec + Fx + OS \\
& \text{(net revenues plus short- and long-term} \\
& \text{funding)} = \\
\textit{Uses} \left\{ \begin{array}{l}
PB + Int + Div + TxP + SD \\
\text{(payments for services)} \\
+ CE + OCEN + Inv \\
\text{(expenditures on goods)} \\
+ FAST + IA + OU \\
\text{(increase in financial assets)}
\end{array} \right.
\end{aligned} \tag{5}
$$

The first and largest source of funds is (TR − OCEO), the difference between total revenues and intermediate oil and oil product purchases. The other sources of funds derive from the change in short-term liabilities (FL) and the sale of debt and equity securities (Sec) and fixed assets (Fx). The remaining term, other sources (OS), is a balancing, mixed grouping.

The uses of funds are organized into three broad categories: payments for services, expenditures on goods, and the increase in financial assets. Payments for services include payroll and benefits (PB), interest payments (Int) to bondholders and other creditors of the industry, dividend payments (Div) to the industry's stockholders, taxes actually paid (TxP) to all governmental units, and the statistical discrepancy (SD) mentioned above. Expenditures on goods are composed of capital expenditures (CE), the nonpetroleum component of other costs and expenses (OCEN), and the change in inventories (Inv). The increase in financial assets includes the change in short-term financial assets (FAST), investments and advances (IA), and the miscellaneous other uses (OU).

The reorganized sources and uses statement appears in table 21. The data are taken or calculated from tables 18–20 above and from other sources within the API publication from which these three tables are reprinted. The top line of table 21 is the total revenue from the API firms' sales. Line 2 is their intermediate purchases of oil, and line 3 is revenue net of these purchases.

Additional inflows of funds, particularly during disruption periods, originate in borrowing and other short-term liabilities (line 4), long-term security issues (line 5), the sale of fixed assets (line 6), and the miscellaneous "other" category (line 7). These sources, particularly short-term borrowing, significantly augment net revenues in 1974, 1979, and 1980, years in which oil prices rose sharply.

Among the uses of funds, the payments for services on lines 9–12 are outlays for productive services by the oil companies: payroll and benefits, interest on borrowed capital, and dividends to stockholders. These funds can be expected to enter the general expenditures stream with no greater delay than would occur in any other industry. If they are not spent abroad, they are thus a clear and immediate offset to the transfer of purchasing power from domestic nonpetroleum sectors. The same can be said, in the first instance, of nondeferred tax payments on line 13. Government's management of its cash balances, including unanticipated increments, is not likely to be less efficient than that of wage and salary earners and other claimants of the oil industry. Government can be expected to turn over additional tax receipts from the industry without delay, more likely than not to reduce the deficits that especially characterize oil disruption periods but characterize most other periods as well. Reduced government borrowing, however, will not immediately be replaced by increased private borrowing and expenditures. There will thus be a temporary net loss of purchasing power and outlays in nonpetroleum goods markets. The treatment of this loss is described under item 6 in chapter 6.

Payments for services, excluding taxes paid, rose 3.8-fold during the 1968–1980 period, less than the 5-fold increase of net revenues. Including taxes, however, payments for services rose by a factor slightly greater than 5.

The second major use category is the firms' expenditures on goods, lines 15–18. Included are capital expenditures, current expenses other than for the purchase of oil, and the change in inventories. Like payments for services, these outlays will tend to be an immediate offset to the transfer of funds from petroleum buyers and any potential oil price drag. Unlike services payments, however, there is a significant foreign component in the expenditures on goods. Approximately 30 percent of capital expenditures is for facilities in foreign countries; on a first approximation, we should probably assign a similar percentage to foreign nonoil expenses and inventory accumulation.[6] Such outlays will not, of course, counter the loss of funds to domestic nonpetroleum sectors. The method of dividing all expenditures, including taxes, into foreign and domestic components is described in chapter 6 in adjustment 3 with reference to table 14. Table 22 reports the foreign component for all goods and services on line 2 and the domestic component of taxes on line 4.

Referring once again to table 21, total expenditures on goods rose 4.4-fold from 1968 to 1980, somewhat less than the rise of the companies' net revenues. Inventory accumulation, however, increased almost

## TABLE 21
### REORGANIZED SOURCES AND USES OF FUNDS FOR THE AMERICAN PETROLEUM INSTITUTE SAMPLE OF TWENTY-FIVE OIL COMPANIES, 1968–1980
(billions of dollars)

| | 1968 | 1969 | 1970 | 1971 | 1972 | 1973 | 1974 | 1975 | 1976 | 1977 | 1978 | 1979 | 1980 |
|---|---|---|---|---|---|---|---|---|---|---|---|---|---|
| **Sources** | | | | | | | | | | | | | |
| 1. Total revenue | 61.18 | 67.48 | 73.50 | 81.30 | 88.58 | 110.35 | 194.36 | 202.12 | 225.54 | 250.40 | 283.81 | 364.83 | 486.61 |
| 2. Intermediate oil purchases | 21.08 | 23.67 | 25.77 | 28.06 | 30.88 | 41.55 | 103.99 | 109.59 | 127.48 | 140.69 | 152.07 | 204.71 | 286.83 |
| 3. Total revenue less intermediate oil purchases | 40.10 | 43.81 | 47.73 | 53.24 | 57.71 | 68.80 | 90.36 | 92.52 | 98.06 | 109.72 | 121.74 | 160.11 | 199.77 |
| 4. Short-term financial liabilities (change) | — | 2.37 | 1.55 | 0.55 | 2.23 | 4.05 | 14.76 | -0.49 | 4.66 | 2.67 | 6.78 | 18.27 | 12.01 |
| 5. Security issues | 2.93 | 1.71 | 2.42 | 1.86 | 0.27 | 0.69 | 2.71 | 3.98 | 4.57 | 3.88 | -0.50 | 1.21 | 3.52 |
| 6. Sale of fixed assets | 0.47 | 0.96 | 0.44 | 0.66 | 0.92 | 1.15 | 1.48 | 1.50 | 1.88 | 1.42 | 1.53 | 2.42 | 3.29 |
| 7. Other | 0.64 | 0.19 | 0.38 | 0.61 | 0.75 | 0.99 | 1.51 | 1.74 | 1.13 | 0.79 | 1.45 | 2.00 | 1.40 |
| 8. Total sources | 44.14 | 49.04 | 52.52 | 56.92 | 61.88 | 75.68 | 110.82 | 99.25 | 110.30 | 118.48 | 131.00 | 184.01 | 219.99 |
| **Uses** | | | | | | | | | | | | | |
| 9. Payments for services (total) | 18.43 | 20.36 | 22.44 | 25.91 | 27.70 | 32.94 | 45.64 | 51.39 | 48.85 | 55.14 | 60.93 | 72.61 | 94.69 |
| 10. Payroll and benefits | 6.59 | 7.20 | 7.75 | 8.77 | 9.41 | 10.04 | 11.53 | 13.63 | 14.67 | 16.21 | 18.34 | 22.04 | 26.40 |
| 11. Interest | 0.76 | 1.01 | 1.18 | 1.30 | 1.38 | 1.51 | 1.72 | 1.77 | 2.05 | 2.94 | 3.60 | 3.88 | 4.19 |
| 12. Dividends | 2.95 | 3.20 | 3.28 | 3.31 | 3.30 | 3.47 | 4.02 | 4.33 | 4.54 | 5.17 | 5.78 | 6.62 | 8.79 |
| 13. Taxes paid | 8.15 | 8.78 | 10.23 | 12.29 | 13.35 | 17.98 | 28.34 | 31.66 | 27.61 | 30.80 | 33.25 | 40.10 | 55.31 |
| 14. Statistical discrepancy | -0.01 | 0.17 | 0.00 | 0.24 | 0.26 | -0.06 | 0.03 | 0.00 | -0.02 | 0.02 | -0.04 | -0.03 | 0.00 |
| 15. Expenditures on goods (total) | 23.63 | 25.88 | 27.61 | 28.94 | 30.76 | 34.59 | 52.01 | 48.29 | 54.67 | 60.50 | 61.53 | 86.88 | 104.92 |
| 16. Capital expenditures | 9.58 | 9.67 | 9.64 | 9.73 | 10.08 | 12.03 | 18.89 | 20.14 | 21.30 | 22.52 | 24.00 | 30.62 | 41.04 |
| 17. Nonoil expenses | 14.05 | 15.78 | 17.18 | 18.71 | 20.58 | 22.37 | 26.00 | 27.40 | 31.87 | 35.17 | 38.02 | 51.18 | 58.75 |
| 18. Inventories (change) | — | 0.43 | 0.79 | 0.50 | 0.10 | 0.19 | 7.12 | 0.75 | 1.50 | 2.81 | -0.49 | 5.08 | 5.13 |

| | | | | | | | | | | | | | |
|---|---|---|---|---|---|---|---|---|---|---|---|---|---|
| 19. Increase in financial assets (total) | 2.05 | 2.79 | 2.47 | 2.07 | 3.42 | 8.15 | 13.17 | −0.43 | 6.79 | 2.83 | 8.54 | 24.52 | 20.36 |
| 20. Short-term financial assets (change) | 0.92 | 0.97 | 1.54 | 0.69 | 2.38 | 7.36 | 11.47 | −2.26 | 4.31 | 0.57 | 6.86 | 17.29 | 9.07 |
| 21. Investments and advances | 0.85 | 1.38 | 0.63 | 0.94 | 0.71 | 0.46 | 1.09 | 1.43 | 1.87 | 1.31 | 0.85 | 7.11 | 9.85 |
| 22. Other uses | 0.28 | 0.44 | 0.30 | 0.44 | 0.33 | 0.33 | 0.61 | 0.40 | 0.61 | 0.95 | 0.83 | 0.12 | 1.44 |
| 23. Total uses | 44.12 | 49.03 | 52.52 | 56.92 | 61.88 | 75.68 | 110.82 | 99.25 | 110.31 | 118.47 | 131.00 | 184.01 | 219.97 |

NOTE: Line 1: Figures are Total Revenue from table 18 above. Line 2: purchases of oil by the API sample firms; series is taken as 60% of "other costs and expenses" during 1968–72, 80% during 1974–79, and 83% in 1980 (see *Key Financial Data*, p. 7, and table 18 above); for 1973, a year not specifically referred to in the API source, the percentage was interpolated at 65%. Line 3: line 1 minus line 2. Line 4: line 20 plus line 18 less the "change in working capital" from table 19 above; some statistical discrepancy is inherent in this procedure, since table 20, from which lines 20 and 18 are taken, yields a level of working capital whose increments are somewhat different from those reported in table 19 (the discrepancy is usually less than $100 million, however; only in 1969 and 1979 is it as high as $331 million and $368 million, respectively); since lines 20 and 18 are first differences of balance sheet data that begin in 1968, there is no entry on line 4 for 1968. Although they are not directly used in the estimate on line 4, the liability items that line 4 approximates are loans, notes, and accounts payable; taxes payable; and other current liabilities. Line 5: "security issues" are the sum of "net long-term debt issued" and "net stock issued" in table 19. Line 6: "sale of fixed assets" is the series "fixed assets sold/retired" in table 19. Line 7: taken from the series "other" under "sources of funds" in table 19. Line 8: the sum of lines 3–7. Line 9: the sum of lines 10–14. Line 10: taken from the series "payroll and benefits" in table 18. Line 11: the series "interest" in table 18. Line 12: the series "dividends" in table 19. Line 13: the series "total taxes" in table 18 less "deferred taxes," derived by subtracting "depreciation, depletion, and amortization" in table 18 from "depreciation and other noncash charges" in table 19. Line 14: "total revenue" less "total deductions" less "net income" from table 18. Line 15: the sum of lines 16–18. Line 16: the series "capital expenditures" in table 19. Line 17: "other costs and expenses" in table 18 less purchases of oil and oil products by the API sample firms; see line 2 for the derivation of oil purchases. Line 18: first differences of "inventories" in table 20; the first entry is for 1969 (see note for line 4 above). Line 19: sum of lines 20–22. Line 20: "short-term financial assets" are the first differences of "cash and marketable securities," "receivables," and "other current assets" from table 20; since the balance sheet data begin in 1968, the initial entry is for 1969; for the 1968 entry on line 20, we simply take the entire change in working capital as reported in table 19. Line 21: the series "investments and advances" in table 19. Line 22: the series "other" under "uses of funds" in table 19. Line 23: the sum of lines 9, 15, and 19; differences between line 23 and line 8 are due to rounding of subtotals.

SOURCE: See notes above.

## TABLE 22
### REPORTING COMPANIES' MISCELLANEOUS DOMESTIC AND FOREIGN OUTLAYS, 1968–1980
#### (billions of dollars)

| | 1968 | 1969 | 1970 | 1971 | 1972 | 1973 | 1974 | 1975 | 1976 | 1977 | 1978 | 1979 | 1980 |
|---|---|---|---|---|---|---|---|---|---|---|---|---|---|
| 1. Expenditures on goods and services (including taxes) | 42.06 | 46.24 | 50.05 | 54.85 | 58.46 | 67.53 | 97.65 | 99.68 | 103.52 | 115.64 | 122.46 | 159.49 | 199.61 |
| 2. Foreign: line 1 × 0.37 | 15.56 | 17.11 | 18.52 | 20.29 | 21.63 | 24.99 | 36.13 | 36.88 | 38.30 | 42.79 | 45.31 | 59.01 | 73.86 |
| 3. Change in line 2 | — | 1.55 | 1.41 | 1.77 | 1.34 | 3.36 | 11.14 | 0.75 | 1.42 | 4.49 | 2.52 | 13.70 | 14.85 |
| 4. Taxes paid | 8.15 | 8.78 | 10.23 | 12.29 | 13.35 | 17.98 | 28.34 | 31.66 | 27.61 | 30.80 | 33.25 | 40.10 | 55.31 |
| 5. Domestic: line 4 × 0.38 | 3.10 | 3.34 | 3.89 | 4.67 | 5.07 | 6.83 | 10.77 | 12.03 | 10.49 | 11.70 | 12.63 | 15.24 | 21.02 |
| 6. Change in line 5 | — | 0.24 | 0.55 | 0.78 | 0.40 | 1.76 | 3.94 | 1.26 | -1.54 | 1.21 | 0.93 | 2.61 | 5.78 |
| 7. Increase in financial assets | 2.05 | 2.79 | 2.47 | 2.07 | 3.42 | 8.15 | 13.17 | -0.43 | 6.79 | 2.83 | 8.54 | 24.52 | 20.36 |
| 8. Change in line 7 | — | 0.74 | -0.32 | -0.40 | 1.35 | 4.73 | 5.02 | -13.60 | 7.22 | -3.96 | 5.71 | 15.98 | -4.16 |
| 9. Value of U.S. oil imports | 1.80 | 2.07 | 2.24 | 2.81 | 3.88 | 7.11 | 25.41 | 24.06 | 31.02 | 40.66 | 38.04 | 54.56 | 71.73 |
| 10. Reporting companies' imports | 1.58 | 1.82 | 1.97 | 2.47 | 3.40 | 6.24 | 22.29 | 21.11 | 27.22 | 34.59 | 33.26 | 51.25 | 60.63 |
| 11. Change in line 10 | — | 0.24 | 0.15 | 0.50 | 0.93 | 2.84 | 16.05 | -1.18 | 6.11 | 7.37 | -1.33 | 17.99 | 9.38 |
| 12. Line 11 × 0.2 | — | 0.05 | 0.03 | 0.10 | 0.19 | 0.57 | 3.21 | -0.24 | 1.22 | 1.47 | -0.27 | 3.60 | 1.88 |

NOTE: Line 1: table 21, line 9 plus line 15. Line 2: see table 14 for derivation of ratio 0.37. Line 4: table 21, line 13. Line 5: the ratio of domestic to total taxes paid, 0.38, is the average for FRS companies in the years 1977–1980; the data were taken from worksheets provided by the Energy Information Administration. The same ratio was assumed to apply throughout 1968–1980. Line 7: table 21, line 19. Line 9: Energy Information Administration, U.S. Department of Energy, *1982 Annual Energy Review* (Washington, D.C.: April 1983), p. 29; data are value of crude oil and refined product imports net of exports. Line 10: data for 1977–1980 are for FRS companies on worksheets provided by the Energy Information Administration; the ratio of FRS company net imports to total U.S. imports on line 9 averages 0.88 for those four years; that average ratio was applied to the entries on line 9 for 1968–1976 to obtain the corresponding entries on line 10.

SOURCE: Authors except as indicated in the notes.

12-fold, whereas capital expenditures rose 4.3-fold and nonoil expenses 4.2-fold. The latter rose quite steadily throughout the period, experiencing a sharp spurt in 1979 and 1980. Capital expenditures underwent a dramatic 57 percent increase in 1974 and rose 71 percent between 1978 and 1980. They tended to rise less than nonoil expenses during nondisruption intervals.

The most obvious manifestation of funds received by the oil companies but not immediately recycled into goods and services is the third use category, the increase in financial assets (line 19). This is evidence of possible oil price drag involving the twenty-five API sample companies. Generally small in magnitude, it is only $2 billion at the beginning of the period but is ten times larger, at more than $20 billion, in 1980. Its components, the change in short-term financial assets (line 20), which includes cash and marketable securities, and investments and advances (line 21), which are mainly loans to subsidiaries and extraordinary acquisitions, are approximately equal at less than $1 billion in the beginning of the period. Investments and advances change little, if any, however, until 1979 and 1980, when they jump suddenly to $7 billion and almost $10 billion, respectively, in response to major acquisitions. Meanwhile, short-term financial assets begin creeping up in 1972, leap to $7 billion in 1973 and to more than $11 billion in 1974, are approximately $4 billion in 1976 and $7 billion in 1978, and skyrocket to $17 billion in 1979. In 1980 they are $9 billion.

The change in financial assets, for use in chapter 6, is entered on line 8 of table 22. Company net petroleum imports are also calculated in the table, line 10, for incorporation in the price drag estimates of chapter 6.

# Notes

1. See Nicholas Gal and Christine Pendzich, *Key Financial Data of Leading U.S. Oil Companies, 1968–1980*, Discussion Paper 017R (Washington, D.C.: American Petroleum Institute, October 28, 1981).

2. Ibid., p. 3.

3. Table 18 appears as table 1 on p. 23, and table 19 as table 3 on p. 29, in Gal and Pendzich, *Key Financial Data*. Table 20 below is identified as table 5 on p. 31 of the API publication.

4. Gal and Pendzich, *Key Financial Data*, pp. 6–7.

5. The Commerce Department does not include lease acquisition costs in its series on oil industry capital investment.

6. Some indication of the range of these percentages is given in the quarterly API release, *Petroleum Industry Profits*, November 8, 1979, May 22, 1981, and August 18, 1981.

# Index

215

216

National Energy Plan (NEP 1), 120
National security, 66
Natural gas, 5, 22, 37, 38, 48, 107, 110
  n. 46, 151 n. 2
Netherlands, 186
Net national product, 8, 51 n. 1. *See also*
  Gross national product
Neveu, Alfred J., 53 n. 18, 54 n. 20–22
New oil, 60
New York State transportation survey,
  33–36, 50, 141
Noll, R. G., 65
Nonproduct costs, 84
Novicky, E., 55 n. 33
Nye, Joseph S., 137 n. 26

Oil companies, API statement, 200–213
Oil import premium, 124–25, 172
Oil price drag, 29–30, 48, 50, 143, 195
  conceptual framework, 44, 153–60
  data sources, 152–53, 200–213
  empirical estimates of, 29–30,
    160–65, 169
  offset by emergency fiscal transfers,
    143
  offset by monetary policy, 165–66,
    169
  what constitutes, 20, 155
Oil substitutes
  least-cost energy strategy, 36–38
  price and output response to
    disruption, 20–23, 42–43, 151 n. 2.
  *See also* Natural gas
Oil supply disruption. *See* Crude oil
  supply disruption
Okun, Arthur M., 151 n. 1
Old oil, 60
Opportunity cost, 11
Options system, SPR, 128–33, 193–94
Oregon, 109 n. 40
Organization for Economic Cooperation
  and Development, 30, 181
Organization of Arab Petroleum
  Exporting Countries, 186
Organization of Petroleum Exporting
  Countries (OPEC), 57, 72, 125, 197
Owen, B. M., 65

Payroll tax reductions, 48, 51, 166-69
Peck, A. E., 54 n. 23
Pendzich, Christine, 159, 213 n. 1
Persian Gulf crisis, 1–7, 190
Peters, Eugene, 151 n. 7
Peterson, John, 55 n. 35
*Petroleum Industry Profits,* 165
*Petroleum Intelligence Weekly,* 198

Petroleum product markets
  crude oil controls effect, 75–78
  efficiency of, 32
  set-asides, 96, 98–99, 106, 178–81
  *See also* Gasoline; Heating fuels;
    Price controls and allocations, in
    petroleum product markets
Petroleum supply disruption. *See* Crude
  oil supply disruption
Phelps, Charles E., 137 n. 25
Phelps, E. S., 52 n. 15
Pikarsky, Milton, 54 n. 31
Pindyck, Robert S., 54 n. 32
*Platt's Oilgram,* 198
Plummer, James L., 55 n. 37, 136 n. 15
Price controls and allocations, in crude
  oil market, 3–4, 59–83
  assessment of, 44–45, 46, 47, 48, 191
  buy/sell program, 78, 80, 102, 103,
    105
  ceiling prices, 60–61, 104
  consumption and welfare effects, 59,
    67–75, 140
  direct allocations, 78–82, 105
  entitlements system, 61–64, 102–5
  equity considerations, 101–4, 106–7
  exceptions relief, 78, 80–82, 102, 103,
    105, 107
  impact in petroleum product
    markets, 75–78
  rationale for, 29, 57–58
  relation of allocations to supply and
    demand, 82–83
  Small Refiner Bias, 61, 64–67, 102–4,
    107
  statutory authority, 59–60
  supplier/purchaser freeze, 78, 79,
    102, 103, 105
Price controls and allocations, in
  petroleum product markets, 83–101
  assessment of, 105–6, 140, 191–92
  and economic efficiency, 94–95,
    97–100
  equity considerations, 101–4, 106–7
  exceptions relief, 96, 106
  gasoline retail market, 85–94, 176
  and inflation, 95, 106
  nonretail product markets, 95–97,
    106
  overview, 83–85
  priority classification, 96–98, 106
  rationale for, 57–58
  set-asides, 96, 98–99, 106, 178–81
  and stockpiling, 100–101, 106
  supplier/purchaser freeze, 96, 97,
    106

Pricing arrangements for crude oil, 197–99
Priority classification, 96–98, 106
Producers' surplus, 14, 15, 25, 49, 71–72, 76–77, 89, 91, 94, 120
Product costs, 84
Product markets
    product shifts, after disruption, 20, 23–25, 43–44, 49
    See also Petroleum product markets
Product quality reduction, 89–91, 92, 94, 95, 101, 105–6, 177
Profit margin, 3, 32, 84–85, 91, 94–95, 105
Propane, 84, 100–101

Rand Corp., 179, 199 n. 1
Rasche, Robert H., 54 n. 32
Rate-of-return regulation, 81, 82
Reagan administration, 111, 123, 126
Refiner buyers' surplus, 70–72
Refineries
    direct crude allocations, 78–82, 102, 103, 105
    entitlements, 61–64, 102–5
    price controls on petroleum products, 59, 83–85
    Small Refiner Bias, 61, 64–67, 102–4
Roeber, Joe, 199 n. 2
Rotterdam market, 198
Rowen, Henry, 136 n. 16

Sachs, Jeffrey, 170 n. 10
Salant, Stephen W., 188 n. 10
Sant, Roger W., 37, 54 n. 24–30
Schink, George R., 46
Schneider, J., 55 n. 33
Schultze, Charles L., 52 n. 11
Schwartz, Warren F., 188 n. 10
Seidman, David, 187 n. 8, 199 n. 1
Set-asides, petroleum products, 96, 98–99, 106, 178–81
Shadow prices, 87–89, 91, 92, 95, 97, 101, 105, 176
Sharing program, IEA, 127, 181–86, 195
Small Refiner Bias, 61, 64–67, 82, 102–4, 107
Smith, Rodney T., 188 n. 10
Smith, Vernon L., 138 n. 33
Social surplus
    and SPR use, 115–16, 117–18
    oil supply disruption effect, 8, 14–20, 24–25, 49
    price controls effect, 69–75, 76–77
    sharing agreement effect on, 184–85

See also Consumers' surplus; Producers' surplus; Refiners' buyers surplus
Soloman, Burt, 199 n. 4
Solow, R. M., 52 n. 15
Sommerfield, Mary, 136 n. 16
Southland Oil Co., 81–82
Space heating. See Heating fuels
Special Rule 1, 78
Special Rule 9, 99
Spot market, 2, 66, 197
Spot prices, 1–2, 129, 197–99
Standby Petroleum Allocation Act of 1982 (S. 1503), 6
State and local governments
    petroleum products set-aside program, 96, 98–99, 106, 178–81
    total expenditures, 151 n. 8
    See also Emergency fiscal transfers
Stockpiling, 2, 26, 28–29, 48, 59, 100–101, 106, 181. See also Strategic petroleum reserve
Strategic petroleum reserve (SPR), 2, 4–5, 48, 133
    benefits and costs, 114–18
    drawdown mechanisms, 127–33
    funding/petroleum import fee, 124–27, 192–93
    1975 plan, 120–21
    options plan for drawdown, 128–33, 193–94
    organizational and budget problems, 121–23
    policy development, 111–12
    private versus government stockpiling, 112–14, 117, 118
    relation to emergency fiscal transfers, 144–50
    size determination, 119–20
    storage development policy, 123–24
    technical problems, 121
Strategic Petroleum Reserve (SPR), Office of, 120–22, 134 n. 2, 3
Stripper wells, 60, 101
Substitute energy. See Oil substitutes
Supplier/purchaser freeze
    crude oil allocations, 78, 79, 102, 103, 105
    petroleum products, 96, 97, 106
Supply
    aggregate supply-and-demand macro framework, 40–49
    crude oil, U.S., 8–11
    gasoline, U.S., 85–94
    price controls relation to, 82–83
Sweden, 56, n. 39, 188 n. 13

220

A NOTE ON THE BOOK

*This book was edited by Marcia Brubeck*
*and by Elizabeth Ashooh of the*
*Publications Staff of the American Enterprise Institute.*
*The staff also designed the cover and format, with Pat Taylor.*
*The index was prepared by Patricia R. Foreman, and*
*the figures were drawn by Hördur Karlsson.*
*The text was set in Palatino, a typeface designed by Hermann Zapf.*
*Hendricks-Miller Typographic Company, of Washington, D.C.,*
*set the type, and R. R. Donnelley & Sons Company,*
*of Harrisonburg, Virginia, printed and bound the book,*
*using paper made by the S. D. Warren Company.*

## SELECTED AEI PUBLICATIONS

*The Deregulation of Natural Gas*, Edward J. Mitchell, ed., (163 pp., paper $7.95, cloth $15.95)

*Energy Security: Can We Cope with a Crisis?* John Charles Daly, mod. (36 pp., $3.75)

*Petroleum Price Regulation: Should We Decontrol?* Kenneth J. Arrow and Joseph P. Kalt (47 pp., $4.25)

*Seminar on Energy Policy: The Carter Proposals*, Edward J. Mitchell, ed. (29 pp., $3.25)

*Oil Pipelines and Public Policy: Analysis of Proposals for Industry Reform and Reorganization*, Edward J. Mitchell, ed. (392 pp., paper $6.75, cloth $13.75)

*Energy and the Environment: Conflict in Public Policy*, Walter J. Mead (36 pp., $3.75)

*Uranium Enrichment and Public Policy*, Thomas Gale Moore (64 pp., $4.25)

*Transporting Natural Gas from the Arctic: The Alternative Systems*, Walter J. Mead (111 pp., $3.25)

• *Mail orders for publications to:* AMERICAN ENTERPRISE INSTITUTE, 1150 Seventeenth Street, N.W., Washington, D.C. 20036 • *For postage and handling, add 10 percent of total; minimum charge $2, maximum $10* • *For information on orders, or to expedite service, call toll free 800-424-2873* • *When ordering by International Standard Book Number, please use the AEI prefix—0-8447* • *Prices subject to change without notice* • *Payable in U.S. currency only*

## AEI ASSOCIATES PROGRAM

The American Enterprise Institute invites your participation in the competition of ideas through its AEI Associates Program. This program has two objectives: (1) to extend public familiarity with contemporary issues; and (2) to increase research on these issues and disseminate the results to policy makers, the academic community, journalists, and others who help shape public attitudes. The areas studied by AEI include Economic Policy, Education Policy, Energy Policy, Fiscal Policy, Government Regulation, Health Policy, International Programs, Legal Policy, National Defense Studies, Political and Social Processes, and Religion, Philosophy, and Public Policy. For the $49 annual fee, Associates receive

- a subscription to *Memorandum*, the newsletter on all AEI activities
- the AEI publications catalog and all supplements
- a 30 percent discount on all AEI books
- a 40 percent discount for certain seminars on key issues
- subscriptions to two of the following publications: *Public Opinion*, a bimonthly magazine exploring trends and implications of public opinion on social and public policy questions; *Regulation*, a bimonthly journal examining all aspects of government regulation of society; and *AEI Economist*, a monthly newsletter analyzing current economic issues and evaluating future trends (or for all three publications, send an additional $12).

*Call 202/862-6446 or write:*  AMERICAN ENTERPRISE INSTITUTE
1150 Seventeenth Street, N.W., Suite 301, Washington, D.C. 20036